sex
in the
south

sex
in the
south

UNBUCKLING THE
BIBLE BELT

SUZI PARKER

Justin, Charles & Co.
Boston, Massachusetts

First Edition 2003

Every effort has been made to fulfill requirements with regard to reproducing copyright material. The author and publisher will be glad to rectify any omissions at the earliest opportunity.

ISBN: 1-932112-16-2

Library of Congress Cataloging-in-Publication Data is available.

Published in the United States by Justin, Charles & Co., Publishers, 20 Park Plaza, Boston, MA 02116
www.justincharlesbooks.com

Distributed by National Book Network, Lanham, Maryland
www.nbnbooks.com

10 9 8 7 6 5 4 3 2 1

Printed in the United States of America

For my parents, Estelle and Billy,
who have always been there for me
with love, support, and understanding

contents

acknowledgments

First, I need to thank the numerous people — named and un-named — who were brave enough to be candid with me about their sexual lives and exploits during this erotic journey through the South. It's not easy to talk about sex in a region where church steeples loom as confessions are whispered. Many brave souls, who believed that this was a worthwhile effort, bared their intimate souls and opened their weekend pursuits up to me so that I could see what really occurs be-hind closed doors.

I would like to thank my agent, Erin Reel, who believed in this project from the first minute she saw it; Stephen Hull, vi-sionary at Justin Charles & Co.; and my editor extraordinaire Carmen Mitchell, with the ultra cool hair, who gave me the freedom to tell the story and the guidance to make sure the creative process flowed in a logical way.

I am grateful to Everett Starling for his always-listening ear and late-night rah-rah calls and e-mails over the last few years about my projects, especially this one.

I would like to thank my wondertwin Glen Hooks who was there from the start to give support, laughter, insight, advice, and the much-needed push to make sure this book became reality. Not to mention the numerous cups of strong coffee during long nights of writing.

Finally, I want to thank my parents, Billy and Estelle, who have always believed in my ability to break down barriers and who taught me to be honest with myself. Their unwavering love and support have always been with me during the good and bad times. They have always encouraged me to forge ahead and follow my heart even if it means getting in trouble sometimes. Their patience during this book and the journey that accompanied it, of which they were a significant part — driving many miles with me through Dixie, reading various versions of the project, especially my mom — was amazing. Therefore, this work is as much theirs as mine.

foreplay

The first time a boy told me that he wanted to fuck me, I was sitting on a pew in the First Baptist Church in Russellville, Arkansas, a small town on the edge of the Ozark Mountains. A chubby blond classmate to whom I had never given a second glance in high school passed me a note asking to do that very thing, earning him my contempt and a withering go-to-hell glance. I never spoke to him after that, and I certainly never accepted his offer. But years later, I was amused — but not entirely shocked — to discover at a class reunion that he had become a minister. That's the South, where what you see is never what you get. Peer behind the hymnals and homilies as I do to find out what really happens when the pastor's not looking. The region is a full-to-capacity carnal playground where the den mother buys dildos, the principal is a swinger, and the preacher is a porn fiend.

This region I call home is a surreal bubbling cocktail of un-bridled desire, über-Bible thumping, and unapologetic hypocrisy. Yankees tell me that if I had a good head on my shoulders, I'd leave and never look back. I tell them sometimes loins speak louder than logic. Actually, it's very easy to understand: The schizophrenic land of Scarlett O'Hara and Rhett Butler slakes my thirsty curiosity more than any big-city Northern romp ever could. No doubt about it — the South is the nation's premier sexual hothouse, be it on unpaved back roads or in covert country club powder rooms. It's a place where an adulterous couple will knock it out as a prelude to church and then spend the sermon exchanging knowing looks across pews while seated with their unsuspecting spouses. Sometimes it's a wealthy businessman and his college-age curvy nanny. But sometimes, more frequently than you'd think, it's a well-known businessman or local politician and the country club's young, male tanned tennis pro.

The deal in Dixie is that everybody does it but no one talks about it. Because no one talks about it, sex is encased in a plain brown wrapper making everything about it taboo, taciturn, and twisted, with just a smidgen of sin to top it off. And there ain't anything that a good Southerner likes better than sinnin' unless it's fornicatin'. If by chance, someone does confront a randy Southerner about a sexual encounter, there's one rule of thumb: deny, deny, deny — unless the romp was with your own spouse. Even then, sex is considered sacred and off-limits in conversation.

But it's okay to gossip about other people's sex lives down here in the land of moonlight and magnolia. If you are a Southern woman, it's perfectly okay to brag about your own sex life as long as you use third person and make damn sure it sounds like it's someone else's — anyone else's — rather than your own. If you don't, get ready for a firestorm of damnation. After all, this is a region where a mighty-steepled church anchors every corner and a Bible occupies every house, where people who aren't even holy rollers are moved to righteous conniptions when sex gets involved.

If you slip up, it's okay. That's expected. God will forgive you and so will your best friend. It's just a matter of the way you play the story. After all, Southern belles like to flirt, and flirting will inevitably lead to some sort of trouble at some point. My longtime friend Julie knows this better than she knows her *Gone with the Wind*, the real Bible for a Southern woman.

Growing up, Julie was given many lessons in acting innocent. Because of those lessons, she created a set of rules to justify any sexual liaison. The magic medicine: She was "swept off her feet" like Scarlett with Rhett. Always have excuses ready:

"Were you tipsy?" Yes.

"Did he come inside you?" No.

"Were you completely naked?" No.

"Did you come?" No.

"See, it doesn't count," Julie says. Presto. Born-again virgin. Sin, repent. Move on.

Southerners must repent, because guilt is pounded into us from the first day of Vacation Bible School. In fact, we thrive on it. But at the same time Southerners like to liberate themselves. And in this land of the rebel yell and Confederate flags, people will sin, repent, and sin again. Perfect example: Bill Clinton showed the world that he could sin (Gennifer Flowers scandal), repent (60 Minutes interview with Hillary after the Super Bowl in 1992), and sin again (Monica Lewinsky). You might call him the patron saint of Dixie, a walking, talking, ejaculating testament to the power of forgiveness.

Even if you don't feel guilty in the South, someone will find something to make you feel that way. Take me for instance. I grew up a whimsical, slightly offbeat, not exactly stereotypical

Southern belle in one of Arkansas's most fiercely Southern cities — Pine Bluff. My hometown was a place taken from a page of an Old South history book where cotillion dances and Junior League membership determined social status as much as your mother's maiden name or the kind of car you got for your sixteenth birthday. I even wore a hoop skirt at age five — the kind Southern girls wear during pilgrimages and debutantes — when I was in my first, and last, beauty pageant. My mom forswore pageants forever after my dad witnessed another parent paying off a judge before the contest. Image is important here, even if it lightens Daddy's wallet a bit.

Pine Bluff was a place where a girl dared not telephone a boy, where conversation about one's period was off-limits, and sex before marriage was the most forbidden of all taboos — and this was in the late 1970s. The long list of proper etiquette would have exhausted even Emily Post. But that life was a prim-and-proper illusion. I knew mothers who made sure their daughters took their birth control every morning before heading off to private school.

I was taught the Southern belle rules — and the consequences of breaking them — even after I became an adult. After all, the same rules apply when you are a woman. It really doesn't matter what you do, but don't talk about it, and make sure you are parked in a church pew at least a few Sundays every month. Good for the image, you see. Rocking the headboard is fine, as long as you don't rock the boat.

Alas, my parents raised an only daughter who pushes buttons, "full of piss and vinegar," my dad says. I learned that, in Dixie, when a single woman like me writes about sex, or in my case, a lava love libation, you can bet your pink plastic dildo that she will get in hot water.

Niagara, a fizzy blue aphrodisiac drink concocted in Sweden to make women tingly, horny, and wet, captured the imagination of Little Rock and the rest of the country in early 2001. For weeks, Niagara was the talk of the city on raunchy redneck radio shows, on local television newscasts, even at the legislature and church. Soccer moms and socialites stood in line for hours waiting to dish out $4.50 for a bottle of the herbal Swedish aphrodisiac. The whispered question on everyone's lips: "Have you had a Niagara night?" Women who hadn't thought about sex in years suddenly possessed a rekindled fiery passion. Niagara's Swedish manufacturer, Nordic Drinks, hired extra staff to make more of the concoction in the little blue bottle. All this fuss was thanks to the savvy marketing of a Little Rock woman who introduced the state and country to the horny pop. It seemed like a good story for a girl reporter like me to tackle. The consequence? I opened my own personal Pandora's box.

When the trouble arrived, I was pondering someone else's sex life rather than my own — that of an ultraconservative Republican United States senator, whose dalliance with a staffer resulted in his divorce. He was the chosen topic of *Arkansas Week*, a weekly snoozer of a political talk show on which I occasionally appeared that airs on the Arkansas Educational Television Network, the state's public television station.

But I never taped that show. An AETN employee called Friday morning, two hours before the show's taping, to notify me that the producers wouldn't need my political banter that day. They had discovered my story and a subsequent *Variety* story detailing Julia Roberts's interest in the story for film. As a result, I was banished from the show.

"We understand she wrote for an adult Web site," said the station's director when the media called him the next day about my banishment. Yep, I had written for an adult Web site, albeit one featuring more erotica than hard porn. The story about me and my boyfriend and a neon-red coming-hard-and-fast orgasm was enough to make Little Rock pause and share a collective blush. That citywide gasp signaled the beginning of a major postcoital hurricane. It didn't take long for the news to circulate in the capital city, which thrives on scandal at least as much as Hollywood. Rumors that circulate in the morning are posted in gossip e-mails well before quitting time. Cell phones may pose as devices for work but everyone here knows that they serve one important purpose: spreading gossip fast and furiously.

By Friday afternoon the press was calling, and I was releasing a statement about a girl's right to share sexual escapades without being burned at the stake. "The reality is AETN can't deal with a woman who writes frankly about sex," I said repeatedly.

Long ago, I had christened myself a Scarlett in this Southern world that divides women into one of the two *Gone with the Wind* characters. A Scarlett is a feisty spitfire, and a Melanie is a meek Milquetoast. A man always desires a Scarlett, but he marries a Melanie. That doesn't mean he forgets about the seductive Scarlett, though. At some point, with luck, he'll have both. While many Bible-nutty Southerners wear WWJD — "What Would Jesus Do?" — gear, I have my own guiding question: What Would Scarlett Do?

On Saturday morning I woke up to face an event-crammed

day that had been planned for a few weeks. I was invited to several parties: a patio cookout hosted by a friend who works at a large advertising agency, a bon voyage party for another friend who had found his calling in San Francisco, and a birthday party for yet another friend who owns a funky art gallery. Shaking off sleep, I sensed that this was a day that would determine my public image for a long time. If I hibernated in my house, everyone would say I was embarrassed and regretted writing about sex. If I appeared, I would be a moving target for catty whispers and crude sex jokes.

Taking a deep breath, I channeled Scarlett and opted for the latter.

I showed up at the advertising guru's house carrying two blue bottles in a brown sack as a housewarming gift. "Good gift," said a woman with bleached-fried hair. "We figured you'd be too embarrassed to show up, you know, with that story and all."

"Takes more than that to embarrass me," I said.

"I guess so. Surely, your parents don't know about this?" she inquired.

"They support me in everything I do," I said, searching for an escape hatch away from this quizzical woman.

"Jeez, what kind of parents do you have?" she said, wrinkling her well-powdered nose.

"Cool ones," I retorted.

During the barbecue of crawdads and chicken, I worked the crowd, preaching about how people in Arkansas should be more sexually liberated and less repressed, especially in this post-Clinton age.

Guests at the next party, thrown in a chain-owned steak house with rustic Australian cowboy gear hanging on the walls, were less concerned about my active sex life and more focused on my eternal damnation. The guest of honor was a religious zealot who I figured was praying for my soul every time I excused myself for the rest room. I felt as if every time he opened his mouth to quote scripture he was also silently wishing that he had been witness to my scorching orgasm. Such is the genus known as the Little Rock Man.

A group of people who think of themselves as pagans and entertain themselves with a renegade (and often crude) theater troupe threw the final party of my whirlwind day. Nearly everyone in this group had slept with each other at one time or another. I had made it through the day and knew a blanket of security would engulf me at this party. I couldn't wait to arrive. But even there, a curiosity bubbled about me. I got the distinct feeling that everyone thought my life and career were ruined — splattered by a head-on collision with inviolate etiquette rules. Surely, it would end soon.

By Monday morning, the story had spread from a local news Web site to state media to national newspapers. I was giving more quotes and feeling as under siege as Atlanta during Sherman's march.

I knew this cyclone of controversy had to spin for a while before it quieted. Sure enough, the winds blew harder. In the midst of my defending my bedroom antics, Pfizer Inc. sued the woman who first sold the drink for trademark infringement. The pharmaceutical giant wanted to halt the selling of the drink with a name that sounded strangely like Viagra, the little blue pill that gives men the ability to go for hours in the bedroom. Spinning like a Tasmanian devil, she called to tell me that my name was in the morning's newspaper with connection to the lawsuit. Pfizer's lawyers told the press that they were looking for me. They needed my story for a deposition, but they could not locate me anywhere.

"They aren't looking very hard," I said. "My name has been in the newspaper every day for five days or so."

My phone rang continuously with calls from friends and acquaintances to tell me what other people were saying about me. Editors of the weekly newspaper even called the Web site's editors to ask if my sexual caper had been fact-checked. Hmmm, no. I didn't send a used condom to the editor for a DNA analysis.

Like any juicy scandal, just when you think you can breathe a sigh of relief, kick back with a good cocktail, or sleep in on a Saturday morning, something happens to bounce it back into the frenzied forefront of life. Two months after the initial quiver and quake of the Niagara scandal, I awoke on a Saturday morning to a knock at my front door. Peeking out, I saw a man standing there, holding some sort of paper. I opened the door and immediately realized the situation unfolding. Covering years of political scandals flashed before my bleary eyes: He was carrying a subpoena to appear in someone's legal torture chamber.

"Miss Parker?" the man asked, studying me as I wrapped myself tighter in the green oversized sweater.

"No, she's not here," I lied.

"She's not?"

"Nope, she's not. Can I help you?"

"I need to see Miss Parker."

"Sorry, she's not here. You'll have to come back."

The guy stared at me as I shut the door in his face. Images of escape routes flashed in my head: a one-way ticket to Mexico, the Cayman Islands, anywhere. The man knocked again on the door, and I opened it. "Are you sure you aren't Miss Parker?" I rolled my eyes in disgust. Busted.

"Yes, I am. Just give me that damn thing." I signed for the document. He tried to ease my anxiety by telling me two checks were attached as payment for my future agony and pain.

I never thought the day would come when I would identify with Monica Lewinsky. We had nothing in common, after all. She was an intern working in Washington. I was a journalist from Arkansas writing about the South. Somehow we both ended up in federal depositions talking about the same thing: sex.

It was a hot June day when I parked my black Saturn in a lot behind a copy store and a restaurant that cooked blue-plate specials. I walked alone into the skyscraper in the heart of Little Rock's miniskyline. As a journalist, I always feel powerful, the pen as my weapon against the world. Even though I am only five-foot-three, I always feel fearless because of my work, taking on the world with one slash of my ink pen. That day, though, I felt small — scared like a little girl going to first grade for the first time.

The elevator opened into the lobby of one of the largest law offices in the state. The décor was the same as I had seen in other law or doctor offices in town: boring and staid with a dark Oriental rug, leather Queen Anne furniture, and unoriginal pastoral oil paintings hanging over twin velvet couches — certainly not the most imaginative décor one had ever seen. I got the feeling this was the look of rich, white men who paid a Junior League part-time decorator, full-time doctor's wife, to give their offices a rich, manly feel. It didn't work.

A grumpy retirement-aged woman guarded the front desk.

"Who are you?" she grumbled.

"Suzi Parker. I have to give a deposition but I'd rather donate plasma with a dirty needle," I joked, but it fell on deaf ears. She wasn't into my gig.

A tall, silver-haired man walked up to me and introduced himself as an attorney for the defendant, the coffee shop owner–turned–love potion goddess. The lawyer apologized, saying he was sorry that I had to waste my time on such nonsense.

"Yeah, me too," I said.

"Hey, but you get money," he said.

In Arkansas, a civil procedure rule exists to compensate witnesses who are deposed for their information. I received $120 for my deposition and my subsequent appearance in court, if the case went to trial. Not enough for my pain and suffering, though.

"They are ready for you," the woman said.

I walked into the conference room, which was filled with white men in conservative suits and ties, and was ordered to the end of the long conference table.

"Miss Parker, can I get you some water?" an aging attorney asked.

"No, no thanks. I am fine."

"You may need some water," the attorney insisted.

"Okay, then, I'll take some."

The aging attorney loomed over me with piercing eyes. I felt like Little Red Riding Hood being fed to a whole pack of big, bad wolves. At the end of the wooden table, a court reporter set up shop with a tape recorder, stickers for exhibits, and a small typewriter.

A short, balding attorney came out of a side door with a smirk on his face. I automatically knew this was Mr. Evil Attorney. He was followed three steps behind by a young fraternity boy, a law clerk.

The men talked about my position at the table as if they were plotting a way to get the money shot in a porn flick. They wanted me to sit in the chair where the best angle of my face would be shown for the videotaped deposition. I gulped. No one said I would be a girl on film. The court reporter rescued me when he said the videographer was caught in a traffic jam. The lawyers grumbled, but finally, a decision: My words wouldn't need to be recorded for a Court TV audience.

Another lawyer entered the room. He looked more pleasant but had a growl on his face that said he would rather be anywhere than in this room. He was an attorney for a third party in the lawsuit — the Swedish makers of the love potion — who had been dragged into the legal mess at the last minute. He plopped down at the end of the table where I had sat earlier, and iciness crackled between the lawyers. I knew this wasn't going to be anyone's finest hour.

The deposition started much like innocent first-date chitchat: my name, education, and job experience in college. My lawyer friends call this "getting to know the witness." I call it "sick foreplay before raping a helpless victim."

Journalists are taught never to hand over interview and research notes for any reason. A good reporter holds notes as sacred material and waits for an order by a judge before giving them up. In the case of many reporters, they opt for jail in order to protect their information. If I had been holding the smoking gun for a military secret that could have launched World War III, I would have considered holding back. Instead, my notebook consisted of scribble scrabble about housewives in warm-up suits buying horny pop — not exactly top-secret classified information. I decided to make it easier on everyone: I'd hand over my notes, and with nothing to hide, I'd quickly be in and out of the deposition and off to have some strong coffee.

But Mr. Evil Attorney had his own agenda: to find out the racy nuances of my sex life. He liked referring to my giddy romp as a "union." He smacked his lips when he said the word, and I wondered, as he sat there imagining me in some sort of sweaty orgasmic frenzy, how many porn magazines were hidden in a locked filing cabinet in his office. The third lawyer broke my train of naughty thoughts when he objected to the line of questioning.

The deposition rocked along like a sinking ship and then I saw something in my scribbled notes that shocked even me. The name Cameron — a pseudonym for my boyfriend — was in my notes. I had picked that name for no particular reason other than I liked it. Then, in my notes, I remembered someone mentioning how Cameron Mathison, a soap opera actor, had received a bottle of Niagara when he stopped in Little Rock on a promotional tour. When he looked at my notes, Mr. Evil Attorney zoned in on those names like a twelve-year-old finding his daddy's porn stash in a closet.

"Who's Cameron Mathison?"

"Apparently a star in *All My Children*."

"Is that the name that you used in your story?"

"Yes," I said.

"Was it Cameron Mathison?"

I wanted to roll my eyes but stared instead right into the attorney's. If this man thought I spent my afternoons bedding New York soap opera stars, he really gave me more credit than I deserved.

"No," I answered.

Mr. Evil Attorney continued to quiz me about how I borrowed that man's name and was the man in my story really named Cameron. I balked and became defensive. "I will not talk about that. I don't see how that is relevant."

"Well, that's really not your decision, ma'am."

The hell it isn't. No one has to do anything in America but die and pay taxes, and talking about my lover certainly didn't fall into those categories. "Do you have notes of that conversation?" he asked.

Honestly, I thought, do most people record their sexual encounters? Hold on, honey, let me get my pen and write that down, hang on, don't come just yet. Got to write down that last gasp. Before we start, let's get the film rolling just in case I want to write about this later, or worse, find myself in front of a grand jury. Yes, get off the bed, I've got to save these sheets as fact-checking material.

"Will you tell me the name of this person that you had identified in your article as Cameron?"

"No," I said.

Mr. Evil Attorney was exasperated, but, hey, a girl's sex life is her sex life. But be warned: A Southern girl enjoying sex is a dangerous thing.

Give up Mr. Evil Attorney, I felt like screaming.

Question after question about my sex life pelted me. I became bored; the law clerk became excited and eventually made an exit but I remained a girl caught in a bad spotlight.

Three hours and what seemed like 850 questions later, I was freed but not for forever. Don't go traipsing off to London or some place exotic; you are expected to testify at the federal court hearing in August, the lawyers said.

Pandora shut her box; I never appeared in court because the lawsuit was settled. I've opted not to drink Niagara again even though I have a whole case stashed away in the pantry. I broke the rules. I wrote frankly about sex, and I got in trouble.

And it shocks people that I even attend church. Surely, a girl like me worships at the altar of some pagan sex goddess. But like all good Southern belles, I know where to sit on Sunday mornings.

So all of that drama got me to wondering: What's hiding in everyone's closets behind the floral sundresses and the denim overalls in Dixie?

Southern states have always had their own way of doing things. The South is where we'd rather secede than surrender, where presidents are born and bred, and where governors stand defiantly in the schoolhouse door. Simply put, we are a cussedly independent people, wholly committed to observing society's expectations but equally committed to eluding those expectations whenever possible (especially in the bedroom).

My mission: to make sure no one ever looks at their neighbor, friend, attorney, doctor, garbage man, mayor — anyone, for that matter — the same way again.

Names have been changed in some instances to protect

the randy, the horny, and the shy. In a few places, location is vague in order to protect people's privacy in their particular community. But nothing has been exaggerated or fabricated. Anyone can find the same stories in their own backyard if they become a voyeur for a couple of hours. This book is an appetizer in the smorgasbord that is the sexual South, an erotic roadmap for the adventurous and hardly-faint-at-heart traveler. Climb aboard and unbuckle the Bible Belt.

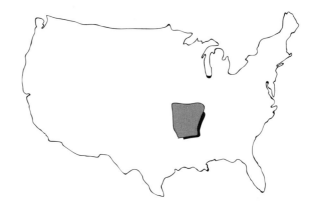

arkansas

dildo-a-rama

Vacuums and Vibrators

MAUMELLE, ARKANSAS — It's hard to focus on the scripture when you are thinking about the EZ Pleaser.

Only in the South would a girl like me go to church on Sunday morning, attend the monthly Methodist potluck after the preaching, and then show up a few hours later at a local hotel to learn the art of selling sex toys to housewives. But after all, this is Arkansas, the land of split personalities, where nobody is ever what they seem.

I gobble down the last bite of Jell-O salad, a frothy green concoction of whipped cream, lime gelatin, and pineapples, before saying my good-byes at the potluck. I don't bother to tell my friends my afternoon agenda — that I am headed to a sex-toy sales meeting at a Ramada Inn.

The motel sits perched on a hill between a chain-owned Mexican restaurant with oversized floppy sombreros on the fiesta-bright walls and a chain-owned Chinese restaurant with jumbo glittery goldfish in a man-made stone pond. I walk into the mauve and beige lobby, and before I even approach the front desk to ask where the sex-toy mavens are meeting, a stern-faced man points down a hall. He obviously knows what I am looking for on a Sunday afternoon — jiggly, wiggly sex toys.

In a small conference room, a group of women — who clearly enjoy shopping at Wal-Mart and prefer casseroles to Donna Karan and personal trainers — bubble with giddy electricity. This afternoon isn't about twelve-inch dildos, fuzzy lavender handcuffs for light S&M, or even vivid violet vibrators. No, it's all about introducing these modern-day salesfolk to a new product: Pure Satisfaction.

Pat Davis, the president of Passion Parties in Brisbane, California, has flown in for this seminar. This, I soon learn, is a big damn deal. She was formerly a motivational speaker at San Diego's Millionaires in Motion before she found a home at Passion Parties. It's not every day the common housewife or beauty operator who sells sex toys on the weekend meets Pat Davis, a brassy woman who tells the crowd she's been married for more than thirty years and a little romance and hoochie-coo never hurt anyone.

It's no surprise that the president of the company would embark on a tour of the South. It's the best-selling area in the country for sex toys. And Passion Parties, hosted by perky Passion Party hostesses (think 1970s Tupperware parties but with rubber penises instead of plastic ice trays) are all the rage in small towns across the region. There's nothing like a bunch of women getting together on a Friday night and giggling naughtily about a piece of rubber in the shape of a dick. Unless, that is, it's on Wednesday night. That's when husbands think their wives are at choir practice at the Southern Baptist church, but then they come home with edible undies and a love swing under their arm instead of the Bible.

The women in this cozy conference room range in age from a bashful twenty-two-year-old to sixty-plus. Some are married, some single.

"Have you tried Pure Satisfaction?" a Big Gulp–sipping woman beside me asks.

I shake my head no. Last time I tried such a sexual aide I got into serious hot water. I prefer to go the natural route now, and if a screaming-banshee orgasm fails to happen, so be it. I'll play it safe for a while.

"Oh, honey, you've got to try it. Make her give you a sample."

I smile and nod. Yeah, sure thing.

Here's how the Passion Party catalog describes Pure Satisfaction UniSEX Enhancement Gel: "An exclusive UniSEX gel for enhanced sexual satisfaction in high demand by today's men and women. Passion Parties is the first to present a safe and natural topical Unisex gel that induces more intense orgasms in both sexes, allows for greater intimacy and maximum sexual fulfillment." You get the picture.

Just in case I didn't get the picture from that description — written by an established romance writer who shall remain nameless (something tells me it's not Danielle Steele) — some of the women in the room decide to give testimonials. Just like church: Time to testify!

"I've always had a fantasy about having an orgasm so intense that I pass out," says a woman in her thirties with curly brown hair.

Damn! I think, suddenly picturing this housewife starring in a snuff film.

"My husband and I applied it to my clit and to the head of his penis. Then you feel it. It's tingling, burning, on fire. He slid into me and banged me until I had the orgasm of my life."

The woman gasps and sweat pops out on her face. Her

eyes glisten at the torrid memory. I'll have what's she having, I think to myself.

"But that wasn't enough so I made him go again, and I came again."

Oh, yeah! I'll definitely have what she's having.

"Then, he just couldn't go anymore but I could. So that's when we got out the sex toys."

Perk! Definifely want me some of that.

"And I came so hard when he kept pushing the sex toy in and out that I passed out. I was gone. I think it scared my husband, but I came to after a few minutes."

Hmmm, not so sure I want what she's having after all. I'm not ready to quasi–meet my maker following a screaming O. But everyone else seems receptive and claps loudly. I'm reminded of an old-time riverbank revival: same passion, different scripture.

Linda Brewer looks more like a Sunday school teacher than a popular in-demand sex-toy sensation. She is a slightly pudgy woman with curly brown hair. She wears glasses that hang on a sparkly chain around her neck. She smokes cigarettes even though she has a lung problem. But she talks about sex instead of the Bible. I couldn't have a more perfect sexual tour guide through this world of Passion Parties. When Linda first started selling items like the Silver Bullet and Pumpin' Peter in the early nineties, she couldn't even bring herself to say the "P" word — that's "penis" for us not-so-shy folk. So instead, to sell her wares, she decided to call that wiggly boy thing a "unit." It's a term she still uses, but these days she's not as bashful about saying penis or even "D'lick-ious," the Passion Party's edible head gel made to enhance anyone's — maybe even Monica Lewinsky's — oral sex life. It doesn't bother her one iota anymore to whip out some fruity-smelling lotion and show a woman how to caress her lover's penis.

Ask Linda why she sells sex toys and she'll tell you she likes educating women about sexual pleasures, either their own or their partner's. Not to mention it's a helluva living. Some saleswomen rake in more than $250,000 a year peddling potions and plastics. In the last few years, Linda has been one of the top saleswomen for the company. In less than six years, she has gone from driving an older model sedan to a snazzy Cadillac SUV — all thanks to the earnings from vibrators.

The women who sell these toys look like quintessential housewives with a smidgen of life's burnout around the frayed edges. There's no pretension, no high glamour, no eye lifts or tummy tucks, no stunning beauty to single out these women from any other Jane Doe standing in a supermarket check-out line. As I look around the room, I realize that this in itself is a savvy business plan. Most women, especially in the proper and often prudish South, feel intimidated in the first place about buying battery-operated cock-shaped gadgets for sexual pleasure. If some curvy hottie who looked like Catherine Zeta Jones stood in front of them and hawked such merchandise, I am sure the intimidation and insecurity levels would jump twenty notches. Buying a blindfold and some Hard-on Cream from Linda is like buying the new fashionable shade of eye shadow from your favorite aunt who sells Mary Kay at family reunions. It's safe and feels okay, not naughty and dirty.

Linda recruited many of the women in this room to the world of Passion Parties, and she knows that many of them keep this aspect of their lives secret from family and friends. It's not easy peddling dildos in the Bible Belt. Some haughty and judgmental women think Passion Parties reek with crudeness and immorality. God didn't mean for a woman to stick a man-made piece of plastic up her private parts.

Law officers, particularly in small towns, enjoy raiding stores that sell such "obscene" products, citing local laws against obscenity. (It's not, by the way, illegal to sell sex toys in Arkansas, unlike in many states.) And it's rare when you meet a Southern woman who actually admits to owning a vibrator. But that's why Passion Parties are as popular as they are and why more and more women — and men — are finding money-making opportunities at these parties. Passion Parties give people a chance to feel and examine intimate objects in a comfortable setting — usually a warm and cozy living room — surrounded by friends or coworkers. Then, at the end of the party, women venture into the privacy of another room with their order forms and exit with a bag full of goodies for themselves and their significant others.

Executives at Passion Parties Inc. realize that "virgins" shop among the seasoned sex-toy connoisseurs. The higher-ups know that an item such as the popular Jackrabbit vibrator, even if it's the centerpiece for a *Sex and the City* episode, freaks out some first-time buyers with its rotating shaft and vibrating ears. That's why Pat Davis is in Little Rock today to promote the Passion Parties new Romanta Therapy collection.

The company's new mantra: Feel sexy first, then buy a sex toy. This new line of lotions, bath salts, and parfums with pheromones is inspired by Aphrodite. She's Cupid's mother, explains Pat, for those who don't know the ins and outs of Greek mythology. Love, beauty, sex, affection — all the attraction that binds hearts together is what inspires this collection. (The anonymous romance writer wrote that, not me.)

Pat launches into her short, but motivational story. Running late to a meeting outside Memphis, she jets through a speed trap on the outskirts of the city. Blue lights appear and so does a strapping police officer. It's not a good day for Pat. But wait, earlier in the morning, she lathered herself in the company's Alluring Body Lotion with Pheromones. It worked. The cop forgot all about Pat's excessive acceleration through his snare.

"I can't say it was the lotion, but I can say it made me feel sexy and that's what is important, right ladies?"

There are a lot of "Uh-huhs" and "Oh, yeahs" buzzing. It sounds strangely like a choir of holy-rolling cicadas chirping "amens."

Passion Parties Inc. has a virtual monopoly on selling bedroom gadgets in the South. That's because, unlike in metropolitan areas on the East and West Coast, there are not many stores that carry Pulsing Orbiters and Honey Dippers.

In Arkansas, and throughout Dixie, there are not even that many stores that carry pornography, magazines or otherwise. In Little Rock, the popular place for such raunch is the 12th Street Newstand, which carries a cornucopia of smut and caters to everyone from construction workers to politicos and preachers. Strip joints are banished to industrial zones or out in the sticks where patrons are just as likely to get shot by a deer hunter as see a naked girl twirling tassels on her tits. Southern women have few choices when they want to buy sex toys. They usually have to venture into a storefront head shop staffed with aging hippies and young, glazed-over cannabis fans listening to Widespread Panic. Upscale sexuality boutiques, or lingerie stores that carry such plea-sure devices, are few and far between. Getting off isn't ex-actly the easiest thing to do in the land of Rhett and Scarlett.

Because of a lingering sexual repression in the South, women like Linda make a lot of money. They also become legends in the housewife world alongside Oprah Winfrey and the cast from *The View*. In her modest home in Sheridan, a small rural town about thirty minutes south of Little Rock, an entire room — a virtual sexateria — is dedicated to the busi-ness of creating good feelings and fulfilling fantasies for women who may be stalled in neutral in the bedroom. Linda has fun with her job, driving all over the Natural State to tell women about "the little man in the boat" — that's clitoris for women who feel squeamish directly referring to their plea-sure point. But Linda also takes her business as seriously as a *Fortune* 500 corporate CEO who has a vested interest in her company's stock listings. Linda can be slightly competi-tive wondering how her sales will rank at the end of the year. But unlike a cutthroat CEO, she's never ruthless. Linda eagerly helps other women establish Passion Party busi-nesses in Arkansas, consistently one of the top-selling, if not *the* top-selling, states in the country for the company.

Once a month, Linda hosts minimeetings on Sunday after-noons at Bobbisox, a local bar near the Little Rock airport. These meetings, similar to the first one I attended, are de-signed to help women get a feel for holding a rubber dick in their hands in front of a crowd of potential buyers.

It's an early spring Friday afternoon. I've downed a couple of Bloody Marys at a quaint Mexican restaurant in Maumelle, a fast-growing white-flight community just outside Little Rock. Maumelle is a picture postcard of suburbia — a never-ending series of look-alike brick houses with land-scaped yards. Yelping dogs scamper around in wooden-fenced backyards, and shrieking kids shoot basketballs in driveways. Many of the people who live here would rather take a beating than live in Little Rock, often viewed as a crime-riddled Gotham. I couldn't pay some of the women who live here to visit a Little Rock shopping mall after dark — too dangerous and too scary with all those black kids in gangs running around, they would say.

Maumelle, which means "breasts" in slang French, could easily double as a movie setting for the next *Stepford Wives* movie. For me, a single girl who likes to think herself pretty fearless, Maumelle is a scary place, as frightening for me on a Friday night as the gang-bangin' hip-hop mall is to the soccer mom in the minivan beside me. That's why I always feel the need to down a few strong drinks before interviewing anyone from Maumelle, especially when the subject matter is sex.

The plan is to meet Linda in a supermarket parking lot and follow her to Donna's house. Donna, a thirty-something housewife with three kids, is hosting a Passion Party while her husband and kids spend the evening playing soccer at a nearby field. It's a little after six when we arrive at the gray brick house in a cozy cul-de-sac that reminds me of the type of place I grew up seeing on *Knots Landing*. Donna rushes out to meet Linda as if she is a long-lost friend. Her Clairol-bottled streaked blond hair fresh from the shower drips on her oversize striped polo shirt. She's not ready for her guests, and she knows it.

"I'm a mess," she says in a panic. "And I've got people coming over any minute."

She may be a mess, but her house isn't. When I step into the open living room, I can tell that Donna has watched a lot of home-decorating shows and occasionally busted out the credit card to buy a faux antique mirror or a pastoral painting on the Home Shopping Network. Her house, like many houses in Maumelle, is neat and clean with a decorating style that's hard to describe — suburban safe, I like to call it. Doubtful there's one thing in this house bought at a flea market.

Donna's bookshelf says a lot about who she is. The occasional Danielle Steele or Barbara Taylor Bradford romance: She likes to be swept off her feet sometimes. A few books about relationships: She likes to work on her marriage or give the illusion she does. A mystery or two: probably her husband's favorites. Then I spot a telling sign on the bookshelf: The Left Behind books — every volume of the popular Christian series. Here's a woman who'll whoop it up with her girlfriends about dildos and Coochie cream but cuddle up with apocalyptic literature at bedtime. Only in Arkansas. Only in the Bible Belt.

The party gets started with a bang as thirteen Chatty Cathys gather in Donna's kitchen to get wasted before Linda opens her suitcases packed with three hours of fun.

The drink of choice this evening is Hi-C punch and rum, but there's blush wine for those who can't handle hard liquor. For these women, this party provides a mega-escape from their mundane married lives of carting kids to soccer practice, making peanut butter and jelly sandwiches, and waiting for their husbands to get home every night. Only one of the women is single, but she has a boyfriend who "isn't into trying out new sex things," and only a few of the women work outside the home. In fact, I get the distinct feeling most of these recipe-swapping women cannot stand single career chicks like myself. I am the single stranger who has landed on Planet Housewife. I know nothing about the ingredients in the cream cheese and chocolate chip concoction served with cute butter cookies in front of me. I could care less about the calories in the fudge and pecan bars on the counter. And I have never penciled in a time to have sex with my boyfriend on a refrigerator calendar. I am a stranger in a strange land.

"We have Nicole to thank for this, you know, girls," says a woman hovering over the pungent creamy garlic dip.

Nicole is a boisterous Amazon in her forties with stark silver hair cut in a severe Vidal Sassoon bob. She loves — *loves* — sex toys and hosted a Passion Party — the biggest one in Maumelle history, she says — a few weeks earlier. The sales from that party hit the $3,000 mark. At that event, her husband, Chuck, surprised the girls by buying a basketful of batteries so that no sex toy went home unable to wiggle.

"He is such a sweetheart," Nicole coos. Clearly, no doubt about it, Nicole wins for having the husband of the year. "He misses me already, I bet."

I'm thinking not, imagining a peaceful man enjoying the silence.

It becomes clear that a silent, sarcastic competition is occurring in this designer kitchen on such topics as husbands, vacations in Branson, Missouri, shopping at outlet malls, and gossip about neighbors — whose husbands are doing whom.

Linda is antsy. She wants to get the show on the road but she knows that suburban foreplay filled with Hi-C cocktails and frothy gossip is crucial to loosening up the women. Inhibitions about spending lots of money on lotions, potions, and playthings simply must vanish before she can weave her magic.

The party herd eventually slides away from the dips and chips to the blindfolds and whips. Linda passes out order forms and pencils with penis erasers on their tips. The women giggle.

"I want a bell, I want a bell," Nicole bellows.

The brass handbells are given to women who have bought sex gadgets at other parties. When Linda brings out their favorite delicacy, they ring the bell. Nicole is all too eager to ring her bell. I'm not surprised. This is the woman who whipped out her broken Silver Bullet from her blue jeans pocket.

"Maybe you used it too much," Linda jokes.

"Ha-ha-ha-ha, yeah, maybe I did." Nicole is not joking.

Everyone sits in a circle, some on couches and some on the floor, while Linda passes around the new romantic bath line. It intrigues some of the women, but I get the feeling everyone is just politely fondling the jars of bath salts. What they really want is to fondle the hardware. Linda, too, knows she makes her money from selling $175 sex toys.

I realize as they continue downing their rummy punch and I sip on straight Coke that all of these women aren't chummy best friends. It becomes very clear that several of them don't even know each other when one woman asks another one what her husband does.

"My husband and Donna's and Carol's husbands all work together. They sell rubber. Get it, wink, wink."

Yes, we get it. It's sophomoric humor like this that cracks me up the most about these women. I get the impression they think this kind of talk is edgy and daring. Maybe I feel like I am superior, worldlier than these supermarket mamas. But maybe I shouldn't — the more rum punch consumed, the more ribald the conversation becomes.

"Their husbands are always kidding mine," Donna explains to Linda. "They walk past him and say 'Is that a Chapstick or you just happy to see me?'"

The women laugh. "We know now why she wanted the extra-big vibrator."

"Yeah, whatever," says Donna. "I swallow and you don't."

"Yeah, we know you do."

Heavens! One minute they babble about perfumed potpourri, the next they confess sucking their husbands' dicks and swallowing what they won't allow on their sheets. But just when I think I am in the middle of a raunchy good time, the women lapse into suburbia speak. They worry about the stains that various lubricants cause on expensive sheets with four hundred thread counts. I didn't even know sheets had thread counts. Beam me up.

"I will not use anything, I don't care how fun the stuff is, if it is going to stain my sheets," says one woman. She's adamant, too.

"Put down a vinyl sheet or a Twister game board," suggests Linda. "Just slide all over the bed. Have fun!"

Nicole, who I pegged as a wild child in the bedroom, looks appalled at the suggestion.

"Are you kidding me?" she asks. "No way."

"Really, think about the mess you'll have to clean up," says another woman. "That's worse than the sheets."

Horrors! News alert: Sex can be messy! I bet none of these women have ever slept in a wet spot in their lives. In fact, sadly, their husbands aren't prone to spewing their spunk wherever the urge strikes. That's why they go wild when the Gigi comes out of Linda's suitcase. Gigi is a pink silicone male masturbation sleeve that stretches to accommodate all penis sizes — from a Chapstick to a Magnum. It's a well-modeled vagina that has a tight opening and is lined inside with ribbed texturing for amazing sensations. Who knew suburban shafts were allowed to feel so good? And it's not messy — a good thing, as Martha Stewart would say. Because Gigi stretches in ways I didn't even know man-made objects could stretch, it can fold over the tip of the penis so that orgasmic juices are neatly contained.

Linda pours a small dab of Slippery Stuff into the Gigi and begins to lubricate the plastic tube as if she is greasing a pan for a Saturday afternoon bake-off at the church. The more lubed the tube the more stretchy the shaft. It's mesmerizing to watch Linda's experienced hands work over Gigi as visions of my boyfriend's screaming orgasms dance in my head.

But Gigi can be a dangerous toy, Linda warns. Once, the story goes, a customer got so wrapped up in sliding Gigi up and down that the tube flew off of her husband's cock and hit a picture above the bed, which fell down on the woman and cut her face. Ouch.

"Oh yeah, oh yeah," Nicole chirps as she rings her bell.

Linda pulls out her sample bottle of Pure Satisfaction. She gives her spiel about the product and tells the women they can have a dab of it. She encourages the women to go into the bathroom and put it on their clit. A few of the woman accept the challenge. One woman looks intrigued, but shy.

"You want to try?" Linda asks.

"It's that time of the month for me. I'll pass, thanks."

Nicole says no, too, because she is an old pro with Pure Satisfaction. "Chuck squirted that stuff out like it was hand soap. I told him he was going to catch his one-eyed monster on fire but he didn't listen," she says.

"Did it?" asks Linda.

"Oh honey, he was on F-I-R-E. But that stuff is expensive. I told him not to use it all in one night."

Hell, I think, too much of a good thing might kill a man in these parts. Curious about Pure Satisfaction, I decide to stay away. Such concoctions often lead me down a troubled path, or into a court deposition.

Denise returns after a few minutes in the bathroom. She is twenty-three, a plain-Jane type with acne and a boyfriend who doesn't like anything but standard missionary-position sex. She is giddy, and her cheeks flushed, as she sits down. "It works fast," she says checking the Pure Satisfaction box on her order form.

It becomes clear pretty damn quick that Nicole must overshadow everyone in the room. If someone has had sex on a trapeze, she's had sex on a tightrope. She also likes to think she is the gossip of Maumelle, spewing juicy tidbits of rumor whenever the chance — or a break in conversation — arises.

"At your party, Nicole, I sold thirty-four bottles of Pure Satisfaction," Linda says.

"That was such a biiiiig party, wasn't it?"

"Yeah, one of my biggest. That one woman bought four hundred dollars worth of stuff."

"Who? Who?" Nicole asks.

"She was the one sitting on the stairs, didn't say much," Linda says.

Nicole ponders this and then releases an "Oooooooohhhh. She works for my husband. Shhhhh, don't say anymore."

"Who is it?" asks Donna, as she sits back down on the floor. She had to excuse herself a few minutes earlier when the family terrier consumed a pack of cigarettes left by some Friday-night wild woman on the deck.

"We can't talk about it," Nicole says, winking at Donna, who nods. She's down with the secret sign. I'm not. I feel more and more like I did the year that I signed up for third-level French in high school. Each day, the teacher spoke for a solid hour in French. I could never translate any of it into English. Just like now. I absolutely cannot translate Suburbanese into Single Girl speak.

There's a book Linda promotes at her parties called *The Complete Manual of Sexual Positions*. The pictures fascinate me, like a sexual jigsaw puzzle, all the twists and turns couples do for pleasure. I'd like to say I've tried half of these 174 positions but I haven't. But I'm certain by this point in the party that neither has Nicole. The tip-off came when she blared: "Chuck says the door is going to be locked tonight."

"He's not going to let you in?" Donna asked.

"No, girlfriend. We are going to tear it up. No kids allowed."

Laughter spills around the room, but I think Nicole is lying. Nicole likes to picture herself this vixen, knowing more about sex than any other woman in the room. She gives the impression that she has sex in places no one has ever considered before — on top of the washing machine in the laundry room, on top of the island in the kitchen, or in the back of the minivan while waiting for the boys to finish soccer practice. And maybe she does in her mind or with someone else's husband. But not with Chuck. My guess: They have gas-bill sex, as my male friends who live in suburbia call it. That's when you have sex as often as the gas bill arrives in the mail — and I don't think shut-off notices count.

Linda is losing control of the party. Some of the women have ventured out to the deck to smoke cigarettes. Some look bored. Others are back in the kitchen eating the wacky chocolate chip dip. Linda passes around the sex positions book.

"Eeew, people do this?" Nicole says. "And who has time for this many positions?"

"Here's what you do," Linda says. "Get the book and put numbers in a hat. Before he leaves for work, make him draw a number. Whatever number he draws is the position you do when he comes home from work. Gives him something to think about all day."

"Who has time for that?" Nicole asks. "We schedule sex on the calendar."

I win my own imaginary bet. Anyone who schedules sex

on a refrigerator calendar has gas-bill sex. No spontaneity allowed.

Linda revs up the show by bringing out more toys — strange-looking ones that pop open even my experienced eyes. There's the Magic Monarch with rotating pearls and butterfly wings for "earth-quaking orgasms." The Super Tongue, a superfly jelly tongue, designed to simulate cunnilingus in five speeds. The She Shell that gently kisses the clitoris. Oohs and aaahs hum around the room. After a while, all the dildos look the same — I figure that's what a hooker says, too, after a rough Friday night.

But then Linda whips out a bizarre contraption. Initially, I think it's a love swing but then realize that it is actually some sort of strap-on gizmo that women, or men for that matter, can wear. Shockingly, it comes complete with a phallic adornment. Soon, it becomes clear that the Venus, as the catalog calls it, can be used for a woman's pleasure or her husband's — if he likes a little back-door action.

Diana sits on the end of the couch, and she hasn't said a whole lot during the evening. She and Donna are friends and for some reason, her husband is staying at Donna's tonight. But Donna's husband and kids will be there. And there's nothing sexual going on at all. At all, she stresses.

"Better not be," Diana caws.

"Please, hardly, no way," Donna says.

Not exactly a bombshell but the idea that Diana protests so much makes my eyebrows raise. But then, she drops the one that stuns everyone: She owns a Venus.

"You mean you, you do it with your husband *that* way?" asks Donna, laughing at the thought.

Nicole hasn't said anything in a few minutes. She's awash

in a rum-punch haze, staring at one toy after another as they come her way. But this question wakes her up.

"I don't understand," Nicole says, genuinely confused.

"You wear it and, you know, fuck your husband," says Martha, an overweight woman who has hardly said ten words the entire evening.

"I don't do that on David. Just because I have one doesn't mean that's what I do," Diana says. "I've cut off all of these little straps. I use it, not David."

"How?" asks Nicole even more confused as she struggles to figure out how the straps work on the Venus.

"I just put it right there in my doo-lolly and let it go to work," Diana says.

As I am trying to contain my laughter — I've never heard that called a doo-lolly before but decide that I'll name mine the Dalai Lama. Then, Tabitha pipes in with an unexpected confession.

"I strap it on and use it while I vacuum," she says.

My eyes pop out of my head like a crazed cartoon character's — aw-hooga! Nicole is stunned. The entire room stares at Tabitha. My assessment: You never know what someone has up their doo-lolly.

"Fire up the Venus Penis and the Oreck Deluxe," says Donna, laughing at her guest's revelation, although she doesn't seem that shocked.

Linda tells me that she has one customer who vacuums her own house, then volunteers to vacuum her mother's and mother-in-law's houses all in the name of pleasure. Note to self: The Oreck Deluxe is the vacuum cleaner of choice in yuppie town, and the attachment of choice, no question, is the Venus.

It's well past nine o'clock, and the evening is unwinding with giggles and horniness.

Most of the dip and chips have vanished. Nicole has rung the happy bell so many times my ears are ringing. And I'm still in shock about women vacuuming while coming like an experienced porn star. It's more than the senses can handle.

Linda is ready to make money and make some women blissful. You can see it in her eyes, almost as if they are saying, "Come to Mama. Mama make you happy." She directs the women into her surreal makeshift sales boudoir, Donna's adolescent daughter's bedroom.

"I like to give women privacy," says Linda. "They may go out there and show what they bought to the room but I think it's nice to let them buy in private. Makes them more comfortable."

The women exit with their plastic bags of plastic prizes, acting like little girls on Christmas morning. "I'll have to stop by the store and get some batteries before I darken the bedroom door," says Nicole. I imagine her husband will already be asleep by the time she gets home with her sack of good vibrations.

Linda later tells me she made close to a grand on this party. Not a bad night, she says. Not indeed, I say, knowing that it's no easy gig working as a suitcase-toting Dr. Ruth to a room full of Southern women.

kickin' it
with **skirtman**

Skirt Lengths and Liberals

LITTLE ROCK, ARKANSAS — For months, Skirtman eluded me.

"You know the guy I'm talking about," a friend insisted. "He has these great muscular legs, better than any woman I know, and wears these really short skirts."

No, I could honestly say I had never seen such a creature. And in Little Rock, someone described like this wouldn't get easily lost in the crowd.

One summer afternoon, at the opening of a new patio for a local restaurant, I spotted him. The first thing that caught my eye was his wardrobe — a silver lamé minidress that would have made Diana Ross and the Supremes pea-green with envy. He pranced around the restaurant in his shimmering getup, his aerobicized tanned legs accented by stiletto heels. He carried a cute vintage handbag that screamed Doris Day.

Every person in the restaurant, and I do mean every one, stopped and stared, but Skirtman walked around as if he was sporting cargo shorts and a T-shirt. He grabbed a packet of sugar and walked back to the table where he sat happily sipping his coffee, his legs daintily crossed. A B-list Hollywood television star with Arkansas connections who happened to be in the coffee shop freaked when he saw Skirtman. Surely, I thought, he had seen such men in La-La Land where he lived.

"You won't believe this, but that guy is famous," the Hollywood star said, motioning to Skirtman.

"Oh yeah?" asked an obviously smitten young woman.

"Yeah, a friend of mine in Paris sent me his Web site. Everyone goes to it," he said. "Here, you've got to take a picture of me with him." The TV star handed a disposable camera to the girl and walked over to Skirtman. He put his arm around him and they chatted for a few minutes. Skirtman took the situation in stride, and I'm not even sure if he realized the actor starred on television. Skirtman just acted like the local celebrity that he is, pausing for a moment to have his photo snapped with a fan.

Skirtman sits at a small round table for two by the front door of Sufficient Grounds, the funky coffeehouse where I first spotted him. Sufficient Grounds is located in Hillcrest, a neighborhood with the most liberal zip code in the state. The colorful former two-story residence is popular among high school students, soccer moms, and lawyers who crave a little hipness but also want to feel warm and comfy while drinking their exotic coffees. This place is also a favorite hangout for Catholic schoolgirls to sashay around in their short plaid-skirted uniforms. Skirtman isn't exactly your typical suburbanite, but he does wear plaid skirts, and very short ones at that. I'm not talking kilts here, either.

With a smile, Skirtman firmly shakes my hand and introduces himself. He looks like a neat and fit Ken doll who enjoyed a wild-and-crazy shopping spree in Barbie's closet. With short blond hair and rimless glasses, Skirtman — alias Dale Miller — could pass for anyone's brother, son, or father.

Well, almost. Silver dangling earrings hang from his pierced ears. Rhinestones dot his gauzy black blouse that is tucked neatly into a micromini pleated dark plaid skirt. Sheer jet black stockings cover his hairless firm legs. Simple black pumps, suitable for the office, complete the outfit. Granted, he's quite the sight to see.

I already know a lot about Dale from his Web site.

Fact: He likes to fly kites.

Fact: He generated controversy at the university where he works by wearing a skirt.

Fact: He's a computer geek.

Fact: His favorite ice cream is Baskin-Robbins Love Potion #31.

Fact: He has lived his entire life in Arkansas.

Fact: If he could be any Winnie-the-Pooh character, he'd be Tigger. Why? He can just enjoy whatever comes along in life.

But questions swirl about this man who prefers skirts to pants. Like, why does he wear one? I'm a girl and I hate skirts and dresses, panty hose and heels. Is Dale a transvestite? He doesn't look like a woman, but more a like a gender-blended centaur. Does he shave or wax? And what exactly is under those skirts? Boxers or briefs?

Dale orders a coffee concoction with whipped cream. "Do you mind if I go ahead and eat my whipped cream before it melts?"

"No, no," I say, never wanting to keep a man away from something creamy and delectable.

This is the biographical info I initially learn from Dale: He was born in a Catholic hospital in Little Rock and grew up as a Southern Baptist in Sylvan Hills, the kind of place that can breed redneck conformity in some and bring out latent desires in others. Like so many kids who later in life hear their nonconformity calling, high school for Dale wasn't the most pleasant of experiences. Dale says that even in high school he longed to wear a skirt, but he didn't.

"I wish I had. If I could go back, I'd do it," he says.

Dale was obsessed with computers before such gadgets were cool. If he had grown up in Seattle, Washington, he could have been Bill Gates's business partner. He admits he was a nerd. Like the majority of the state's high school students, he went away to the big campus in the Ozarks — the University of Arkansas in Fayetteville, home of the Razorbacks. His time there was limited to two years because he studied less than he partied. Dale tried on his first skirt in Fayetteville when he was nineteen but, shy and not yet confident enough, he dismissed his notion.

Dale moved on to the University of Arkansas campus in Little Rock, still wearing pants, and earned a degree in computer science. But while he was there, Dale performed some groundbreaking computer wizardry. He helped create a computer program that linked several universities in the state to each other — a forerunner of what we now call the Internet.

A bad marriage encourages unusual behavior in folks, and Dale is no exception. With his relationship disintegrating, Dale, in his midthirties, searched for an escape route from matrimony. He found it in the home of Mickey Mouse and ska and rap groups — Anaheim, California — at a computer convention surrounded by science-fiction buffs and computer know-it-alls.

"If you are going to try something, try it at a conference full of nerds. They are the least judgmental group you'll ever see," he says.

Among the kinder and gentler love of the technology geeks, Dale discovered his identity. He explored a new side of shopping, dismissing the men's department and finding a fresh exciting universe in the woman's department. Piece by piece, he morphed into Skirtman and walked boldly into the southern California computer conference.

"I figured no one was going to care, and they didn't," he recalls with a shrug.

Even if his fellow computer geeks didn't give a damn about his attire, his wife certainly did. When Dale arrived home from Anaheim wearing a skirt when he exited the plane, his wife had a hissy fit. She couldn't, wouldn't, deal with it. And Dale? Having reached the point of no return in the relationship, he just didn't care about saving his marriage anymore.

"She was a good little Southern Baptist girl, and it didn't work that way. This is not how men dress down here," Dale says.

Indeed, not. Men don't prance around in skirts and heels in Dixie. They wear Brooks Brothers business suits and Cole Haan shoes. They like plaid flannel shirts and jeans on the weekend. They prefer collared polo shirts and starched khakis at the country club. If they are more Bubba than banker, men may wear a NASCAR or some other sports-themed T-shirt and camouflage pants with work boots.

In Dale's early days as Skirtman, his wardrobe was a tad more conventional. He often wore a man's dress shirt, a tie, and a blazer with his skirts. It looked like he just accidentally picked up his wife's skirt instead of his pants on the way out the door to the office. While his top half looked guy-normal, his bottom half was slightly off-kilter, commanding a double-take from those who passed him. He calls those days his frumpy conservative days.

"I lost a bunch of weight so that opened up a whole new way to dress," he says.

Boy, did it.

Nowadays he wears what he likes to see women wear — tight and revealing skirts and blouses. He calls his wardrobe "tacky," and he loves it, especially in summer.

"You can wear less and I do," Dale says.

Sitting in the coffeehouse with Dale, I notice more women say hello to him than men do. Some young college guys who look as if they could be in a garage band also say hello to him. He's a java fiend, and so are they. His friend Julia sits at a nearby table working on her college homework. Once, the pair dressed up in matching sequined dresses that laced up on the sides and went out on the town. The sexy dress posed a problem for Dale. The outfit, a creation with slits and straps near the panty-line area, just didn't lend itself to a thong. Dale didn't let that little snag deter him.

"I wasn't sure what to wear under it, so I made an over-the-shoulder thong that hid everything and made it look like I was wearing nothing," he says. "I'm a fan of thongs."

So the answer to that boxers or brief question: thongs. Of all varieties. I'm glad that's settled. Another cup of coffee, please.

Wearing a skirt when you're a Southern man generates its own kind of adventure, er, trouble. Dale likes to push buttons and make people look twice, or thrice on a good day. While he has gotten used to the doubletakes, especially in Little Rock, he also often finds himself in a more serious pickle while trying to defend his dress.

Dilemma number one: church.

For years, when he was a married man, Dale attended Immanuel Baptist Church, a historic downtown church and one of the largest congregations in Little Rock. It's also the home church of Bill Clinton. The minister at the church often defended and prayed for B.C., as I like to call the former prez, during the turbulent days of scandal and impeachment. Many well-to-do people and society wanna-bes attend Immanuel Baptist Church, which has recently undertaken a mammoth multimillion-dollar construction project in a ritzier area of town to create one of the largest houses of Jesus in the state.

Because of his high-tech savvy, Dale enjoyed serving on the church's television ministry and making sure the sound and visual equipment were in tip-top working order. Dale also set up scripture and titles at the bottom of the screen. He often went to the church to make sure everything was ready for Sunday mornings. One Saturday, he popped into church wearing a skirt. He attended to the technology matters and left. The next day, he went to church wearing pants and ran the television switcher. None of the congregation seemed the wiser to Dale's preferable type of attire as they shook hands and said hello. But he received a call a few days later from a prominent well-known Little Rock personality and Immanuel Baptist Church member.

"You need to separate yourself from the television ministry," the businessman told Dale. He also instructed Dale to return a set of keys to the church office.

Dale, who once taught children Sunday school in his pre-Skirtman days, thought, Who cares what I wear, God doesn't? But apparently someone did.

The next Sunday, Dale, a little perturbed by his church dissing, entered the church just like he did any Sunday of any week, but this time he wore a skirt. People looked, a few said hello, but most just pretended he wasn't in the sanctuary. Thinking that church members were understanding, Dale attended church the next Sunday in a skirt, and this time, an usher stopped him in the foyer. Soon, an associate pastor appeared and requested that Dale not attend church in a skirt.

"What bothered me was that he took time to alert an usher to stop me when he had had the entire previous week to talk to me about it. He had my cell phone number, my home phone, work phone, pager number, e-mail . . ."

Dale trails off shaking his head. Needless to say, Immanuel Baptist officials say they don't remember this at all, and Dale doesn't go to church anymore, saying organized religion isn't for him. He's visited a few churches around the city, but more and more, Dale just doesn't bother with religion.

"Jesus wore a robe. I wear a skirt. What's the big deal?"

The big deal, many people say, comes from the Bible, Deuteronomy 22:5. "The woman shall not wear that which pertaineth unto a man, neither shall a man put on a woman's garment: for all who do so are abomination unto the Lord thy God."

Dale points out that in the same chapter, it states not to wear garments of mixed fibers such as cotton and polyester or leather and lace, and to build parapets around the edges of your roof so that no one can fall off and hurt themselves.

He's certainly done his homework in this area.

Dilemma number two: Hooters.

Dale likes to look at pretty girls just like any other straight American guy. That's why he likes Hooters, the chain restaurant and bar with waitresses in supertight T-shirts. But when a guy who has better legs than some of the servers struts in wearing heels and a miniskirt, watch out. Dale was a hit among some Hooters chicks and many of them posed for photographs with him. He was a happy guy who wanted to show his pictures to the world, and so he posted the pictures on his Web site.

Uh-oh.

Trouble arrived in the form of a letter written by the chain's attorney with lots of legal mumbo jumbo. Dale had violated some sort of copyright laws by featuring the pictures on his personal Web site. Never mind, he says, that he actually bought the pictures from the restaurant. He fired a letter off to the attorney, rejecting her claims, removed the pictures for a while, and went on with his life.

"I think it was because I had a skirt on," he says.

Probably because his legs looked better, I say. Women will put up with a lot from a man, but they draw the line at being out-gammed.

Dilemma number three: college.

Dale works at the local university as a computer systems programmer. A few years ago, after he launched his personal Web site with pictures of himself in skirts, he started wearing them to work, and some students in this conservative city didn't like it. Both male and female students said that there was nothing to gain by a man wearing a skirt. Other students said Dale wore skirts for attention.

The chancellor said he received complaints and some callers to the university expressed disgust with a man wearing a skirt. Dale was criticized by college officials for standing in front of a university sign in a skirt for a newspaper photograph. The university asked Dale to rethink his workplace attire. So he did. He now wears slacks and shirts just like any other boring American male in the South, so as to not intimidate the populace.

It was during the university controversy that Dale became known as Skirtman when a local television station coined the term, and his life hasn't been the same since. His business cards even have SKIRTMAN printed on them, and his credit card has a picture of himself in a skirt.

One who enjoys stirring the pot, I decide to invite Dale to spend Valentine's Day with me. He seems sad that he'll be alone on Valentine's Day, because after all, he tells me, he is a romantic at heart. Women, more times than not, can't get into the way Dale dresses. Honestly, some women like to be the one in the family to wear the dress. They don't like competition.

Friends of mine, liberal Democrats, are hosting the party, but I decide to keep my Valentine's date a secret from them. To give Dale the attention he deserves, I opt for black velvet pants and a long velvet coat with a fur collar. Hopefully, it won't take away from his Valentine's surprise.

Dale and I meet again at his favorite coffeehouse before heading out to the party. Dale sits in the spot that he likes by the large plateglass window, because he can watch girls while reading under the nearby lamp. Walking in to meet him, I'm not sure what to expect, but whatever I was thinking it wasn't what I see when I arrive. There he is in an above-the-knee red skirt with a diagonal ruffle highlighting the split. A white rayon tank top with a red heart and the word "Love" highlighted in rhinestones snugs his chest. White pumps and a matching handbag complete the assemble. Indeed, quite the getup.

"I know it's a no-no in February to wear white shoes, but I don't care. I can wear white shoes if I want, if I am wearing a red skirt and a tight tank top," he says.

I laugh. Chatting for a few minutes, I mention there is a drag show at Vino's, a pizza dive downtown. Interestingly enough, Dale says he doesn't like drag shows, but he is ready to head to the party. Skirtman doesn't like drag shows? Go figure. Too much competition, perhaps? Dale drives a sparkly silver sports car with a vanity license plate that reads SKRTMAN. Cute. One thing can be said about Dale: He likes who he is.

The party, held in a box-shaped World War II-era home in a part of town known for its Dick-and-Jane quaintness, is in full-throttle when we arrive. A few men in their early twenties gawk at Dale as we walk up the concrete path, but they say or whisper nothing. Once inside, everyone smiles and introduces themselves. It doesn't take more than ten minutes to realize one thing: Dale will be the hit of the party.

My prediction is correct-o-mundo. The women love him like he's Santa Claus or the Easter Bunny. They ask him about his outfit, gush over his funky little tank top, and pepper him with questions about his wardrobe. Nearly every female in the room wants her picture taken with Dale. He obliges, gobbling up every second of the attention like a PMSing woman devouring chocolate kisses.

A newly elected male legislator who is learning the political ropes of Arkansas keeps staring at Dale with goofy wide eyes but doesn't really talk to him. Not a good way to get a vote, even from a man in a skirt. A few other boy guests shake his hand and chat him up like he is the next political hotshot. Dale flirts and floats around the party like he is Zeus, and I stand around watching, munching on some fruit and cheese. He passes out business cards and makes a lot of new friends. By the end of the night, Dale owns the party. I half-expected someone to be appalled. Perhaps that would have happened if I had taken him to a Republican shindig.

"I've never been scared in my life, but I try to avoid the Bubbas, say in a bar or at the mall," Dale says.

The Park Plaza Mall isn't a pleasant place for Dale to go. He doesn't like it because groups of young male teens who haven't yet discovered their own fetishes in life harass him. They follow him around, laughing at him and cackling mean jokes. Dale is comfortable with himself and says frankly he doesn't need that kind of heckling when he's shopping for a skirt at The Limited or Express. If there is something he is dying to buy at the mall, he goes when the bratty teenage punks are in school.

Obnoxious teenage boys aren't the only ones who question Dale's sense of style. He's had clerks in dress shops around Little Rock refuse to let him try on clothes. But honestly, Dale doesn't like to pay retail for clothes. He prefers hunting for bargains at local used clothing stores and on eBay. The automatic perception, says Dale, is that if you see a man who likes women's clothing, he must be gay or he is in some transgender mode trying to decide if he is a woman or a man. Since he's not gay and doesn't wear makeup or wigs with his skirts, he can't be put in a nice little box with a label. That's exactly how Dale enjoys life: by keeping people guessing, even his dates. He dated one woman for nearly three years, but the relationship failed because she wanted only one of them — preferably her — to wear a skirt or dress. Dale preferred to dress the way he wanted, and so eventually the relationship faded.

Another time, Dale and a date both dressed in skirts while they were in Dallas. The date, who looked babelicious in her micromini and sexy high heels, stood at the bar waiting for a table. Dale was standing near a couple of guys listening to them talk about how hot his date was. When the hostess called their names for the table, Dale and his date connected and walked away together.

"It totally threw them off. They weren't expecting that at all," Dale recalls, laughing.

Still, if Dale lived in a more progressive non-Southern city, his dating prospects might be more open-minded and tolerant of his dress habits.

"Most women in Arkansas haven't been out of the state, so

to them I'm that weirdo," he says. "I like the way I dress, but it's definitely hurts my ability to get a date. Down here, the male is the one who asks for the date, not the female, and I'm bad about meeting people."

That's why Dale has posted his dating resume online. His qualifications?

- *Capable of compiling lists of why women should go out with me.*
- *It does not bruise my ego to have a woman do something that is traditionally considered "man's work."*
- *I am gainfully employed and have a comfortable lifestyle.*
- *Too honest for my own good.*
- *Willing to be strict or a pushover as necessary.*
- *Able to write Web pages that make women laugh.*
- *Not usually thought of as a "boring and unattractive blob of organic matter."*

If women saw Dale's legs, they certainly wouldn't consider him a blob of anything.

How short of a skirt can a man get away with wearing?

That's the question of the night in Dale's house in the middle of the woods near Chenal, a tony area of town where new money likes to park its Lincoln Navigators and a Lexus or two. Dale's house is not one of the nouveau castles with a three-car garage. Instead, his modest flat-roofed house blends in with the woods around it. Behind the house sits a machine shop owned by Dale's landlords. Without looking really hard, no one would ever find this secret hideaway. An array of candles sits on the mantle in the den while a clock ticks off the minutes. A couple of computers rest on a desk near a patio door. The screen saver on one of the computers is a tanned naked beauty with long blond hair running on the beach. Three cats scamper around Dale's bare feet. His wardrobe this evening: a blue T-shirt and tight blue-jean hot pants with a carpenter loop on one side.

Dale thinks if someone is comfortable with their body, they shouldn't let fashion rules dictate their wardrobe nor let what others think have an influence. Take his slinky black halter dress, a throwback to the golden disco days of Studio 54, made from stretchy fabric with a hip-high side split and a plunging neckline. A small rhinestone clasp holds the dress together. Once again, Dale engineered a black thong to hide his private parts before he wore the dress to the coffeehouse. Two different women, both relatively thin, approached Dale and said the same thing, "I wish I could wear that dress."

"I said you can wear this dress, but they didn't think they had the body to pull it off. Of course, they could have worn it," he said. "Some of my outfits just wouldn't work on someone a size 28W. In other cases, it is simply that they have been conditioned to think that only someone with a perfect body should show it off. I think our culture tends to make women insecure about their bodies. I wish that was not the case, because I like to look."

Dale says he thinks some of the women like what he wears and find it sexy. But in their real lives, they wouldn't dare strut about town in his getups for fear of being labeled slutty. Other women tend to be more practical than Dale, who is as far from that as I am from starting for the Razorback football team.

One of Dale's shortest skirts is twelve inches from waist to hem. Yes, that's shorter than the skirts go-go dancers used to wear on *Laugh-In*. His latest purchase from eBay makes me look twice and giggle. It's a pink sweater skirt with knitted white hearts at the bottom and a matching pink sweater vest with knitted white teddy bears on it. White teddy bear buttons accent the ensemble. Dale is giddy about the purchase.

"If I am going to stir things up, I might as well do a good job," he says, holding the small skirt — a junior size 11 — up to himself.

If the pink girlie outfit doesn't make people look three times, certainly Dale's swimsuit will — a skimpy red suspender one-piece thong with a cup for his private package. Dale wears the suit wherever he can get away with it, but seldom at a public pool, he says. Initially, the swimsuit was a shocking hot pink, but Dale thought that was too wild for even him. He decided to dye the garment red before going to a foam party at a local club. Dale goes to foam parties? The thought boggles my mind. Pulling clothes from his closet, I feel like I'm visiting Auntie Mame instead of a university teacher with a penchant for skirts.

Soon, it is time for me to leave Dale's house. As I get ready to leave, he flips on the porch light and watches me walk to the car to make sure I get in it safely. He stands on the side patio, waving, just like my mom and dad, until I am out of sight. It's a reflection of normalcy, I think on my drive back into the city lights, of how Dale Miller aka Skirtman is like any other Arkansan. Albeit with better legs.

there she is, miss gay america

Drag droppings, Divas and Charlie Rose

LITTLE ROCK, ARKANSAS — I have never felt less feminine in my life.

As I walk up the metal steps to Backstreet, a lesbian bar next door to Discovery, the most popular gay club in Arkansas and one of the largest in the South, the heel on my black mule somehow gets hung up. Clumsily, I fall up the stairs. It's not really the coolest thing to showcase my inability to walk in heels when I'll soon be surrounded by drag queens who effortlessly strut around in stilettos as if they were flip-flops.

My search at the moment is for Dominique Sanchez, Miss Gay America 2003. I've seen his tiara-topped picture on the Internet in full-on drag-queen regalia, and he's gorgeous. Walking into the dark club, I tell a man that I'm looking for Dominique.

"Follow me," he says, leading me to a back room that features a round stage adorned with black velvet and gold satin curtains, a long bar, and a disco ball, natch. He waves at a willowy black man with a short ponytail who is talking on a cell phone.

"That's him, right there. He'll be with you in a minute," the man says, turning to walk away.

Dominique waves to me. If I ever get in trouble and decide to make a run from the cops, remind me to get a drag queen to do my makeup. The transformation from glamour diva to plain-Jack, everyday dude is amazing. I'd never recognize Dominique in his civilian gear.

"Hey there," he says, shaking my hand. I immediately notice his long fingernails. Mine have never been that long in my life. "Just have a seat. It'll all get started in just a while."

Dominique invited me to attend the Miss Gay America Retreat 2003 so I can get a feel for what the pageant is like. This retreat offers pageant promoters, contestants, and a handful of the curious a chance to learn all about MGA — that's short for Miss Gay America. The room buzzes with a lot of Gap and Banana Republic fashionista men, hugging each other like long-lost shipmates. Beside me, another woman sits at a small round table. Across the room, another woman — or is that a man? — stands in deep conversation. It breaks down to 2.5 women (I'm just not sure about that one person) and about twenty-five gay men.

I plop down on a high bar stool at a table. In the time it takes to say Liza Minelli, a man passes out red folders decorated with a sticker of Dominque's glam MGA picture. Oooh, the juicy, dishy secrets about the pageant all lie within these folders, filled with an agenda and pageant rules. I can't wait. Rock and roll!

Drum roll, please! There he is. Norman Jones — also known as Norma Kristie, Miss Gay America 1973. The owner of Miss Gay America, he's an elusive chap who looks more like he is about to set sail on a yacht than lead a discussion for pageant poodles. If he ever got tired of promoting pageants, Norman could definitely find work as a Ralph Lauren model. A fiftyish man with tanned skin, Norman wears jeans, leather clogs, a white T-shirt, and a baseball cap. Under the cap, he's tied a bandana, but a lock or two of gray hair peeks out from beneath it.

Norman sits smack-dab in the middle of the long conference table in front of us, with Dominique on one side of him and a bespectacled man on the other. Because she's the most recent Miss Gay America, Dominique speaks first.

"This has been the most incredible journey of my life," she says in a drawl. "It's not an easy job. You have to be well-planned and well-organized. People will critique you to hell."

With that warning about the hard life of a pageant princess, the afternoon kicks off. Norman invites everyone to introduce themselves.

"Who are you, little darling?" he croons, looking my way.

Why do I always have to be the one to go first? Jeez-freakin'-Louise. I introduce myself, and everyone smiles at me before moving on to the next introduction. Good, they're a friendly bunch.

The pageant folks have two bitch sessions a year, and this is one of them. The retreat's focus is on hashing out issues in the Miss Gay America pageant system, such as crown standardization, rules for creative costume, and prop size. These are intensely critical issues for pageant promoters and contestants, who spend thousands of dollars participating in preliminary pageants around the country before competing in the big enchilada. The topic on everyone's mind this afternoon is crowns. In a room where image is everything, this crown business is serious. And honestly, what drag queen doesn't want a big-ass, sparkling bejeweled crown?

But the concern on the table is cost. Crowns are expensive, especially the ones Norman wants promoters to buy for preliminary pageants. Horror of horrors, we soon learn that some crowns out there are made of nothing more than cheap wire with a rhinestone in the middle.

"So what?" says one promoter. "I'm losing money by having to update crowns. For thirty years, we didn't have any standardization and now to throw more money at a promoter and tell him to buy crowns that look better, it's not fair."

That comment starts the party in a flamethrowing way. The debate rages about some winners wearing expensive crowns with sparkly high-end stones, which catch colors of the prism and shimmer so much more nicely than the dreaded crystals other winners are forced to wear. Norman suggests that promoters buy one high-quality crown and pass it on after each pageant to the new winner, instead of letting the outgoing winner keep it.

To look as professional as the Miss America pageant (the one with swimsuit honeys), every pageant from the ground up needs a nice crown that fits the standard rules set by the MGA board. Find a way to afford them, says the panel.

Norman suggests following the lead of a local MGA preliminary pageant in Arkansas. That promoter sold twenty-five-dollar sponsorship certificates to people who wanted to support the pageant. He raised more than one thousand bucks out of the endeavor.

"Don't say that's so tacky, or that's so Arkansas. Don't

scoff. It works and increases the level of support," Norman says.

On and on, the queens rage about this crown issue. I've entered a mind-boggling universe of crowns, scepters, glitter, and glamour with more rules than the Homeland Security Department.

Break time. Whew. You could cut the diva tension in here with a nail file.

Little Rock may seem an odd choice for the headquarters of a pageant dedicated to recognizing the best drag queens in the nation but, surprisingly, this city has a large population of gays and lesbians. Both Backstreet and Discovery could rival dance clubs in Los Angeles and New York City. These two places, the largest dance club and gay entertainment complex in Arkansas, are popular classy nightspots for gays and straights, but it's clear to the heteros who dance the night away that gays rule these places, so no redneck gay bashing allowed.

Norman Jones is an enigmatic fellow who owns Discovery, Backstreet, and the pageant franchise and doesn't have time to sit down and tell the curious about his life. Through careful research, though, I've gleaned a few details for my dossier about Mr. MGA. He's from a small town in south Arkansas but grew up in Malvern, the same place that bred Billy Bob Thornton, which is only a hop, skip, and a jump from Hot Springs, where Bill Clinton spent his teenage years. Norman served in the Navy during the Vietnam War and ended up living in the nation's capital for a few years. After the military, he returned to his native state and earned his teaching degree from Ouachita Baptist University, the same place that our Southern Baptist governor Mike Huckabee earned his degree. Norman taught school for a while but couldn't handle the unruly kids so he went to work for the state. Later, he saw the light and bought a nightclub. Then over time, Norman bought more and more nightclubs, eventually creating the empire he owns today.

As for Miss Gay America, Norman was a visionary. His interest in female impersonation and entertaining began when he was serving his country in Washington, D.C. From there, he entered the Miss Gay America pageant in 1973 in Nashville, Tennessee, at the Watch Your Hat and Coat Saloon, and right out of the chute, Norman won and was crowned MGA. He knew a good thing when he saw it, and latched on to the contest's rights from the original owner in 1975. The pageant has caught on over the years with more than sixty contestants sometimes participating in the annual pageant, and both gays and straights delighting in the delectable dish of drag.

Break is over, and it's time to get back to work. That is, as soon as everyone stops oohing over a collection of sparkling supersized rings and flashy bracelets made by a drag queen from North Carolina. I'm not sure how the crown issue was resolved, if it ever was, because it's all queenspeak to me. One thing is certain, though: Standardization of the crowns must happen.

The Miss America pageant — the one in Atlantic City — doesn't have a "creative costume" category, but MGA does.

It focuses on a theme, a character, or haute couture. Forget about evening gowns, Las Vegas showgirl attire, sportswear (tennis outfits or riding gear), or business suits. All of those choices mean one thing: yawn. Three minutes of music and a story accompany the creative costume presentation, and the two elements should harmonize to create a wickedly cool persona never before seen by the human eye. That's some heavy creativity that has to be ginned up in a drag queen's mind.

At issue with the creative costume topic: props and music. Occasionally, the mistress of ceremonies reads the story over the music during the presentation. Sometimes the contestants record the story over the music on a compact disc. Some of the stories in the past have been crappy babble and the promoters want to make sure everyone is on the same page about the fact that the concept and music should mesh.

Everything being batted around in this room is so inside baseball that I don't have a clue to what anyone is discussing. But my friends don't call me spy girl for nothing. I nab the thick booklet of rules for the pageant and look to it for answers.

What are judges looking for in the ideal Miss Gay America contestant?

According to the booklet in hand, a well-rounded contestant who has good taste in clothing — what they wear and how they wear it — for competition (Fifty percent of the score will be what you wear and another fifty percent on how you wear it and model. Work it girl!). The interview is also important, because whoever lands the coveted crown will actually work as Miss Gay America, traveling to preliminaries all over the country and representing the pageant.

Better not show up in some ragged evening gown, either. Contestants must wear a gown of appropriate length that fits properly, sport matching accessories and shoes and a flattering hairstyle, and possess graceful modeling skills. That "graceful modeling" thing would cost me points since I can't even walk up steps.

Creative costume: crucial. Talent: even more critical. If a drag queen is going to lip-synch Shania Twain, she better make sure she knows every word. Mistakes are not tolerated, and entertainment is a must. Don't bore the audience. Conjure emotions and let the audience ride the emotional roller coaster, too. If Miss America winners had to do all of this, the pageant would have gone by the wayside long before Bob Barker did.

Contestants must be twenty-one. Drugs are a big no-no. No pot, no cocaine, no drugs, period. Break this rule, and disqualification occurs immediately. This is not Studio 54. It's a rigid professional pageant system. Any talent is acceptable except use of fire. (No Great White impersonations allowed, obviously.) No stealing or contestants will hit the door. Norman doesn't want any contestant demeaning the pageant with sarcastic words. Utter something blasphemous about Miss Gay America and a contestant can kiss the scepter good-bye.

Titleholders must act professionally, not cause problems for promoters (i.e., act like a diva bitch), never become too intoxicated while representing the title, never participate in an argument except as a mediator, and try to solve all problems in a peaceful manner. Good rules for all of us, I muse, remembering similiar rules from Sunday school and kindergarten.

Dominique Sanchez loves nachos.

Sitting in a Mexican joint, bareface in work-out clothes and hair pulled back, Miss Gay America 2003 looks like the average thirty-something black guy. So I have to wonder — how did Chris Williams (Dominique's real name) transform into the gay beauty queen of the twenty-first century?

When: Early 1990s.

Where: A pizza place.

Why: Dominique was working to make money while in college.

Who: A customer told Dominique about the drag pageants at Discovery.

Looking for adventure, Dominique decided to participate. Immediately, he was hooked and figured he could do this female-impersonation thing for a while and maybe even make money with it. But a friend who ventured into the world of drag with Dominique around the same time fell into a deadly pit: believing the hype that people fed him.

"He'd get 'You're so talented, you're so pretty,' and then he'd be like 'I want more, I want more,'" Dominique recalls.

While his friend basked in the adoration, Dominique, who really didn't have anyone supporting his drag aspirations, just kept trying.

"I knew I was talented, but no one told me so I had to do it to prove myself. I had the drive to do it," he says. "I've surpassed that friend ten times over."

I guess so, since he holds the Miss Gay America crown.

In 1996, Dominique decided he just might have what it takes to become Miss Gay Arkansas. He entered two big pageants before getting his act together enough to represent Arkansas in the big showcase showdown. After he tried and lost the Miss Gay America title, Dominique decided he didn't have the drive to go for it again. He sat out for two years, pondering which direction he needed to take for his act to wow the judges and score winning points. When he reentered competition, the Susan Lucci syndrome struck. For two years, Dominique was good, but just not good enough. He came in second runner-up, not once but twice.

"I thought, 'This is it. If I don't win, I don't want to do it again,'" he says.

He spent more money for pageant gear than he had in previous years, and his expenses paid off with the glorious jackpot win.

"I had more of a fire than in previous years. I thought, 'I can't let anyone stop me from taking it but me,'" he says.

It didn't hurt that he practiced like he was training for the lead in *A Chorus Line*. Two months before the pageant, Dominique, who worked as a cheerleading coach before winning his title, practiced four out of seven days a week on his entertainment. Two weeks prior to the face-off with the judges, Dominique practiced his dancing from nine in the evening to one in the morning with his backup dancers, who were attending school at the time. They were dedicated to his cause to make every leg kick and arm sway clean. And they were.

Entering Miss Gay America comes at a hefty price. A rough estimate of the price tag for Dominique's crown:

Evening gown: $2,000–$3,000
Shoes: $30–$40, another $20 to dye them to perfectly match evening wear

Creative costume: $700
Five dancers in costume: $200–$300
Talent set decorations: $600
Talent costume: $700
Fingernails and hair: $300–$400
Travel to Dallas for costume fittings: $300 or more

Unlike pageant girls who compete in events like Miss Black Eyed Pea or Miss Arkansas, drag queens can't really go to a car dealership and ask for a sponsorship. The money comes out of their own pockets unless they find someone to help them, like friends or a family member.

"You really hope you make it in the top three and get some money back," Dominique says.

One contestant, Dominique says, has a rich boyfriend who allows the drag queen to spend thousands of dollars vying for the Miss Gay America spot. So far, the title has eluded her.

Dominique swears that the judges for the Miss Gay America pageant are much tougher than the Miss America judges. The MGA judges look at every minute detail, from a string hanging from a hem to beads missing on an evening dress. Frizzy hair will make a contestant lose points, and so will shoes that don't match a dress. If the dress is cobalt blue, the shoes better be the same exact shade.

Judges record their opinions on evaluation sheets and the honesty can be agonizingly harsh. Say a talent was good but not exactly entertaining enough to pull in the audience? Too bad, the judges will say so. Costumes look tacky? That, too, will be written down.

Just like in pageants everywhere, cattiness reigns. Dominique has her own tale to share. During her creative costume, in which she was attempting to transform into Plavalaguna — the opera-singing blue-skinned diva with flesh dreadlocks from the movie *Fifth Element* — things began to fall apart. Literally. That created a problem. If a contestant thinks she may make the top ten, she has to replay the creative costume portion the next night. Dominique spent all day with a hot-glue gun, attempting to salvage the costume.

"I was like, 'Oh my gosh, I can't believe this is happening.' I didn't win the creative costume portion," she says.

Dominique's loss made some bitchy contestants happy, but they said nothing — that is, nothing that Dominique could hear.

Evening gown and talent were the next night's categories. First up, evening gown. Dominique nailed it.

"They all started bitching then," Dominique says about some of her fellow contestants.

Second: talent. Once again, Dominique won.

"That's when they blew up. You can't imagine how bitchy these contestants are. I think when they know that someone has a good chance of winning, they are just a little more sarcastic."

At the pageant's finale, rest assured that pitching tantrums and throwing makeup brushes are as common for the losers as wearing the crown is for the winner.

I never thought I'd see Charlie Rose in a gay bar in Arkansas.

Okay, so he's on television.

On three screens, Charlie Rose has replaced some techno

dance babes for some unknown, and strange, reason. My best friend, Dylan, is killing time by making up a nonsense song about Charlie Rose, and I can't stop laughing. The entire scene is dreamlike: Dylan, straight boy that he is, surrounded by a room full of gay men; me, straight chick, trying to decipher who that guest is on Charlie Rose; and drag queens walking around air- kissing each other's cheeks. All a prelude to the Miss Gay South Regional America Pageant, a preliminary, that starts at midnight, about twenty minutes from now .

Dylan, his hazel eyes twinkling with silliness, is still adding verses to his original, creative song about Charlie Rose when the familiar notes of the theme to *Gone with the Wind* begin. No other song would be more appropriate than this one for such a pageant. Scarlett would be so happy that her appeal crosses sexual lines.

Victoria West, a blond creature in a tight technicolor dress that flares at the bottom, walks onto the stage with a big smile.

"Hi y'all," she drawls to the audience that continues to filter in as the pageant begins.

The current Miss Gay South, Rachel, joins Victoria onstage in a black satin dress with a cape edged in fur tails.

"Anyone want any tail?" Victoria asks as Rachel prisses off the stage. The crowd laughs, and I get the feeling I am at a bawdy Rotary club meeting.

Then, there she is Miss Gay America. Dominique doesn't at all look like the guy who chowed down on nachos with me a few weeks ago. The transformation amazes me. Dominique could pass for a girl better than some girls I know. In her green swirly dress with padding in just the right places,

Dominique, with her crown all aglitter, is sexy enough to give Jennifer Lopez a run for her money.

Time to meet the contestants. Just because it's called Miss Gay South doesn't mean all the girls are from Dixie. Contestants can enter any preliminary, and many of them strategize to see which preliminary would give them the best shot at winning and then entering Miss Gay America. Only four contestants have entered this preliminary: Angela Dodd from Phoenix, Arizona, who was a top ten finalist in MGA 2003; Tionne Iman from Little Rock; Christina Carruthers from Annandale, Virginia; and Aaron Davis from Corpus Christi, Texas.

The four divas emerge from the stage's wings wearing stunning evening couture. Angela wears a deep red velvet dress with ostrich feathers floating all around its edges. Tionne floats in a blushing lavender dress, Christina a green strapless dress, and Anna, the largest of all the contestants, wears a bold leopard skin–print dress. If I were a betting woman, I'd say Angela's dress impresses the judges more than the other three.

Because only four contestants are vying for the title, it's up to Dominique and some other drag queens to provide the entertainment during costume changes. Dominique struts out onto the stage wearing a black and white–print coat and breaks into a frenetic version of "Conga." As the salsa-driven beat pounds through the club, Dominique strips out of her coat to show black and silver tight-fitting bell-bottom pants and a black and silver sequined bra.

Fans in the audience line up next to the stage to bestow Dominique with dollar bills and kisses. It's very similar to the way men act in strip joints, but with much more class and less overt horniness. The dollar bills are actually handed to the dancer, not thrown up on the stage in some rude, cheap manner. The money flows in for Dominique in a hurry. The wad of cash is so large she has to take a step over to the side of the stage to dump the dollars and keep dancing.

Dancing with high kicks and sharp turns, Dominique's moves would make Britney Spears, and even a Rockette, look twice. The Energizer Bunny doesn't have as much energy as Dominique, who ends her act with a dramatic collapse onstage. People may say that drag queens are transvestites who don't know if they want to be male or female, but drag queens put a lot of practice hours, money, and talent into becoming female impersonators who can entertain. Dominique has all it takes to electrify a crowd.

Throughout the night, many eyes have been on the shirtless bartender, who the drag queens have proclaimed a stud. I've been slyly studying a table of three overweight fiftysomething lesbians, one of whom just hollered that the bartender's got nice biceps. The more booze that flows at the table, the wilder they become. One of the lesbians has no teeth in her mouth. I guess she left the dentures at home. I'm not exactly sure why these women find the drag show so sexy but they clearly do. The redneck Rubys seem out of place in a room of upper-class gay men, many of whom wear bigger diamonds than Elizabeth Taylor.

At a nearby table something more curious brews. A black man in a straw hat, tan linen pants, and a safari type shirt holds court.

"He looks like a pimp," Dylan says. "I think he is one. He acts like the gay black godfather."

Oddly, he does. Dylan has a way of calling a pimp a

pimp. Every black man who enters Backstreet immediately walks up to the man and kisses him in a manner that shows respect. In return for one kiss, the godfather licked one of the men's nipple. That's one way to make an offer you can't refuse.

Back on the stage, an audience member points a camera at Victoria West and Dominique.

"Don't aim a camera at a homosexual. They'll pose in two point two seconds," Victoria cracks.

Alert: There are drag droppings on the stage. Drag droppings? Sequins, threads, beads, feathers, and any other object that might fall from a drag queen's costume. On the stage, they can become dangerous, tripping queens as they strut their stuff. After a speedy sweep of such evil trash, the show goes on.

Goody! It's time for the evening gown competition. Angela, a five-foot-six-inch-tall petite queen with red hair and hazel eyes, steps out onstage in a most stunning gown, perhaps the most beautiful creation I have ever seen in my life. The lime-green beaded and sequined dress shimmers and catches more light than the average dress thanks to hundreds of tiny silver and gold seed beads woven between shades of green. A front split shows a deep green satin accenting the gown's lining. The beads form an elaborate brocade pattern, and a small train and high vampire collar bestow a regal look on the gown. Angela's lime-green pumps tie up the outfit in a perfect package. The interesting thing about Angela? She was enlisted as a serviceman in the army for four years. Now she's a hair stylist.

"I think I got a nipple hard-on," Victoria West jokes as Angela leaves the stage.

Tionne, a short black woman who is the hometown favorite and works at Kodak, walks onto the stage in a high-collared black sequin dress with gold trim accenting the three straps in the back. While the dress is pretty, it's hard to compete with Angela's beaded fantasy from a few minutes ago. She doesn't quite have the confidence Angela does, either.

Christina, a nurse at a veteran's hospital in Virginia, looks like an Amazon, but her stats say five-foot-eight. High heels do wonders for drag queens. She wears a vibrant red wig in a tightly teased coif on top of her head. Her orange beaded dress with silver flames around the bodice grabs my attention, and her silver-orange sequined shoes are a perfect match.

Dylan looks awestruck at the drag queens. Of course, it is late and PBS has changed its programming from Charlie Rose to some sort of "how to raise a baby" show. Odd choice to play in a room full of gay men. The family values council would have a conniption if they knew this was airing in a gay bar.

The last contestant, Aaron, looks like Divine was her heroine. She wears a lavender dress with silver beads and chiffon accents around the bodice. Tight curls float on top of her wig, resembling the 'do of a 1967 prom queen.

"She's one hundred seventy delicious pounds," Victoria West tells the audience.

She's a whole lotta woman, that's for sure.

Entertainment time again.

Dominique busts onto the stage to En Vogue's "Free Your

Mind," and boy does she make an impression. She sports a long black latex dress with six-inch heeled thigh-high boots and a black collar around her neck highlighted with large hooped rings. Black netting graces the side of the dress's skirt. She works the audience into a frenzy, mingling with them, lip-synching, blowing kisses, a drag queen fantasy come to life. The music melds into a song by Hole, and Dominique gives the audience all she's got.

"Tie me up by my heels and spank me," Dominique tells the crowd when she's done. "I feel like I'm getting ready to go to one of those S&M clubs." The crowd loves the naughtiness, and I wonder how many of them have ever been to a dungeon.

The crowd in this place continues to intrigue Dylan and me. An older man in a dirty baseball cap, Wrangler jeans, and a long wallet chain continually walks to the stage to give the entertainers money. He's the type of redneck guy at the 7-Eleven who I would normally think was checking me out as he backed out of the parking lot in his beat-up truck. Instead, he apparently spends his Friday nights giving drag queens money and buying drinks for guys in little Gap shorts. Maybe all of this time, guys like him who check out girls like me were looking at my jewelry and makeup with envy instead of wanting to take me to bed.

Watching a Miss Gay America pageant is like watching a 1960s variety show. You just never know what you're going to see next, especially if the category is creative costume.

Angela — our serviceman gone drag — pays tribute to the United States military in a red, white, and blue breathtaking fantasia. Two sailors in white suits with sparkly sequins on their hats march out with Angela in the middle of the two flags they carry. It soon becomes apparent the flags are actually part of the costume when the dancers unfurl them to reveal Angela in a costume of dazzling stars and stripes. She wears her original name tag from her days in Uncle Sam's army. The music has an overlay of Angela reading her desire to shed the don't ask, don't tell policy and open the military to all sexual orientations with no hidden secrets.

In a patriotic swoosh, Angela unveils another layer of costume, a white pantsuit with a red, white, and blue coat that looks like a creation from a *School House Rock* cartoon. Red and blue stars that jut out from her head highlight the matching red and blue streaks in her blond wig.

She ends the spectacular show with, "I'm proud to be an American man and an American queen."

Frankly, I'd be shocked if anyone could top that. During wartime, even the drag queens go patriotic.

Next up: Tionne. Her costume, a silver creation with a Spartacus headdress, looks like something that went awry in a microwave experiment in a science lab. While Angela had her movements down with the music, Tionne's don't quite gel. I feel sorry for Tionne, following Angela who has obviously trained for this pageant like an Olympic gymnast.

Eek!

Freaky furries always shock Dylan and me, and on the stage, a big white bunny and a gray rat prance around with Christina, who is dressed like a psychedelic Mad Hatter who has had way too much acid. Pink, violet, and green plumes poke out of her large purple velvet hat, which hides a short purple wig. Fabulous gold shoes match the Mad Hatter's gold scepter. The motley array of colors and patterns on Christina's spandex getup would give somebody with color sensitivity a seizure.

After Christina, Aaron's up. I can see her on the side of the stage, lying down in what looks to be a mermaid costume of some sort. After her introduction, she wiggles onto the stage with her hair in a wild straw and fabric medusa arrangement. Then, I see her tail and realize she's no mermaid at all. She's some sort of crazy snail creation with a beige tail like an inchworm and a gold corset. Aaron slithers around the stage, erecting her tail in the air to the beats of the music. I can say that I have never seen anything like it before. Chances are, I'll never see anything like this again.

Hard to say who is the winner of this rodeo. Both Aaron and Christina created costumes that let the mind roam to fanciful places that would make the most die-hard surrealist get a creative charge.

Dominique doesn't like it when people talk when she's on-stage.

In the back of the room, at the bar, a bunch of people chatter with no regard to the fact that a pageant is occurring while they are trying to flirt.

"You people are out there talking like it's a Yahoo! chat room," Dominique says. "It's rude."

A hush falls over the room. Dominique commands a presence, and don't you forget it, girlfriend. It's time for the entertainment competition.

Angela knows how to woo, and I'm getting the strong impression that she wants to win this pageant very badly. She hits the stage in high drama fashion with a blue robe edged in blue and white feathers. Angela's talent number begins with some gay ranting and from there evolves into a power-dance number while she lip-synchs to Christina Aguilera. Her backup dancers, the same two boys from her other act, wear blue satin basketball shorts. In a blink, Angela strips out of the robe and shimmies in a blue fringed minidress, white boots, and a sequined bra. Angela's dancing and rhythm captivate the judges.

On any other night, if I saw Tionne in a dance club, I'd think that girl's got rhythm and she can dance. Not tonight. Not when she has to follow Angela, who looks like she's been teaching Jennifer Lopez a dance step or two. Tionne can pop, sizzle, pop, shimmy like Janet Jackson but the hometown girl just doesn't have what it takes to clear the memory of Angela's performance.

Drag queens change their wigs with their costumes to keep things livened up. It almost makes me wish I owned a personal wig collection. Christina appears for her talent number in a blond one — think 1949 Joan Crawford — and long black gown. A thin man in a pinstriped suit joins her and together they tap dance a soft shoe number before another man joins them for a faster paced ditty. Christina disrobes to reveal a black and white zoot suit, fishnets, and black dance pumps. Everything is going along splendidly until Christina breaks out into "Vogue" by Madonna. An audible groan goes up through the room. Yawn. Who hasn't seen a gay man vogue before?

One thing I've learned tonight: Aaron knows how to shock. After the inchworm-snail performance, she decides to tone it down, wearing just a simple black dress with an interesting sheer slate-gray vesture with ostrich feathers floating about it. Dramatic silver makeup with dark lipstick accents her face. She lip-synchs a raspy version of "All By Myself" that sounds like Eartha Kitt. The judges are clearly entranced by this drama queen. Who wouldn't be?

Victoria West is back, and this time she's dressed like a pink cotton candy bath mat. Her latex bustier is just the beginning of this creation that has a long skirt with pink furry dots of various tones. It's a crazy confection that makes Victoria, with her blond wig with twigs of pink hair sticking about in it, look like a colossal Barbie doll. She dances about, singing a song that encourages the audience to kiss her, kiss her. No thanks.

Dominique, though, always charms and looks as if she just stepped off the catwalk. For her final number, she wears a gorgeous lavender beaded dress that looks like something Halle Berry would wear on the red carpet. She performs "True Colors" by Cyndi Lauper and spellbinds the crowd. It's easy to see why she was chosen as Miss Gay America. Her act is flawless.

Suddenly, at the end of her number, a group of guys have appeared in the bar wearing black underwear, white parody T-shirts that say "I prefer Dicks to Hooters," and black laced-up boots. They like giving Dominique money and she likes taking it. As the entertainers perform one last time and the clock closes in on three A.M., the crowd is ready to learn who will be the new Miss Gay South. Dominique and Victoria walk out with bouquets of roses.

"I want a flower," bellows one of the redneck lesbians behind me. "I want one of those damn flowers."

Time for the big-biceped bartender to cut this woman off.

The four queens prance out onto the stage. Angela wears a rusty orange velvet dress cut in dramatic swoops around the waist and shoulders. I didn't know they made velvet in this unusually gorgeous shade. Tionne wears a white sequin dress that would have made one of Charlie's Angels happy in 1977. Christina chooses to close the night in the same gown in which she began the night — a green dress that looks like a dinosaur. Aaron, large and round as she is, shines in a brazen red sequin dress that only someone with balls could wear.

The first runner-up and the winner of the pageant will head to the Miss Gay America pageant in a few months. Who will they be? First runner-up: Aaron. No doubt, wearing that medusa inchworm creation and slithering around onstage generates a winner. The winner? Angela, Miss Military, in the expensive gowns and patriotic fusion of stars and stripes.

It's late, closer to four than three, and as Dylan and I leave, all the pageant contestants kiss and hug just like the girls do in Atlantic City. A techno version of Sister Sledge's "We Are Family" blasts. For a moment, before the cattiness kicks in, sisterhood prevails.

florida

the life of an iron belle

Biceps, Triceps, and Cereal Boxes

TAMPA, FLORIDA — Do not ask for whom the Iron Belle tolls, for she may pick you up and swing you over her head.

No kidding.

I'm not particularly fond of the Rambo look of bulging muscles that could whisk me up like a flimsy piece of rope. Many of my girlfriends have wilted at the sight of hard-as-rock biceps and triceps, but not me. I'd choose Edward Norton over some rippled guy in a tank top any day.

But what about muscle women? No, they don't do it for me either, but there are certainly plenty of men in the world, especially in the South where women are often ultrafeminine, who get their jollies by worshipping the rippled and tanned sirens known as the Iron Belles. Tough, buff women, they know how to put a man in his place. That is — if he wants to be put there, and plenty of men do.

Dakota lives in the tropical setting of Florida. She is a transposed Yankee who likes the sunny warmth more than the frigid cold, which can limit showing off one's muscles. If I had muscles like Dakota's, I might flex a little too. At five-and-a-half feet tall, Dakota has a 42-D chest. Impressive, but it's these numbers that stun me: She can bench-press 315 pounds, do 70-pound dumbell hammer curls, 120-pound hamstring curls, 315-pound squats, and 1,300-pound leg presses. This is a woman I don't want to mess with at all.

Men, on the other hand, beg and pay their hard-earned bucks for Dakota to spin them above her head. It's all part of being an Iron Belle, a group of ladies who can bench-press more than Arnold Schwarzenegger and who indulge in bringing fun, fantasy, and semicompetitive activities to those who enjoy toned physiques.

Women like Dakota just might put the svelte dominatrices in the Emma Peel leather catsuits out of business.

On a spring morning, Dakota wakes up early and boards a plane to New York City. She's not exactly fond of the Big Apple. The city's constant buzz and hum distract her, and the never-ending gray cloud of smog affects her voice. But she routinely leaves her tropical palm-tree paradise to make money — lots of it — in the city that never sleeps.

As Dakota boards the airplane, settles in and prepares herself for the two-day marathon that is about to begin, no one on the plane knows why Dakota is headed to New York. No one would even suspect she's about to fulfill some fantasies. To the average flier, she looks like a business-woman off to a conference. Little do they know what she'll be doing in about twelve hours.

When she arrives in the city, like almost every visitor to Gotham, she gathers her bags at JFK, hails a taxi, and heads to her hotel. Stuck in traffic, she watches the minutes vanish, and the luxury time Dakota envisioned for herself while waiting at the baggage claim is evaporating. In the backseat of the cab, she tries to get into the proper mind-set to work, but it's hard when she's worried about the traffic around her that won't move, won't even budge, so that she can get to her destination. By the time she arrives at her upscale hotel, Dakota, frazzled and already tired from travel, has two hours to get ready for work.

In her room, Dakota throws down her suitcases and heads out to get enough food and water to last for the next day or so. She won't be leaving the room, and she won't want room service intruding on her work. Rushing back to the hotel, Dakota has just enough time to take a breath before applying her makeup, styling her hair, and putting on her costume — a red string bikini. She's tired and her first customer hasn't even knocked on the door.

It would be easy to assume that Dakota works as a high-class escort or a prostitute — someone like Julia Roberts's character in *Pretty Woman*. But Dakota is not even close to that. She's a weight lifter, a body builder to the extreme with bulging muscles, tits made of iron, and legs that would make Superman kryptonite-green with envy. Men — everyone from CEOs to cops to the average Joe on the street — have saved their pay to make their Amazon hard-body dreams come to life.

Dakota created a schedule before she left the Sunshine State. For weeks, she's booked men to see her while she is in New York City. Even while she sat at her desk, penciling in the finance attorney, the deli worker, and the stock broker, Dakota knew that some clients would back out, fail to show, or appear at her hotel door late. Such schedule changes bother her, but she has learned to take them in stride. You have to when you do this kind of work, she says.

It's 5:30 in the afternoon and while most New Yorkers are headed home after a long day at work, Dakota's day is just starting. Her hotel telephone rings.

"Come on up," she says.

The CEO for a sports marketing company appears at her hotel door. Dressed in a black suit and purple silk tie, the CEO likes wrestling, particularly when Dakota pins him down under her while he begs for mercy like a scrawny second-grader fighting off the school bully. Dakota is just the one to do it. The wrestling session lasts thirty minutes. In between clients, Dakota reapplies makeup and tries to get in a bite of a snack.

"You are basically an entertainer," Dakota says. "It can be mentally draining." I imagine so if you are having to constantly feed fetishes.

"The only thing that is glamourous is how much cash you have in your pocket on your way home."

Money always makes everything seem better.

Dakota sees twelve clients in a day and half, roughly thirty-six hours, and that's plenty for her.

"I don't know how girls go for a week," she says when the adventure is over. "I just want to go home and veg. It's all too weird."

Uh, yeah, crushing cereal boxes between one's thighs is just a tad bizarre.

That's one of the requests Dakota has gotten during her years as an Iron Belle.

"The box looks like a bow tie when you are done. The guy likes to hear cereal, the sound of crunch. One box exploded and went everywhere," she recalls.

Another man wants Dakota to dress up in a policeman's uniform. Okay, that's an understandable fantasy. Wait. The man likes to dress in a tutu.

Hmmm. I may have to dig out the Psychology 101 textbook for that one.

Dakota says another client brings a shopping bag filled with fruit — watermelons, cantelopes, and peaches — for her squeeze. Another guy likes for her to step on bugs. Still another one has an even gutsier fetish: He likes Dakota to place a glass on his chest or stomach and then walk on it, crushing it with her six-inch heels. Sure, he bleeds, but he doesn't care. He's checked out, living in some other head-space and associates the entire experience with pleasure. Yeow!

Dakota says that the men who visit her in hotel rooms across the country have some expendable income. They aren't wealthy, but they're doing all right. Some of them aren't just sweet on Dakota. No, some of them will see every girl who visits New York, Fort Lauderdale, Memphis, Dallas, or any other city that the Iron Belles travel to. Iron Belles, I learn, seldom visit my hometown, Little Rock. There's just not a market for the fetish in Arkansas. Other clients like certain ones who provide variety in looks or abilities.

Who are these men?

Lonely ones, surmises Dakota. They aren't happy with their

current station in life or who they are in relationships with in the real world. Others just like the naughty nature of doing something edgy without telling their significant others. One of Dakota's clients is married to a wrestler. She hasn't nailed what makes him visit her.

Even more common, some are powerful men who want to give up control. Many of the Iron Belle's clients are cops, lawyers, stock brokers, investors, and real estate guys — the type of man you see in the airport who carries an expensive leather briefcase, holds a pager in one hand, and talks into the headset of his state-of-the-art cell phone.

Still, I have to wonder. If these men find pleasure in brawn, could they possibly be closeted gay?

Bingo, she says.

She thinks that some of them wish they were with men and these hunky women give them that feeling without all the guilt.

There are also the men who like to dress up in women's clothing and have her spank them.

"Yes, it's very bizarre. I think it's the crazy world we live in; people need stress release. It's like a drug fix and once they get it, they feel okay. As long as no one gets burned, it's okay," she says.

A lot of the men tell Dakota that their fetish for muscles stems from a desire or fascination with old girlfriends, teachers, or an aunt. It's not a fetish they cultivated, like a love for fine wine. Instead it just happened.

Call Cheryl Harris the mother of all Iron Belles.

Around 1995, during the baby steps of the Internet,

Cheryl, who was living in Atlanta at the time, saw a way to band together a lot of the female body builders who freelanced as muscle fantasy girls. She created Iron Belles, a twist on the Southern belles concept, which seemed logical at the time because she lived in Atlanta, where she had moved in 1986 from the North. She worked in real estate and, to keep her body firm, she turned to body building. After seventeen years in Atlanta, she had had enough of the traffic congestion and the melting-pot morosity that haunts the city as more and more non-Southerners move in and erode the traditional Southern hospitality, so she moved to Tampa, Florida, a coastline oasis of kink.

Iron Belles, then and now, focus their attention on men who love beefy babes, the kind who can lift a grown man upside down and make all the blood rush to their heads. When the women banded together as the Iron Belles and put their show on the Internet, the business began to grow.

It wasn't that Cheryl created the idea single-handedly. For years, muscle girls had been freelancing, many underground, as private wrestlers for men who bought muscle magazines and lusted for women with oversized biceps, hard-as-steel calves, tits firm like bowling balls, and necks as big as Vin Diesel's. In body-building circles, women knew the secret to making extra money: flexing in private for men. Cheryl just happened to be the one who saw the major money-making opportunity and brought the women to the Internet, creating video stars who also tour the globe.

"There's not a lot of money in the sport of muscle building, but there is for private wrestling or posing for pictures," Cheryl says. "Men like seeing the girls right here before them live and in person."

Men who like brawny women don't necessarily want to make mad passionate love to the Belles. Their fantasies lie elsewhere: wrestling, muscle worship, dominant muscle worship, fantasy role-playing, light domination, flexing, submission, lifts and carries, personalized training, massage, lingerie, posing and modeling, oil wrestling, and fantasy and cuddle wrestling. If they want more, say a roll in the hay, forget about it, says Cheryl.

"We aren't a full-service organization. If some girls do it behind closed doors, I don't want to know about it. If that's how they are going to be, then they deserve to be busted. It's muscle fantasy and that's how it should be in their mind. If they want to go further, they shouldn't."

Some men like to wrestle a Belle and feel the power that exudes from years of body-building training. Some men just want to feel dominated, but not in a whip-and-handcuff kind of way. Others want to be lifted toward the sky like a bag of chicken feed, twirled around, and thrown down on the bed. Still others just want to watch a woman flex and pose while he snaps a few photos. Whatever they want, the fantasy doesn't come cheap. Thirty minutes begin at two hundred dollars. The next hour can be anywhere from three hundred to five. For men who fly their Belle to a town for a visit, the cost rises significantly. Excluding airfare, a muscle-hungry man can count on paying at least one thousand dollars for a session. Usually, the price is significantly more. Muscle babes who hustle the circuit can make seven thousand smackeroos in two days of touring. But that means forty hours filled with back-to-back sessions, much like Dakota's adventure in New York City. Not easy work, but if you've got the muscles, flexing can certainly pay the rent.

So you wanna date an Iron Belle?

You can do it.

By "date," the Iron Belles really mean date. Their definition? "Date means an actual date in all terms of the word," says Cheryl Harris. "You take the girl either to dinner, a show, a sports event, et cetera. The length shall be determined by how much fun the two of you are having, anywhere from one to three hours in length."

Wacky. I know a lot of guys who would have loved knowing about this when they were in college. At least a twenty-four-hour notice is required for a date, and a name, occupation, physical description, and the location of the date must be given to the Iron Belles corporate headquarters. A date's not cheap with the beefcake Belle of choice: $250 dollars per date with $50 up front when the date is made. That's not counting what a gentleman will spend on his date.

But it's worth the expense if a fantasy involves dating someone who looks like the Terminator's baby sister.

If a date sounds intimidating, there are other ways to feed the fetish. Fans can buy calendars, catalogs, photo albums, and memberships to the Iron Belles Fantasy Theater, where viewers can subscribe and watch online videos. Cheryl Harris has even created an audio project called Strong Words available on compact disc or cassette. Now that's innovative. What does the tape contain? "Four sexy audio stories of strong, superior women," says the CD cover. "Cheryl Harris, whose years as a wrestler and dominatrix make her uniquely qualified for this project, reads tales of love, power, dominance, and submission." That should be enough to keep truckers who love listening to porn while driving awake on the country's interstates and back roads.

I feel so mischievous watching porn on the Internet. But what's a girl to do? I want to see an Iron Belle flex her biceps. On the Web site, demo clips are available to entice those who might want to join the Iron Belles Fantasy Theater. In one clip, a woman licks her bulging bicep with her tongue. Another clip shows an Iron Belle smothering a man with her thighs. The clip of the month is a montage of Iron Belle images: a topless woman with a pink bikini bottom teases her bikini line with her finger and then touches herself; a blonde woman lifts a barbell in a weight room; a leg muscle flexes; a man licks an Iron Belle's leg; two woman on a green mat wrestle, and one of them puts the other in a leg lock.

Iron Belles don't like to let voyeurs like myself watch their performances regardless of how charming the voyeur attempts to be.

Thank goodness for VHS.

I've enlisted four twenty-something men to watch an Iron Belles video with me. We are in a cozy little conference room in a downtown Little Rock office building way after hours, watching something it feels like we probably shouldn't. The four single men act as if this is the most naughty adventure they have ever undertaken. Perhaps for two of them it is. The other two, I'm sure, have done a few things that would make L'il Kim blush.

Ernie is a recent college grad with an eye on business school, who I suspect masturbates a lot. Carl is a law student and politico who fancies himself edgy, but in reality I think

he'll be disturbed by what he's about to see. Whitt is an at-
tractively rumpled ne'er-do-well who never kisses and tells.
That leads me to think that there isn't anything Whitt won't try
at least once. Sam has spent the last ten years working in the
restaurant business. I think underneath the T-shirt he could be
a wild man, but I can't quite get a handle on him.

"I can't wait to see what you have drummed up for us to
watch," says Carl.

I haven't told any of the four men what to expect. Shock is
good for the soul.

"Oh, just something I find intriguing," I say.

Whitt laughs. "You're always intriguing."

Is he flirting with me? Slipping the tape into the VCR, I
can't wait to see their reactions. Let's go, boys.

The premise of the video? Cheryl Harris — yes, the very one
who owns the business — isn't taking anymore crap. Move
over Terminator. Cheryl has had enough of power-happy
airport security. It's too exhausting to deal with anymore. Her
solution? Take it out on an airport traffic controller.

When Cheryl appears on the screen, the guys in the room
gasp.

"Daaaaaaaaamn, wish I had biceps like that," Carl says.

Ernie laughs. "She's one healthy woman. She could suffo-
cate you with those legs."

"What the hell is this shit?" Whitt asks, laughing.

"Iron Belles," I say.

"What is an Iron Belle?" Whitt asks, staring at the woman
on the screen.

I explain the concept and the fetish: how some men want to be picked up and twirled in the air like a baton. Whitt shakes his head and drinks his Guinness.

"Not for me," he says. Nope, didn't figure so. Whitt is a man who likes to control a situation, not be controlled.

Cheryl sits on the man's face and he begs her to get off of him. He says something about how large her thigh muscles are. "What do you feed them?" he mumbles as Cheryl straddles his head with her legs. Bizarre-o.

Sam laughs cautiously. Does he like what he sees or is he disgusted by it? Hard to tell. On the screen, the overweight man doesn't stand a chance against muscle-mistress Cheryl. It's a brutal game of mercy that's about to be played out, and I don't think it will be pretty. Obviously filmed in a motel room, the video isn't sleek or high-quality, but does it really matter? No, because it's all about sinew jollies. Winning an Academy Award is not a priority.

"You guys bored, want to stop watching?" I ask, half joking.

"God no, I want to see how this thing plays out," Carl says.

"Same here," Whitt says.

Ernie laughs. "Strangest damn porn video I've ever seen."

He's got a point there. Oof! Cheryl slams her body down on the man's face. That has gotta hurt. Unlike some wrestling, I don't think this is fake. The guy is probably getting a hard-on while Cheryl kapows him with a headlock. She doesn't let up with some serious belly flopping — a horizontal fall across the guy's belly. Locking the guy's neck in a scissor hold, Cheryl twists his head ever so lightly with her bulging calves. Flexing harder, she makes him wince. A series of more headlocks and trampling — Cheryl walks on him like he is a well-worn carpet — and the video is over.

Whitt sits back in his leather chair and surveys the situation. His facial expressions betray none of his emotions, if he feels any at all. But Sam is another story. As I study him a little more, I decide the boy is aroused. No question. I really think he is. No wonder he is sitting there quietly.

Question on the floor: What would you do if you had an Iron Belle for the day?

"You serious?" Carl asks.

"Well, yeah," I say.

Carl laughs. "I don't think this is the kind of woman I wanna fuck. Really, you serious?"

"Yeah, I am. I don't mean fuck her. You didn't see any of that on the video, did you?"

"No, it was kind of a bore. I mean sorta like watching WWF or some redneck thing like that."

"I'd have her carry me into the Capitol Bar," Whitt says.

"Really?" Carl asks.

With Whitt, you can never tell if he is serious or not. He seems to be this time.

"Yeah, how cool would it be to have a woman carry you into a bar? Way cool, I think."

"Everyone would stare," Ernie says.

"Yeah and that's what would be cool."

Carl laughs. "You're weird."

"What would you do?" Ernie asks.

"Wrestle her. I know I could take her. Wonder what you get if you beat her?"

"I don't think you can beat her," I say.

Sam agrees. "She's got incredible leg muscles. Your biceps are nowhere near to hers. I mean just look at them."

Sam likes Cheryl, no doubt.

"Yeah, but she's no match, I mean come on," says Carl.

"What the fuck-ever, this woman could take us down. I'd use her to cart me around town," Whitt says.

Everyone is laughing, but I can see respect and a hint of fear behind the bravado. For the first time, perhaps, these Southern men have seen a woman who can undoubtedly kick their collective ass and take their money while doing it. Mission accomplished.

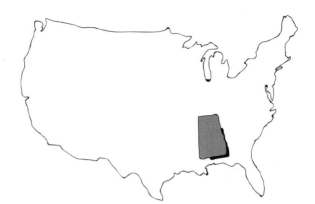

alabama

sticks and stones, whips and chains

St. Andrew's Crosses and Cocktail Weiners

ANYWHERE, ALABAMA — Enemies should be chosen carefully. That being said, it's probably unwise to choose a group of adversaries who are adept with whips and floggers. Alas, that's what initially happens when I begin my adventure to find the truth behind the deep underground BDSM scene — that's bondage, domination, sadism, and masochism for the novices — in Dixie. Just like in my first cotillion class, I started off on the wrong foot.

The Internet serves as the perfect place to find all-things sex so it was on my laptop computer that I came upon a group in Memphis called the Impact Institute. The snazzy red and black Web site features pictures of a dungeon replete with all manner of intriguing contraptions. An events calendar provides the careful BDSM planner with a list of future activities such as "KingDom" and "Wicked Women." Because the group apparently wants new friends to join their kinky circle, they provide an e-mail address.

My mother raised me to be honest and straightforward, so I contact the group about spending a Saturday evening with them observing their tricks. I don't pretend to know the ins and outs of tying up a lover with black electrical tape. I'm just a curious journalist. Honesty can't hurt, right?

Wrong move.

The return e-mail flatly refuses my request, citing a strong need to keep such events private for the sake of anonymity.

"The fact of the matter is, we are not ready to 'come out of hiding,' so to speak," the e-mail reads. "The main reason we have been able to build a great community here in Memphis is that we are very, very quiet. No advertising, strict rules on discretion, etc. Otherwise, we would suffer the same fate as Nashville, whose club was recently raided. They were one of the first clubs to have articles written about them in their local paper. It is regrettable that our society isn't as free as we would like, but this is why we are unable to help you out at this time. When the social and political climate changes here in Memphis, perhaps we can be more out than we are now."

A minor setback. Never one to put all my sex toys in one doo-lolly, I search out another group in Memphis. Maybe they will be more friendly to my request to explore a Southern dungeon on a sultry Saturday night? And they are. Returning home from dinner one night, I find a nice e-mail in my box from a man with "Master" before his initial. He'll talk. "Call me," he writes, offering his celly digits.

When I make contact, the master is in a restaurant and can't talk. He'll call me back. Easy avoidance tactic, I assume. Surprisingly, he calls me back within minutes to tell me he would be happy to talk to me.

"Memphis has a healthy scene," he says. "There are a variety of smaller groups. We all know each other."

The Memphis Master tells me that he can connect me with some people in the scene. He sounds fiercely serious in his tone. "Have you talked to anyone else in the scene?"

I mention in all honesty the rejection I received from the other group.

"Oh, yeah, well that's a different group," he says in a snobby tone. "We all know each other." Who knew there were cliques?

The Memphis Master and I talk again a few days later. He tells me he has been in the scene for five years, when he began an online group for kinky folks before deciding to take it off-line and have face-to-face connections with kinky people like himself. He informs me that anyone interested in joining their group must undergo a screening and meet with the committee. That, he says, is to out anyone who is only curious or interested in seeing if their neighbors are into whips and riding crops.

In his deep voice, the Memphis Master tells me he just ended a twenty-four seven master-slave relationship, but is newly involved with a new submissive who he's training to be in a relationship. He plans to "collar" her — whatever that means — in the next few weeks at a ceremony.

"It's like a BDSM wedding. None of this is legal," he says.

Of course not, I say to myself.

"People come in and think it's role-playing. This is not make-believe," he intones firmly. "We really live the lifestyle."

If I am nice, he says, I might even get to visit the local dungeon, which the group shares with the Impact Institute. Woo-hoo!

The next day the Memphis Master sends an e-mail to me and his listserv.

I'm sure she would love to get the scoop on the Scene, in the process (how much she gets is discretionary, and up to us/The Community). Ms Parker told me she spoke with "T" at Impact through eMail. (I asked her if she had contacted any other groups in Memphis and she said No.) So I feel she's doing her homework. I do not know if she is in the Scene currently or if she has ever been, in the past, but I recognize now that this is actually an important Question. And, in fact, one I should have asked last night but didn't.

In the "scene"? Eh, no. Once for Halloween, I dressed up like a dominatrix with a touch of disco diva mixed in for a glitter effect, but that's about the extent of my foray into the "scene." Oh, and somewhere tucked away in a random drawer, I have a pair of silver handcuffs. But that's it.

The Memphis Master tells me to answer the questions in the e-mail and let the group know who I am.

"I can do that," I reply. Once again, I answer the questions honestly. When will I learn? Honesty doesn't always pay.

The Memphis Master avoids my calls and e-mails for days. Finally, he tells me he's been busy over the weekend — training his submissive, I'm told — but that he doesn't think now is a good time to talk to me. The community has had a meeting about me. A meeting? I became an agenda item at a BDSM meeting? Who knew such things existed? Not only has the Memphis Master talked to his group about me, he has contacted other groups in the leather scene to ask their opinion. The consensus: Don't talk to her.

A curious girl's gotta do what she's gotta do. The gloves are now off.

As a child, tales of Nancy Drew, Emma Peel, and Charlie's Angels going undercover to find the truth or a bad guy entertained me for hours. I loved glamour mixed with a dash of danger and a shot of adventure thrown in for intrigue and drama.

"We're going undercover to a bondage club," I announce to Dylan.

"We are?" he asks, an eyebrow slowly rising.

"Yes," I say, mischievously.

"But Memphis won't work. Those people are on to you," he says. Not to worry, my dear boy.

My plan gels when I discover a weekend dedicated to fetishes and the BDSM lifestyle in Alabama, featuring workshops on how to succeed as a couple in the scene, vendors selling mysterious torture goodies, and a latex-leather fantasy ball. There's no question — we're there. Eagerly, Dylan makes online reservations, including paying the sixty-dollar registration fees through the Internet. Who knew bondage people use PayPal?

"What are we going to wear to the ball?" I ask Dylan about twenty times a day. "I want to look like this is the kind of event we attend every Saturday night."

"I think we should say we are bondage virgins but curious about the lifestyle," Dylan says. "It'll take stress off of us having to pretend we know everything."

He's got a point.

The group's dress code screams strict. Latex, leather, rubber. Fantasy wear such as sailor, geisha, or prisoner costumes are okay but should be mixed with fetish wear. Do not wear costumes that are likely to offend other guests, such as Nazi uniforms. Makes perfect sense to me. Nipples, aureoles, and genitalia must be concealed at all times. No exposed butt cheeks. No jeans or T-shirts. Adult infantilism is acceptable as long as it is a complete outfit. A diaper, bonnet, or pacifier is not adequate.

Abracadabra, a large magical costume shop, sits in a part of North Little Rock that hasn't changed much since the 1950s. Hole-in-the-wall beer joints and drive-in dairy bars line the wide street. Two days before the fetish ball, Dylan and I spend the afternoon at Abracadabra attempting to find our fetish. Harem girl? Sailor? Geisha girl? Vampire? It's hard to figure out a fetish in an hour, but a big part of deciding involves finding a costume that fits. A pair of ultratight latex pants looks sexy but lack of circulation isn't my gig. A French maid costume with a frilly petticoat calls my attention. Comfortable and sexy. Dylan settles on a black leather cape and a wicked black vest with leather trim that goes with a Robin Hood costume.

"I'm a count, Phantom of the Opera, Batman. They'll let me in. It's leather," he says when I shoot a look of doubt. The cape does rock.

The invitation said that the "fashion police" would be at the door monitoring outfits. I imagine a leather-hooded executioner with a paddle standing guard. If the outfit fails to pass inspection, twenty licks. Ouch!

"Stop worrying, we'll get in," Dylan says.

Maybe, I wonder, but will we make it out?

Seven hours of drive time, and we've made it to Anywhere, Alabama. GET AN EYEFUL says the large billboard greeting us as we roll into the chain hotel's parking lot. The large eyeball is a fitting welcome from the unwitting merchant.

"I wonder if that'll be prophetic?" Dylan asks.

"You can bet it will be," I say. "Maybe two eyes full."

A sign in the hotel lobby with the group's acronym points us to the library for registration. Dylan and I look at each other and grin knowingly. The curious thing about this event is how ordinary it seems. The organizers have the same standard procedures as a convention of podiatrists. The group has booked a block of hotel rooms for guests at a popular chain hotel, rented out a room for attendees to pick up registration packets, and even designed souvenir T-shirts for the weekend. Money raised will be donated to a medical nonprofit to help research a disease from which a member of the group suffers. According to the invitation, even a silent auction will be held. Jeez Louise, throw in a banquet and goodie bag, and this could be an insurance conference.

For miles across three state lines, Dylan and I have asked the same question: Who attends one of these events? Aging baby boomers? Goth chicks? Trailer trash? Drug addicts? Wal-Mart supershoppers? CEOs? People we know from Arkansas? Alien life-forms? As we head down the hotel's corridor, the answer isn't far away.

Two hefty women greet us from behind the long registration table covered with manila envelopes. A bearded man wearing a black leather vest and jeans stands nearby smiling at us. He looks like a motorcycle enthusiast who has a tale or two to tell.

"Is this your first BDSM event?" the man asks.

"It's mine. Is it yours?" Dylan asks me.

Of course, if Dylan and I are a couple, we should have talked about our forays into Kinksville. I shoot a look at him.

"Yes, it is," I say timidly.

Less than five minutes into role-playing and Dylan and I don't even act like we know each other. Memo to self — acting lessons for Dylan. The man introduces himself as Mr. Jack.

"How many people are you expecting?" Dylan asks.

"Probably close to eighty. There are fifteen states represented, even people from as far away as Massachusetts and Texas."

"Anyone else from Arkansas?" Dylan quizzes Mr. Jack hopefully. We've been joking about the judges and journalists we're dreaming of running into in Alabama.

"Nope, you folks are the only ones," he says.

So much for discovering some secrets about people we know in our city.

"Be sure you have two blue tickets for entry into tonight's and tomorrow night's events," recites one of the registration women. "You'll find a pin to wear, too. Be sure to wear it," says one of the women at the desk as she hands us our much-coveted T-shirts. Dylan, a T-shirt collector, couldn't wait to get to Alabama and receive his free shirt, which turns out to be a simple black tee with a city scape on the left-hand breast. Not the best logo ever, but it's our first BDSM convention shirt to treasure. Ahh, the golden moments.

"See you tonight," Mr. Jack says as we head to our room.

In the hotel room, a yellow slip of paper falls out of the packet. More rules.

> *This is a closed and confidential event. If you see anyone you suspect may be a representative of the media, television, press, radio, or newspaper, or anything unusual, immediately contact any security or board person; DO NOT attempt to talk to them. The locations of*

this event are confidential. Do not out yourself to others by being careless. Remember to contact a security person should anyone attempt to ask questions that may lead you to suspect they are the press.

Gulp.

"I hope I can pull this off," I say, worriedly.

"You'll win an Academy Award for your performance," Dylan reassures me.

In the packets we also discover a major change to the agenda. The Friday night social with a special drag show, the workshops, and the fetish ball will not be held at the hotel, but rather off-site at a popular gay club. A sudden eeriness creeps into the weekend. There was a certain comfort to being at a standard chain hotel. The safety net is quickly disappearing, but we'll press on.

A white-hot adrenaline rush exists in the unknown, and the rush is even more intense if there is a chance of getting caught. About two miles from the hotel, a large wooden lodge sits on a hill surrounded by apartment complexes. Pink, red, and blue Christmas lights accent the large round windows. A couple of people stand outside, smoking cigarettes and greeting guests. We've arrived for our first baby steps into the scene.

"Guess we should plunge in," Dylan says, jingling the car keys.

"Yep, let's go," I say, hoping my black velvet pants and black satin shirt fits the dress code. We're undercover at a bondage convention hundreds of miles from home, but all

I've been able to worry about is wardrobe. Scarlett O'Hara would understand my distress.

As we walk up a series of wooden steps, two smokers — one we recognize as Mr. Jack — welcome us with open arms.

"Have fun," says Mr. Jack, beaming at the newbies.

Dylan and I walk up to a counter where we hand over our blue tickets for entry.

"Do you have your pins?" the man behind the counter asks.

We flash the small lapel pins on our shirts. As if the pins symbolize a secret handshake, the counter guard lets us pass into a long, dimly lit hallway lined with faded red carpet. The stairs snake up a tunnel, and loud dance music lies on the other side. So does a buffet lined with raw veggies, chips, dip, and, strangely enough, cocktail weenies and sausage balls. A feast fit for a VFW Saturday night hoedown or . . . a fetish weekend for two.

"Balls and weenies, I'm cracking up," Dylan says. Such a boy.

A giant television screen shows a basketball game while disco music blasts through the club. A few people are playing pool in the back. A lot more people hug and kiss like long-lost friends at a class reunion. Most folks are dressed like, well, random grocery store shoppers. Normalcy pervades my field of vision.

"Hi!" says a squatty fifty-plus woman with highlighted blond hair in a tousled cut. She's dressed conservatively in a long black skirt, black pumps, and a scallop-sleeved lacy black and gold blouse. It's a look that's equally at home at the country club, church potluck, or a cocktail party. Surpris-

ingly, the fashion also works well at a social for bondage en-
thusiasts. "I'm Anne. Are you the folks from Arkansas?"

Nodding our heads like dodo birds, we introduce ourselves and marvel at the BDSM grapevine. Word zooms
when a couple travels several hundred miles to attend a function like this. I mess up and say my real name, but Anne just
smiles. "This place is such a special place to me. My master
proposed to me on that stage during a drag show three
years ago." Anne's eyes shine with the memory.

Dylan and I both try to contain our amazement, shock,
and laughter. This grandmother-type has a master, who
popped the question while surrounded by queens? It's becoming rapidly apparent that appearances are deceiving. I
look down at the floor, and the urge to laugh passes.

"Enjoy yourselves," she says, floating off.

"There are a lot of old people here," Dylan remarks, cast-
ing his gaze around the room.

Indeed, he's right. These are folks who would remember
the Beatles' first appearance on *The Ed Sullivan Show* and
the lunar landing the year I was born. Equal parts leather
and Grecian Formula. Ordering two Cokes, Dylan and I
head to a table near the stage to settle in for the night. We
aren't alone for long. Anne waddles up and introduces us to
her master, Leon, who sits down on a bar stool beside us. A
large man with a Santa Claus–white beard, he is both jovial
and mysterious. Leon initially seems a tad curious about why
two people would drive so many miles for their event. Good
question. Hmm.

"We looked in Arkansas for some events but we just
couldn't find any," Dylan responds. "We are new to the
scene and we like to road trip so we said what the hell."

"So here we are," I interject. As I learned from giving depositions: Only answer the question, then shut up.

"Glad to have you," Leon says, opening up. "This is a good scene. Nice people and a great place to learn and feel welcome. This scene may or may not be for you but it's a good place to learn. This is a good group. I'll get you some e-mail addresses to people in Arkansas so that you can have a connection back there."

Leon tells us he's been in the scene four years. On the side, he makes dragon tails. Dragon tails?

"Long pieces of leather that unfurl," he explains.

For spanking and whipping, I gather.

"Y'all should read some books like *S&M 101* and *The Loving Dominant* to learn more," Leon explains.

Anne walks over and stands by her master, as if awaiting any possible request. Her wait isn't a long one.

"Could you get me another drink?" he asks.

"Yes, sir," she says, scurrying off to the bar to follow orders. The title of respect isn't lost on Dylan, who is clearly trying not to make eye contact with me.

"You guys are coming to the party after this, right?" Leon asks.

Bondage party! Should I be worried? Probably.

"We don't know anything about it," Dylan says.

"I'll get you directions. It's an erotic art show and reception. It's not associated with this weekend's events, though," he states in full legal disclaimer mode.

"Okay, yeah, we're game. We'll go," Dylan says.

I nod like a good servant should.

When Leon leaves to visit bondage buddies across the room, Dylan and I move down the table to a trio of interesting folks: Lena, Jackie, and Harold. Lena, a roly-poly blonde in her late forties, smiles sweetly, looking like she belongs behind a counter wrapping gifts in a Hallmark store. Jackie, a thin woman in her late fifties wearing a burgundy turtleneck sweater with a silver-studded leather vest, sits across from Lena. She's much more severe than Lena and takes long drags off her cigarette. Jackie wears her auburn hair in a short spiky 'do. Beside Jackie, an older man with a permanent scowl and a craggy face sits slightly humped over, listening intently to Jackie and Lena.

After a round of introductions, I find out that Jackie works in the medical field in a major Southern city. What her patients probably don't know is that on the weekends, she's all about some knife-playing. Jackie travels around the country attending leather and BDSM conferences and conventions. She's an expert on the scene, no doubt, and speaks with the timeworn authority of someone who's been around the BDSM block a time or two.

"In Las Vegas you have to be careful," she lectures. "Out there a lot of stuff we do may be viewed as prostitution even if there isn't any sex or assault. But like, say, in Memphis anything goes," she tells us in a cool, serious tone. Jackie doesn't crack a smile and it doesn't take a doctorate degree in bondage to know she's a dominatrix. The attitude shows.

Between puffs on her long cigarette, Jackie tells us about the time she went through a metal detector at the airport. The security attendants took Jackie to a side room and basically made her strip. Finally they discovered what made her buzz: her nipple piercings. Lena appears enamored of Jackie and through bits and pieces, the story comes together that Lena and Jackie have spent some wild weekends together.

"One minute we are talking, the next minute this guy's tied to a chair on the balcony on the Gulf Coast," Lena recalls of one adventure. "Hotels can be fun. I like to be tied to the closets in the hotel but you have to use thin cord to get it to thread through the hinges right." Jeez, this is just like a bunch of guys talking about having the right tools for home improvement. Bizarre-o.

Jackie enjoys creating knife art on Harold, a veteran with a fancy military insignia on his windbreaker.

"I was doing this sunburst design on his chest and all of a sudden he's bleeding a lot like a stuck hog, and I'm having to get all of these paper towels," Jackie says, finally cracking a throaty laugh.

"I'm taking aspirin, you know, for my heart," he says.

"Makes his blood thin," Jackie says. "And boy, was it messy, and it was hard to explain to the doctor what happened to him. Now I just carve him up around his doctor's appointments because of the blood."

"Yeah, I had to tell them she's got really long fingernails," Harold says.

He laughs heartily, and Jackie takes a sip of her drink. Ahh, the perils of middle-age BDSM.

A thumping dance song signals the start of the drag show, which isn't as splashy as Miss Gay America, but the performers know how to dance, slither around on the stage, and work the audience. One thing Dylan and I note: A lot of overweight women have attended this social and appear to be involved in the scene. A woman in a tight red dress with stiletto heels and her brown hair in a mound on top of her head fawns over one of the dancers, clamping money between her teeth and teasing one dancer to take it from her mouth. Her female companion looks on and smiles. During the disco beat ballet of transvestites, a petite woman who looks and acts like a schoolteacher passes out orange flyers with directions to the art show.

"Do y'all have one?" she asks.

"No, we don't," Dylan says.

"Oh, I'm sorry, here, here," she says, making sure we each have one. "I'm Cathy. If you need anything, let me know. Be sure to have this invitation with you. Remember, this party is not officially part of the conference."

The flyer announces that the show is located at a place with more than five thousand square feet of gallery and play space along with separate social, smoking, and play areas. Only an hour into this shindig, I've figured out that play space is just that — a romper room for adults to whip and spank and get off.

When the parade of dancers have flittered offstage, no one lulls around the club for another round of drinks. It's time to go to the erotic art show, which we've figured out will include some playtime. Everyone bolts as if their curfews are up. Dylan and I are lost. We have no idea where the art show is or how to get there from here even though directions are stated on the invite.

"Do you guys know how to get there?" Cathy asks.

"No, no we don't," Dylan says.

Cathy, in a swirl of Dixie hospitality, finds us a couple to follow to the party. Off we go.

Driving down an avenue lined with suburban businesses — a drugstore, a car lot, a bowling alley — Dylan and I can't wait to see what lies ahead. The four-door sedan in front of us pulls into a 1920s–style brick building near a residential area. A light glows in the front room of the building with a sign advertising home furnishings. We enter and are greeted by two women who look like they don't make a habit of refusing dessert. The couple who brought us here say adieu.

"You aren't staying?" I ask.

"No, no, we just brought you guys here," the woman says. "See y'all tomorrow. Good night."

They leave us with the strangers who have a silver money box on their table and a curious look in their eyes. Suddenly, it feels as if it's feeding time in the lion cage, and I'm the steak.

"Hi. You guys are new?"

"Yes," we say. Guess it shows.

"You'll need to read and sign these," one of the women says, handing us consent forms.

It soon becomes clear that this evening isn't about nude art and refreshments at all. On one side of the paper is a Release of Liability Waiver with seven aspects for permission. On the other side are the Rules of Conduct. Glad to know that Dylan, standing beside me reading his list, attended law school and earned his attorney's license. I feel like I need one before scribbling my Suzi Hancock on the piece of paper. The waiver includes the following:

- *I acknowledge that I wish and desire to voluntarily participate in and/or observe BDSM activities and as such am expressing something I consider to be a spiritual activity or sexual preference and understand to be protected under my first amendment rights.*

It's like yoga, which I don't do, but I understand that when people are meditating, to them, it's sacred, quiet time. Apparently so is getting one's buttocks slapped silly. I can dig that.

- *I understand that BDSM activities involve certain real and unpredictable risks.*

No secret that hanging upside down by the ankles while being doused in hot wax is dangerous.

- *I understand and agree that any bodily injury, dismemberment, death, or loss of personal property and expenses as a result of my own intentional or negligent act(s) is my responsibility and I accept same. I also state and acknowledge that the activities associated with BDSM involve risk of injury from or resulting in bruises, contusions, lacerations, scalding and burning, and severe contortion of the human body, and the forgoing list of possible injuries acts is neither complete nor exclusive.*

Dismemberment? Holy riding crop, Batman. How tight do these people have the handcuffs around their wrists?

- *I understand that accidents may occur, mistakes may be made, and equipment and devices may fail or malfunction, and that the premises in which I desire to participate in BDSM activities do not include medical facilities, and that injuries may be aggravated by delay in receiving medical attention.*

Wonder if a first-aid kit is nearby?

- *As partial consideration for being permitted to participate in and/or observe BDSM activities, scheduled, planned, unscheduled, or unplanned, I hereby release from any legal liability and agree not to sue, claim against the property of, or prosecute, and to indemnify and hold harmless the host and/or place of business, their associates, agents . . . for any and all injury or death caused by or resulting from my voluntary participation in BDSM activities.*

Am I about to join Cirque du Soleil?

- *This Release of Liability shall be binding upon me, my heirs, my estate, assigns, legal guardian, and my personal representatives.*

So much for my heirs becoming rich if I get tangled up in some lethal electrical tape.

- *I have carefully read this Release of Liability and fully understand its contents.*

I sign on the dotted line without plans to participate in the impending kinkfest. But stranger things have happened. I hope that the next hour doesn't find me begging for mercy like a scrawny accountant getting pummeled by an Iron Belle.

The Rules of Conduct pique the curiosity even more.

- *BDSM play shall be safe, sane, and, above all, consensual, as defined by the individuals who are directly involved. Guests are expected to be responsible, courteous, tolerant adults. Behavior that is perceived as dangerous, offensive, threatening, abusive, coercive, illegal, or harassing by other members or guests will not be permitted.*
- *Alcohol, illegal drugs, and poppers are not allowed — period!*

(According to a BDSM dictionary, poppers are volatile nitrites, such as amyl nitrate, butyl nitrite, isobutyl nitrite, and alkyl nitrites, used for inhalation. They are said to increase sexual pleasure, relax muscles, and decrease sensitivity to pain. They are often labeled as incense or room deodorizer.)

- *No guns or illegal weapons. No unsheathed knives or swords except during a scene.*
- *Cameras, video recorders, audio recorders, or other recording devices of any kind are not allowed.*
- *Anal intercourse, vaginal intercourse, oral sex, and fisting are not allowed. Dildos and other plugs may not be used.*

Oh my. Fisting? Egad. I'm not sure which is more disturbing — the thought of fisting or knowing that a prohibition on such things has to be spelled out in writing.

- *Remember that "No" means NO, not "maybe" or "yes."*
- *Ask permission before handling or using someone else's toys or equipment. Ask permission before touching someone.*

Good rules to have in daily life, too.

- *Talk quietly when near a scene, and keep your distance from players and play space.*
- *Do not join a scene unless you're invited first.*

Guess it wouldn't behoove someone to get in the mix of a bunch of people wielding weapons.

- *If you think a scene is unsafe, don't interfere, but do talk to a Dungeon Master.*

I haven't talked to a dungeon master since junior high when some of my friends were into Dungeon and Dragons. Pass the twelve-sided dice, please.

- *Use street-appropriate dress and behavior when you are in public areas.*

That means slip some denims over the latex if you want to step aside for a smoke.

- *Dungeon Master (DM) decisions are final. No appeals, arguments, or whining allowed. If a DM says to stop a scene, the scene must stop immediately.*

Would you really argue with a man who can wield a whip better than Zorro?

- *Dungeon safewords are "Red" and "Safeword." Use of either means "Stop doing what you're doing NOW!" Do not use these words in a prank or joke.*
- *Don't hog the equipment or play space. Limit space to thirty minutes or less when others are waiting.*

Just like children's playground rules.

- *Clean play equipment after use with paper towels and disinfectant. Dispose of used sharps in biohazard containers.*
- *No cutting, breath play (choking, breath control, bondage around the neck, etc.), water sports (urine), or scat play (feces).*

One word: Gross!

- *Check with a Dungeon Master before a scene that involves piercing, fire play, waxing, or suspension.*

Someone's going to die here tonight.
Dylan and I hand over the forms.
"Tickets for one night, or two?" one of them asks.
"Two," Dylan and I say in unison.

"It's twenty-five dollars for a couple for two nights if you want to come back tomorrow night," the woman says.

One night certainly won't be enough to see everything. Dylan and I glance at each other and smile, placing twenty-five dollars on the table. In a matter of seconds, we, the giddy voyeurs, will be entering a spanking wonderland. Through the looking glass we go.

In the reception area, charcoal and pastel prints on torn newsprint line the white walls. Bottles of soda and two bags of chocolate chip cookies sit on a round table. Two sets of chairs form half moons around the art, and a boom box plays an eerie New Age tune that reminds me of something from a 1970s horror movie. Dylan and I peruse the art as if we are buyers looking for an S&M Picasso to hang in the foyer. The bag of cookies entices Dylan.

"Don't eat one, you don't know the rules," I hiss-whisper.

He ignores me and eats a cookie just as a parade of people bustle in through the door. They roll in suitcases on wheels and carry brown gun cases along with flat silver and black music instrument cases. Some people say hello, some walk past focused on another door in front of them. No one looks at the art. It's simply a ruse, a cover, to protect everyone.

"Let's follow them," I say.

"Let's!" Dylan echoes, still munching.

We walk through another small area with a blue floral sofa and a curio cabinet holding faded silk flowers, a social area with leftover furniture from someone's redecorated house. A steep stairwell greets us and we follow the stiletto and leather-booted crew up the concrete stairs. It doesn't take James Bond to figure out that this is not a true, medieval-type dungeon since we're going up stairs and not down into a dark, torch-lit stone strong cell. Like a fuzzy camera becoming focused, our location becomes clear: a dance studio where tutu-tushied tots practice in the afternoons but bondage babes in shackles play at midnight.

We walk into a waiting area that features a futon, a big-screen television, and a poster of the Rockettes on the wall. To one side, a low massage table sits with plastic wrapped around it. A few chairs sit around the room's perimeter. Two white double doors are closed in front of us. Get me Monty Hall — I want to know what's behind Door Number One. As if the dungeon folks can read my mind, the doors open.

Mirrors line one entire wall for the benefit of ballerinas and bondage queens. Two wooden "X's" — a black one and a red one — lean against a wall. We quickly learn that these are St. Andrew's crosses. Two other pieces of equipment stand in the middle of the wooden dance floor. A silver bar connected to a wooden frame with buckled handcuffs stands near the two doors. Next to it, further down the long room, is a more primitive contraption called a rig, with slots for arms. I haven't been this clueless about equipment since my brief flirtation with gymnastics.

Dylan strikes up a conservation with a woman whom he had chatted with earlier in the evening, and she gives him an impromptu tour of the equipment.

"She's looking for a new submissive," one of the men tells me. "She's a master with the whip."

Uh-oh. Dylan's getting interviewed and doesn't even know it. For a nanosecond, I imagine a shackled Dylan getting his butt spanked like a five-year-old by this fierce dom, but the thought quickly vanishes when we are ordered back into the front room. A limber, petite-framed man who looks like he could twirl better than Baryshnikov reviews the rules that we signed before entering this master-servant Disneyland.

"Let's play, let's have a good party," he says, sounding like a boxing referee urging a good clean fight.

A quick tour of the equipment follows as three dungeon masters brag on the craftsmanship of the pieces. Some of the creations can hold up to seven hundred pounds. Word must have quickly spread through this group that we are visitors from out-of-town because the welcome wagon is chugging along at full force.

"You guys are new, right?" a large man named Lance, wearing leather boots snatched from Napoleon's closet asks after the tour.

We nod affirmatively, and he says, "Well, if there is anything you want to try or have questions about just ask. You want to see how anything works, we can do that. We have a brand-new violet wand you might be interested in," he says.

These people are über-friendly and sincere. They could easily give welcoming lessons to a country church congregation. We don't know what a violet wand is but we sure want to know.

Earlier at the social, Dylan and I had met Greg, a thirty-something clean-cut blonde guy with a silver chain and small padlock around his neck. He welcomed us and praised the group of people involved. Greg said he had been living the lifestyle for a few years and had actually met his new mistress at his son's daycare. That remark boggled our minds for at least two hours. Now, Greg has shown up in the dungeon with his mistress, Laura, a diminutive sexy blonde with curves in the right places, a dazzling smile, and stunning aquamarine eyes. Easy to imagine her at daycare, this leather-clad sexpot.

"Let's get someone to try the violet wand for you guys," says Lance. "Greg, you want to demonstrate it? He hates it, but maybe he'll do it."

Greg, who seemed like a perfectly strong and independent man two hours ago, whimpers and looks at Mistress Laura. "Go ahead," she purrs. "It'll be fine." Laura urges Greg to take on the challenge.

"He really hates it," Lance says to us, a trace of sympathy in his voice as he unpacks the wand from a briefcase lined with foam.

I feel bad that these people are making someone lie down and be tortured for our benefit. But Greg does as his mistress says, shedding his black silk shirt and lying down on the workout bench for our crash course in Violet Wand 101.

The violet wand, also known as a Tesla Coil, is very similar to a Van de Graaff generator, the popular science museum exhibit that makes hair stand on end. A purple electrical current zaps through a glass lightbulb that slides quickly across a person's body. Within a minute, red streaks glow on Greg's back.

"You okay?" Lance keeps asking Greg. His tone is caring, almost tender.

Greg mumbles yes, forcing the words through his gritted teeth.

Lance explains how the lightbulb attachment can be swapped out for a smaller glass piece resembling a chandelier bulb. He exchanges the attachments and begins to

stroke Greg's back again. Then, he exchanges that bulb for
a flat-head round glass attachment that creates a glowing
purple circle.

"It's like the one dermatologists use," Lance explains.

He rubs the attachment on Greg's back for another minute
or two. Greg whimpers as the electricity crackles.

"Y'all want to try it?" he asks.

I see lawsuit written all over this so I decline. So does Dylan. We haven't lost our minds. Yet.

Then, Lance hands Greg a small silver barbell with a yellow cap on one end and a red one on the other. "This will
allow you to run your hands over him and generate your
own electrical current on his body. I like this because it's a
little more personal and I can control it," Lance says as he
starts to run his large hands over Greg's back.

"Try it," he insists.

Okay, I cave in. Running fingers down Greg's arm, a purple electrical arc zings through my fingertips like I'm a wiz-
ard. Greg flinches as Laura watches him. After about ten
seconds, Lance says, "That's enough."

Greg rises from the bench and kneels in front of Laura who
caresses his head as if he is a puppy. He stays in that position as Laura coos reassurance in his ears. The stripes down
his back are sunburn red. As Dylan and I turn to find the next
adventure, the smell of burning flesh sears our senses, and
my fingers still tingle.

A hypnotizing techno beat engulfs the dungeon while
voyeurs and participants whisper. Dylan and I plop down on
the long wooden bench across from the mirrored wall and

wait to see some action. Greg and Laura hit the contraptions first, going for the silver suspension bar. Greg takes off his shirt and Laura snaps his wrists into red cuffs, seductively running her hands over his body. On the side of the contraption, Laura opens her large brown suitcase and checks out the playwares. Greg looks straight ahead in the mirror as Laura orbits him like a satellite circling a planet. Strutting in front of him, she moves her hands across his bare chest. In a swift move, she unbuckles his black leather belt with silver studs, unbuttons his pants, and pulls them quickly to the floor. His bare butt shines at us, and his penis looks chubby in the mirror's reflection. A glint of silver catches my attention.

"Is his dick pierced?" Dylan whispers.

"Cock ring," I say with ease and expertise, as if I see such things every day.

"Ah," Dylan says, focusing on the scene in front of us.

Laura begins by striking a black leather riding crop on Greg's firm butt. Within seconds, she's mastered a spellbinding rhythm in time with the pulsating beat. She strikes Greg's butt as if she is whacking a drum, and his butt turns red as she continues to rap and tap for ten minutes. She stops for a split second, switches her pleasure device to a thin rattan cane, and without missing an erotic beat, resumes her punishment, striking Greg's butt and upper thighs repeatedly. After about ten more minutes, when Greg is warmed up like a piece of beef on a hot grill, Laura switches devices once again, this time choosing a thin wooden paddle that packs a punch. Out of all her torture goodies, this one thwacks the worst. It gets Greg's attention, too. His whimpers get closer to howls.

Before Laura finishes with Greg, Anne and Leon take to

the floor for their S&M tango. Her contraption of choice? The black St. Andrew's cross. Leon carries a silver briefcase, which he sits on the floor and unlocks, showing enough high-tech equipment to make the CIA look twice. Without a grain of modesty, Anne, with her back toward us, strips out of her skirt and lacy blouse. Exhibitionism is not lacking in the room. A black thong slices up her butt, which would be a perfect canvas for a liposuctionist. With her master's help, Anne secures her wrists into the cuffs on the cross, and then Leon places some space-age sunglasses and silver head-phones on Anne's eyes and ears. He puts his own pair of earphones on, and with the ease of an experienced circus trainer, begins flogging Anne in time with some mysterious beat only the two of them can hear.

Leon maneuvers a pair of floggers against Anne in a pre-cise robotic revolution like a baton twirler. While Anne and Leon get busy, a twenty-something girl with a body as thin as an umbrella handle, dark hair, and a pink kitten collar walks to the sidelines. Dressed in a black latex merry widow and thigh-high stockings, she turns and reveals two large blue-blackgreen bruises on her butt cheeks. "This isn't her first rodeo," whispers Dylan.

Master John, a six-foot-four-inch shirtless grizzly of a man, moves a circular tie-rack stand next to a bench, where his topless wife kneels over a beam like a good Catholic schoolgirl waiting for her communion wafer. He meticu-lously places a dozen whips, floggers, and other leather goodies onto the rack and wastes no time punishing his wife who, by the look and sound of things has been a very, very bad girl.

Around one in the morning, we leave the leather clan at the dungeon and head back to the hotel. Dylan and I are rendered speechless by what we've seen and by the ease with which we discovered the secret password into this kinky wonderland.

"Everyone is so normal; these could be anyone's parents or coworkers," he says. "And they are so nice. Who knew pain people would be so friendly. I feel kinda bad for going undercover. It's like I'm lying to my mom or something."

"I felt like a bug-eyed weirdo girl. I felt like my eyeballs were out on stilts and I was the weirdo, because I don't want my ass spanked in public."

Dylan is still hung up on the niceness. "It was like being at a new church with everyone welcoming you and making sure you have what you need. It was graciousness and Southern hospitality to the nines," he says, amazed.

"Yeah, I almost feel a little guilty we snuck in," I say.

"I know what you mean," he says.

By morning, that guilt vanishes and curiosity returns with a vengeance. We can't wait to return to the club where the drag show was to get a look at the playthings for sale from the vendors.

"So y'all decided to come back. We didn't run you off," says Mr. Jack, standing outside smoking a cigarette.

"No, we had fun last night," I say. And that's no lie, we did.

"Well, you should learn a lot today," he says.

"That's what we're hoping," Dylan says.

Vendors hawk everything from whips and feather ticklers to glass dildos and glittery maces with spikes that look like some sort of medieval weapons — for massages, I'm told. Yeow. Each vendor has business cards just in case I want to order something later. In his spare time, a minister — yes, a Christian one — forges iron shackles to sell at events like this one. Anne's master, Leon, makes dragon tails and tongues (shorter versions of the tails) — in various colors of leather — red, teal, yellow, blue. Also for sale at the show: riding crops in all sizes and prices, harnesses, chain mail gear, vibrating rubber duckies, candles, knives, leather gloves, and dental picks. I didn't ask what those are used for in the play space. Is this where the sadistic dentist in *The Little Shop of Horrors* browses?

"There's coffee available on the bar," Mr. Jack says, walking up to us. "Don't forget the silent auction."

Oh, yes, like at any good nonprofit fund-raiser, there's a silent auction, but this one is different than most. The auction items read like a must-have list for the bondage fanatic. Low-burning candles for wax play (à la Madonna in *Body of Evidence*,) a chain mail collar, erotic black-and-white photographs, a thirty-minute caning session, leather wrist and ankle restraints, a slapper. Dylan makes an offer on the candles and the slapper. I open the bid with five dollars for the chain mail collar because it would look nice with a black turtleneck sweater.

More people arrive on Saturday morning. Everyone appears to be good friends. The cozy atmosphere around the vendors generates a good environment for education. After all, if we're going to use candles, we should know how to use them properly. If we want to play with fire, we should know how to use matches. If we want to tie each other up, we should know how to tie a good, strong knot.

A fiftyish couple — Rick, a former professor, and Ruth, a health care worker — serve as the educators for the first seminar. Rick and Ruth look like they belong more at a *Star Trek* convention than at a BDSM weekend. Dylan and I are the first to wander over and start asking questions. Just like in the real world, shy people exist in the fetish world. Many people still mingle around the vendors, so the session becomes an informal discussion about how to survive as a couple in the scene.

The first thing Rick wants us to remember is "Your kink is not my kink, but your kink is okay." It's a mantra for people in the scene who may not like what another person does — like rope play, for instance — but agree that those fetishes should be accepted. Certainly any one kink shouldn't be criticized or judged. Rick gives an example. He wasn't into an age play scene with a partner who liked pretending she was a teenage girl, but he went with it.

"It turned out to be very hot," he exclaims, slightly frothy with the memory. "The point is free your mind, give stuff a try. If you don't like it, tell your partner, but try it first — you might just like it."

Rick likes to use the term "vanilla" to describe ordinary, conventional life, both sexual and otherwise. He talks over everyone's head like the scholar that he is. I eventually tune out and focus on an overweight woman across the room in a prim and proper white lace dress walking out of the vendor fair with a riding crop. Eventually, Ruth tells Rick to hush and let other people express a thought or opinion once in a while.

Master John, who we last saw whipping his wife at the play party Friday night, sits across from me. He wears a big silver S&M belt buckle and a black T-shirt with black jeans. His wife, who says she works in health-care, wears a black t-shirt that says I LIKE PAIN. WHAT'S YOUR EXCUSE? John has something to share with the group.

"I'm sitting drinking coffee the other day and my teenage daughter comes in and says she needs to talk to me about alternative lifestyles. D'oh! I'm thinking Did you find something in my library? But she hadn't. She wants to tell me she is gay. At first I was like, Kink must run in our family. Then I was relieved. I don't have to worry about her getting pregnant now," he says, chuckling.

The group laughs as the subject turns to being into an alternative lifestyle and living in the Bible Belt. The consensus: It ain't easy.

"It's a secret-society lifestyle down here," says a man beside me who looks like he shops regularly at the Banana Republic. "Everyone wants to know your business in the South."

Rick, who now lives in New England, says, "What's curious down here is how the first question anyone asks someone when they first meet is 'Where do you go to church?'"

True, but in my experience if you are a woman the first question is Where does your husband work? Then the second question is about church.

"Yeah, you have to be more down-lo down here. Everyone wants to know their neighbors and what their neighbors are doing. And some of these people may not really want to know what happens behind their neighbors' four walls," says Master John. The circle laughs again.

Rick says it's time for the South, and the rest of the country for that matter, to stand up and admit to kinks. "It only takes one person to stand up and admit to having a kink, especially in the South."

A chorus of amens follow his advice but my money is on Master John not wearing that belt buckle to work on Monday morning and telling his coworkers what he did this weekend.

It's rope time!

Goodness gracious. The master rope man is a hippie cracker with a mullet and a beer gut who talks in a monotone about Japanese bondage rope tricks called shibari. He makes his own rope using jute, and he babbles endlessly about the fibers of such natural materials. The droning makes my mind roam. Where do these people come from? Do they live and breathe this lifestyle twenty-four seven? Or do they kick back once in a while and watch the Cartoon Network? And who do I know in Arkansas who likes the violet wand for foreplay? Certainly, there is my married friend Nick who has told me through instant messages about his fantasies to be a servant. He's even offered to wash my car. But whether he owns, or even knows about, the violet wand, will have to be explored when I return home.

Rope man's submissive, a thin barefoot woman who must wear an A-cup, sits in jeans to the side of the wooden frame, which has been moved from the play space of last night to the club. She gets up once and walks to the bar to retrieve a soda for him. When it's time for her part of the show, she unzips her blue jeans and slips out of them. A black leotard covers her body. She whips her long red hair into a ponytail and positions herself in the middle of the frame.

The rope guru smiles and jokes with the woman as he starts to wrap the rope around her as if she is the frame for a macramé masterpiece. Within seconds, he has her wrapped in rope with elaborate secure knots, her arms behind her back, and her ankles tied to her arms. She sways like a tire swing on an oak tree.

"I just want to ride her," Dylan whispers.

In this workshop, I've learned how to tie a secure knot and hoist up my lover, or a sail if I find myself stranded on a yacht.

Lena arrives at the seminar late but smiles and rushes over to us as soon as the shibari god finishes his lecture. She settles in next to us and starts getting chatty.

"You guys having fun?" she asks.

"Yeah," we say.

"Good. It's a lot to take in but if you need some help or anything, let me know," she says.

"Can I ask you some questions?" Dylan boldly asks.

"Sure, of course. I'm here to help," she says smirking.

"Are you more a submissive or a dominant?" he asks.

Dylan knows how to ask the pertinent questions.

Lena is very open about her S&M life. "I like being a submissive. But you know trust is the foundation of all of this. You have to find someone who is worthy of your trust because the dom has all the power, and it's all in the negotiations, too. Like my stepmother humiliated me when I was growing up, so I can't take humiliation. I have to explain 'These are the things you can't say to me.'"

Before a scene, we've learned, negotiations occur. Sometimes they are more complicated than those between the United Nations and the White House.

Some people have these six-hour negotiations where one person says, "Can I do this?" The other person says yes or no or I want you to do this or don't do that. Sometimes people are more into the negotiating than the scene itself.

Lena tells us that seven levels exist in the BDSM world.

1. Dominant: An individual who accepts the submissive's power and uses it for their mutual pleasure.
2. Submissive: An individual who gives up power in a BDSM relationship for the mutual pleasure of those involved.
3. Top: A person who in play delivers the stimulation but does not require the submission of his or her partner.
4. Bottom: Someone who engages in stimulation play as the receiver of the stimulation but who does create a semblance of submission as part of his or her play.
5. Sadist: An individual who enjoys causing pain in a nonconsensual manner or regardless of the presence or absence of consent. That term comes from the writings of the Marquis de Sade.
6. Masochist: An individual who derives pleasure from pain.
7. Switcher: A person who enjoys both the dominant/top and submissive/bottom roles.

She tells us that the play scenes we saw on Friday night were nothing compared to some things she has heard about or seen. There's a mistress, the best of them all, in another part of Alabama who is the goddess of caning. On her slave's ass and legs, she created a basket-weave pattern that lasted for days. Lena has even heard about a woman in New Orleans who had her vagina sewn up with needle and thread in front of everyone. I'm shocked by this bit of information. Surprisingly, Lena likes edgier play — with fire.

"Fire?" I ask.

"Oh, goodness, yes. That is so erotic. I had it done to my back. You have alcohol rubbed on your arm or your body and then someone lights a cotton swab and traces the swab along the alcohol and their hand is right behind the flame to snuff out the fire. God, it feels good."

Yeouch!

How did a seemingly vanilla girl like Lena get involved in the scene? It began with a teenage fantasy of being tied up. She says she had always fantasized about bondage and a couple of years ago she began dabbling in bondage forums on the Internet. From there, a group invited her to a "munch," a weekly or monthly gathering at a vanilla restaurant like an Applebee's or an Olive Garden to get to know people in the scene in a nonthreatening environment.

"I sat in the car for fifteen minutes mustering up the courage to go in," she says. She's glad she did. The adventure has afforded her avenues of delight she never knew existed.

"I've met terrific friends in the scene, but it's odd. If you see someone from the scene in public aside from a munch, you don't acknowledge them. It's important to protect privacy."

Anne bops up and joins the conversation. "Tell them about your collar," Lena urges.

Anne giggles like a schoolgirl and touches the silver necklace around her neck, which I had failed to notice because it looks like a standard silver collar necklace. "Master found it at a gun show. He said, 'I want to see that one,' and the woman says 'You mean the collar?' When she called it a collar, Master knew he had to get it."

Anne tells us that when she gets up in the mornings, she takes a shower, makes coffee, and fetches Leon's pills before heading back to bed. By that time, he's awake and Anne leans over the bed, at which point Leon takes the collar from the headboard and places it around her neck.

"I wear it to work. Then, at the end of the day, he takes it off of me and puts it back on the headboard. I never take it off myself. I'm not allowed to do it. It's his job," she explains.

"What do you do when people ask you about it?" I ask.

"I tell them it's a gift from my husband because it is."

Anne and Leon met, not surprisingly, on the Internet like so many people here do. Both of them were coming out of thirty-plus-year marriages. They developed a friendship on-line, took it offline, and then . . . Master dropped the bomb.

"He mentioned he was into this lifestyle and I, well, I freaked," she recalls.

That was it. Anne decided she didn't want anything else to do with this man. At all. Forget about it. She cried for days. Sometimes, though, attraction, regardless of the perils involved and common sense telling us otherwise, is undeniable.

"I didn't want to lose his friendship. I figured he could keep that part of his life separate."

Compartmentalizing didn't suit Leon, though, and he soon talked Anne into attending a BDSM event with him.

"I was just a little country girl. I didn't know anything like this existed," she drawls, her eyes twinkling. "I thought it would be whips and chains in a dirty old dungeon." She certainly didn't expect to enjoy such things as spankings. But, oh, how she does.

"I need someone to control me. I can be bad. I need to do things for someone, to feel needed. I really can be bad. I really can," she says, grinning impishly. I wonder what she does that is so bad that she would need whipping. But in this topsy-turvy lifestyle something as benign as forgetting to ask permission to go to the rest room could be considered reckless disregard for authority.

Anne fell in lust with the lifestyle and in love with her master. She ended up marrying him not once but twice in two separate ceremonies — one, a traditional wedding with family attending, the second, a bondage-style wedding at the play space. At the fetish wedding, two bridesmaids, including Lena, flanked Anne as she took vows promising to be her master's servant.

"I cried," Lena says, smiling and hugging Anne. "It was beautiful."

When all the promises were made and vows exchanged, the minister, a real-honest-to-God one, told Master, "You may now spank the bride."

"I hiked up my skirt and he went at it," she says, grinning like a preteen sneaking a smoke behind the schoolhouse.

She shows us a ring with the symbol for BDSM, a swirly emblem that looks like a fan blade, which Leon gave her during the fetish ceremony. At the vanilla ceremony in a church with a Baptist minister and her children present, he gave her a gold wedding band. Does she feel like she is living a double life?

"Well, yeah, I do, sometimes. I mean you have the life out there, paying bills, going to work, doing everything that has to be done, but what gets you through the day is knowing that you come home to your real life after all of that."

I've always wanted to see a real-life in-the-flesh dominatrix, but Lady Chiffon isn't the dom of my fantasies. Not by a long shot. Lady Chiffon is not svelte. She's doesn't wear latex. There's no dark kohl around her eyes or crimson cherry lipstick on her lips. No funky goth jewelry adorns her neck. Thigh-high boots? Nope. Instead, she's a little on the curvy side with the roundness accentuated — and not in a good way — by a black polyester dress. She wears not a smidgen of makeup. Her scuffed black pumps have seen better days. But she has a scary demeanor, and I wouldn't dare express my opinions to her. She could easily kick my ass. Or at least wallop it good and hard.

Chiffon isn't here to explain the art of dominating. She will tell us all about how to be a submissive because she's been one damnit, and she wants to share her knowledge about how to be a perfect, nonannoying slave. Nothing irritates her more than a subordinate who doesn't know what he is doing.

"It took me a long time to get where I am. I learned, I begged to be taught," she says in an over-the-top clipped tone. "It took me three — count them, three — years to be able to even lie beside my master. I earned the right. Earned it."

Chiffon quickly informs the crowd — the biggest one of any seminar so far — that those days are o-v-e-r. After nine years of being someone's footstool — literally — she saw the light of dominance and transferred to the other side.

Now, she's Charlie and someone else is the angel doing the dirty work. Remember this: Servitude is no nine-to-five gig, no ma'am. If ever there was such a thing as working twenty-four seven, slaves do it. They don't just retrieve a glass of water or a pair of slippers for their master or mistress. They do much more, even going so far as seeking permission to eat at the kitchen table, and, like in lovemaking, an art exists in the sphere of slavery.

For instance, slaves must hold their hands a certain way. Palms out is a good way; it shows reception, willingness. And for goodness sake, do not — and Lady Chiffon means *do not* — make jerky motions.

"You should be constantly thinking, staying fluid, moving. Do not make me notice you. I do not want to notice you. If you come into a room where I am, keep moving. In two minutes you will blend in and I will not notice you," she emphasizes. "I do not want to notice you."

Message received.

"You are there to serve me," she says. "It's all about me and it should be about me. Do not get into my personal space. Do not hover around me."

Can we say e-g-o?

Not that the thought has ever crossed my mind prior to this moment, but Lady Chiffon is about to tell me how to be a human footstool. "I need a volunteer. How about you?" she says, pointing to . . . whew, Lena who is right beside me. No way in hell do I want to volunteer for this demonstration. Lady Chiffon offers Lena a chair. Lena, usually a submissive, seems strangely out of place and says so: "I feel like I should be doing this for you."

"It's okay to be in power now," Lady Chiffon says, validating Lena's nervousness.

Lady Chiffon gets down on her elbows and knees in front of Lena, as if she is praying toward Mecca. "Now put your feet on my back. Go ahead, it's okay." Lena obeys, reluctant to place her submissive footsies on the back of a dom.

"See, it's comfortable for me, if I have my back positioned just so. I could stay like this for hours," Chiffon says, but she doesn't stay in her submissive position for very long.

Chiffon's mannerisms dictate a person who has a few, shall I say, issues. She talks about how she's a busy person and her servant should walk behind her, matching her stride so that if Chiffon needs a folder on the way to a meeting, she simply reaches back and in magical step-in-time her servant will know just the precise moment to hand it to her. I hate to break the news to her but Chiffon's world is nothing novel. Political aides do that very thing all the time. Thought: Maybe the whole world is made up of doms and subs, but we just call them by different titles.

Between seminars, Dylan keeps a close eye on his silent auction item. So far, he's lost the candles, but he's winning the slapper — a leather paddle with flaps of leather. I've lost the collar. It's up to thirty dollars and I don't care to bid higher. I bought an erotic novel that Lena highly recommends. The author is the Danielle Steele of the BDSM world, and giddiness reigns because she has actually graced the conference with her presence.

"Anne Rice tried writing about bondage clubs and all but

her stuff is so not real. That's a fantasy world she made up. Julia writes about the real stuff," Lena says.

The Julia seminar is held in a faded area of the club that has seen better days and desperately needs redecorating. No one cares because there she is — the author of several books about erotic bondage and hot sex. At first glance, I can't believe it's her. While Anne Rice presents a dark, gothic image for her fans, Julia has no such presence; she's just a writer wearing some casual slacks and a blouse. In fact, she looks dowdy, but her words captivate the audience, especially the parts about how to live a master-servant life in the real world.

Say you are in Wal-Mart buying lawn furniture. No way can you say "Yes, master, no, master" without causing a stare or two. But you can say, "Yes, sir." Anything with a title of respect. Some couples who live this lifestyle actually have cute code words they use in front of their vanilla friends, who are none the wiser. "Whatever you say, you're the boss," is one such phase. Heavens to Betsy! I know tons of couples who say that to each other. Now, I shall forever be curious about these people. And not in a good way. Curiosity was always the devil on my shoulder, anyway.

Julia often talks in BDSM lingo that is both foreign and peculiar. She mentions a slave school in Arizona, where masters send their servants to learn protocol. If a third party — a slave — is coming into a relationship, both parties should be happy and know the roles of the slave. The slave is not merely about sex. No, sir, it's all about servitude. It's hard being a master.

"You always have to think for the slave and that can be exhausting," says one participant.

Cathy, the meek hospitality queen from Friday night, in her starched jeans and fetish ball T-shirt, likes being a servant. "I like doing stuff for people. It makes me feel worthy, like I have some self-worth. But sometimes I get upset that I am taken for granted." She almost looks like she could cry. She's a submissive with self-esteem issues. Who would have thought it?

That can be a problem, but I don't hear how to solve it because my mind is mired in a bondage traffic jam caused by too much eccentric jargon. And then I learn . . .

The author's been branded — yes, the same process that cows undergo. To make sure her brand was raised, she kept picking at the scab for weeks. Okay, I need a barf bag and a time-out. Thank the bondage gods that's the last lesson of the day.

The French maid costume makes me look like a frilly meringue.

In the hotel, I peek out into the hallway when doors slam. Everyone leaving wears evening clothes, sequins, or black cocktail dresses. No latex for miles. No leather in the corridor. Dylan, in his black leather cape, and I will arrive looking like the freaks we are. Typical and not surprising.

"Don't stress, let's just go and have a good time," he says.

When we arrive back at the club, there's latex aplenty. Somewhere between the hotel and club, a Superman-type phone booth must exist so that the bondage gods and goddesses can transform. By this time, Dylan and I are old pros at showing the secret pins and handing the blue tickets to the doorman. We greet everyone as if we are the new prom king and queen on the scene.

"I won the slapper!" he says, returning from the silent auction table. We are silly in a not-so-cool way when a man with a long silver ponytail approaches us.

"My mistress would like to touch your cape. May she?" asks the man.

"Yes, of course," Dylan says, granting permission.

"Oooh, that's nice," the woman gushes.

That's the start of numerous compliments on Dylan's rented cape.

"People are so nice here," he whispers to me.

Indeed, no one touches anyone or anything belonging to someone else without asking. It's a nice throwback to a time when manners and chivalry meant something.

Greg and Laura greet us with big smiles. She looks like Elvira in a latex dress with widow peak sleeves and a long black wig. Her black leather boots match perfectly. Greg wears typical clubbing gear — leather pants and a long, flowing brightly colored shirt with his chain and lock around his neck.

"So, have y'all decided which one is the dominant and which one is the submissive?" Greg asks.

"No, no, we haven't," Dylan says.

"No, we can't make up our minds," I say.

"It's okay to switch," Greg says.

We nod.

"Would you like some more wine, ma'am?" Greg asks Laura.

"No," she replies.

"I'd like to get another beer, is that okay?"

"Yes," she says.

"Would you like anything?" he asks me.

"No, thanks."

While he disappears, Laura lays her story on the line. The two thirty-somethings met four months ago at a daycare where both of their children attend. Laura and Greg have both been married previously. Greg, who works as an architect, came into the scene a few years ago. Laura, who works in technology, never suspected Greg's lifestyle. When she visited his five-thousand-square-foot house and saw the chains and cuffs on the wall, she knew something was amiss. Indeed, Greg hosts monthly parties at his house for people in the scene, including Anne and her master.

"I'll try anything once, so I did, and here I am," she says.

Laura admits that it's hard to be a mistress because she is continuously thinking for Greg, telling him what to do next. Draining, she says. When Laura visits Greg at his house, he won't let her lift a finger. Literally, pouring tea for her, picking the cup up when she is finished and taking it to the sink. He even offers to hold the cup while she sips. She drew the line on that action.

Mr. Jack waves hello and greets us.

"Having fun? Have you two figured out who's the dominant?"

The question of the night.

"No, we haven't," we chime.

"How did you get into the scene?" Dylan, ever investigatory, asks.

Jack's story begins in the 1960s with a prostitute in Vietnam. Before sex one night, the Asian vamp slapped Mr. Jack. He returned the slap. To his surprise and later delight, she enjoyed it. Mr. Jack soon learned that his hooker had been a submissive for a French military officer when France controlled the country. She learned her tricks from the officer; Mr. Jack learned his from her. There was no going back after that. Thirty years later, Mr. Jack is still hooked.

The fetish ball is a mere formality, a gathering to have a few drinks before the play party, which is all anyone seems to care about. Like everyone else, Dylan and I can't wait to see more of the same from last night. We roll into the front doors this time like old friends of the ticket takers, pass the cookies, and head right up the stairs to the play space. Friday night was like *Sesame Street* compared to the Saturday night action. On the big-screen television, a bondage scene rolls with a striking Asian woman with an edgy bob, dressed to the hilt in latex and fishnets. Unlike Lady Chiffon, she's the kind of dominatrix I've always imagined. Her name is Fetish Diva Midori, a legend in the BDSM world, and on the screen, she's giving a severe whacking to a man with a ball gag in his mouth and his balls wrapped tightly in saran wrap.

"Diva Midori is wonderful," Gail, yet another overweight woman in her forties, says dreamily. "She's coming to Kentucky sometime soon for a demo. I've got to see her do one."

The guy beside her looks like a plumber or the bug man who visits my apartment. An average nonthreatening Joe, but for the evening, he's got power because he's a dungeon master, designated as such by the red sash around his waist. Gail watches the video while giving us the skinny on bondage in the South. In Memphis, anything goes. Total nudity. Butt plugs. Dildos. Hanging upside-down torture, hot wax, and metal gadgets. In Nashville, about the same, slightly not as hard-core. In Alabama, things are a tad more conservative, but bondage clubs dot the state from the Gulf Coast to the Tennessee stateline. Heck, she says, in Alabama, the state still has a law on the books that says anything other than missionary-position during sex is illegal. If what I've seen is conservative, get me Jerry Falwell on the phone.

Once the rules are repeated for the participants, the group cuts loose. Tonight is like no night before. Whip-crazed abandonment! Riding-crop fiends rule the evening. The people in this room have discovered the sweet pill that makes butt cheeks glow with passion. Boys and girls, it's time for needle play.

In the front room, Master John has pulled long needles out of his duffle bag, along with a biohazard container and rubber medical gloves. His wife lies face-down on the plastic-covered massage table. Master John starts piercing needles under her skin, creating a pattern on her back. Note to self: Don't stand near this woman during an electrical storm. Underneath the needles, she squirms but mostly seems to enjoy herself.

In the other room, Lena has already stripped down, showing the crowded room her black thong. She's cuffed face-first to the black St. Andrew's cross with a black leather mask covering her eyes. And who is spanking her? Jackie! She's dressed in a long, flowing shiny-red latex evening gown, eight-inch stiletto heels, and a rhinestone tiara perched on her head. With extreme precision and magical rhythm, Jackie whips, flogs, and then strangely caresses Lena. In a fast ninja-like move, Jackie grabs a knife with a deadly blade and starts to run it over Lena's back, making red marks but oozing not one drop of blood. Between the seductive knife moves, Jackie caresses Lena's breasts. I feel like I'm invading someone's fantasy, a voyeur looking where I shouldn't, but my eyes won't dart away from the scene. That is until a crazier scene emerges.

A woman in a black thong with a tiny white bow at the top faces the other St. Andrew's cross. Her master, a man in leather pants and a flowing leather shirt, takes his riding crop and slaps it aggressively against her back, legs, and butt cheeks. Within minutes, her body reddens from the leather heat. In a strange twist, the master pounds her back like she is a boxing punching bag. The dungeon masters study the scene, and I think for a minute they might stop it, especially when the woman begins to cry and whimper. But they don't. He keeps torturing her, and she cries. The scene continues as he whips her with a long bullwhip. With each crack, she hollers loudly, and the master occasionally presses his body next to hers and whispers sweet BDSM nothings in her ear. Bizarre doesn't begin to describe this. Like a spectator at a tennis game, my eyes bounce between watching Lena and Jackie and this scene. The master keeps punching at his servant until he unlatches the cuffs and turns her around to face him. Just when I think it can't get any kinkier . . .

The master takes an array of colorful hair clips and places them all over the woman's fleshy body. Several are pinned around her breasts and two on her nipples. She seldom flinches. With his bullwhip, the master flicks off each one of the clips — about twenty or so — from her body. When they don't pop off with ease or speed, he walks up and rips them off her body. Freakin' A! That has to hurt. I feel the pain and I'm across the room.

After a scene, the two players usually cuddle in the safe area. Sexperts say it's crucial that players cool down in a safe area after a scene. A scene takes participants into some sort of erotic headspace that takes awhile to escape. The dominant leads the submissive to the area filled with soft pillows and warm blankets and spends some time comforting the injured one. During my daze at watching the whip crack, Jackie and Lena have wrapped up their scene, and Jackie leads Lena, who appears to be crying in some sort of post-coital way, to the safe area. Sitting Lena down gently, Jackie engulfs her with blankets, transforming her into a papoose with only her head sticking out from a green and white throw. Jackie coaxes and holds Lena. It's the strangest thing I've ever seen.

"With that tiara, Jackie looks like a Sweet Potato queen," I whisper to Dylan.

He starts giggling, and he can't stop. Infectious laughter overtakes me. We are punch-drunk, but I focus my attention back to the flicker guy. When he's finished with his whip cracking, he loosens the cuffs. The woman collapses into an orgasmic mess onto the floor. Moaning and gasping, she kneels before the man. Usually, the dungeon master clears away play items and lets the couple head to the cooldown area. Instead, the flicker guy makes his slave gather up the whips, clips, and paddles and put them in the large case. No cooldown for her.

Across the room, an overweight woman leans against a ladder-type contraption. A Blackbeard look-alike spanks her with his huge hand. The smacks echo so loudly Dylan and I can hear them over the other whacking and chatter. When Blackbeard gets tired of spanking her ass, he starts spanking and hitting her sagging breasts. After about thirty minutes of this, the woman's butt is redder than a Macintosh apple. How these people sit down the next day remains a mystery to me.

In the front room, Master John has upped the ante to more electric play, placing long needles around his wife's breasts. He takes the violet wand and begins to send electric shocks through the needles.

It's like a three-ring whips-and-chains extravaganza.

"Want to try the headphones and glasses?" Leon asks us.

"Sure," I say.

I sit down in a chair while he hooks me up. After I put the headphones on, Leon helps me slide on the silver glasses.

"Close your eyes tight. You'll see pulsating light. Do not open your eyes at all."

I nod. Within a minute, the same electronica music from the night before begins to play in my ears. A few seconds later, the orange, blue, green, and red lights flash in my eyes, creating my own private rave — minus the ecstasy — in my pupils. I can only stand the intensity for about two minutes. Dylan tries it after me, and his trippy experience lasts about the same amount of time.

"Whoa," he says. "That was wild."

Leon shows Dylan how the glasses and music work in time. Across the room, Anne is curled up on a futon, dozing, oblivious to any action around her. In the dungeon, a young man in his twenties, wearing a bowler and kilt, caresses his submissive, who is a head taller than he is, before taking off her dress. She's completely nude. It's the first time we've seen any real tenderness between two players before a scene and the first complete nudity, but strangely it aggravates us.

"What is this, bondage light? Looks like they're about to shoot a video for VH-1," Dylan says.

"Hush," I say, weary and about to laugh again. The later it gets, the more scenes evolve, but it's time to call this surreal weekend a wrap.

As we check out of the hotel the next morning, we run into Mr. Jack, who encourages us to attend a booksigning for some BDSM authors, but we pass on his offer. As we load our bags into the car, the giant eyeball looms over us, asking if we want to get an eyeful. No, thanks, I think, we've gotten enough to last a decade. Back home, it's hard to shake off what we've seen. Even harder is to look at anyone around us, friends or strangers, without wondering what kinky dance they did last weekend.

magically delicious
southern charms

F-stops and G-spots

PELL CITY, ALABAMA — I roll into Pell City late, and there are no Southern Charms to be found anywhere.

Checking into the Hampton Inn off of Interstate 20, I'm greeted by two young desk clerks, one lanky like Beaker from *The Muppets,* and the other short with black hair and a crooked smile.

"I'm late. I got into the most hellish hailstorm. Hail as big as golf balls pounded my car," I say, hoping they haven't given my room away. "It was horrible."

Honestly, it was the worst storm I had ever experienced. Right there in the Bible Belt with hail coming down in sheets, I wondered what was next? Frogs? Locusts? Red plague? Was God sending me a sign about this weekend? I'll keep a look out for Charlton Heston.

One of the clerks hands me the room card, and as I turn, I spot a hot-pink poster that says SC BASH written on it in black ink.

"Do you know where this group — the Southern Charms, this modeling group — is now?"

The pair look at me quizzically with slight smirks. They think I'm a Southern Charm! Go with it.

"I don't think they're exactly a modeling group," Beaker says with hesitation.

"They were sitting over there for a while. I guess they probably went to dinner," says the other one. "They've been gone a long time, though."

"Yeah, a long time," Beaker echoes.

Dinner, ha! The Southern Charms have snuck off to a hideaway somewhere near Pell City for a meet and greet with each other and, since I was late, I don't have a clue as to the location of the function. More bad news: My contact for this adventure, Ms. Cindy Charms, isn't answering her cell phone. Her husband doesn't answer his, either. For now, I'm here in Pell City, being ogled by desk clerks and waiting for a Southern Charm to call me.

Southern Charms, which began in 1994 as a BBS, claims to be the largest amateur porn site on the Internet. With more than 550 women at any given moment, the Web site gives men what they want: normal, average women who are willing to bare it all, from tits to coochie — for a minimal membership fee, of course. According to their Web site, Southern Charms averages 5.59 million page views and 101.54 million hits per day. To download the entire Southern Charms site on a standard 56.6 modem, it would take 4,500 hours, or roughly 187.5 days. That's because the Web site has more than 1.1 million pictures. On average, 1,175 pictures are downloaded every second of every day. The average Southern Charms customer looks at 6.84 pages, downloads 715.9 kilobytes, and stays on the site for sixteen minutes.

What does this mean for America? A whole lot of men are

a) not working; b) not paying attention to their significant others; or c) actively exploring the idea of getting a broadband Internet connection.

Cindy Charms, who has traveled from Texas for the bash, calls around eleven o'clock to tell me that she and her husband have returned to the hotel. The bash was held out in the sticks, somewhere between Pell City and Anniston, and Cindy's cell phone had no service.

"Come see us," she says, giving me her room number.

Usually I don't venture into strangers' hotel rooms, but I've talked a lot to Cindy on the telephone, and in recent weeks, we've become pals via e-mail. She's an overprotective mother to a five-year-old daughter, so how spooky could she be? Not very. Still, standing outside her hotel door, I hesitate for about five seconds before plunging headfirst into the Southern Charms universe.

"Come in, come in," Cindy says with gusto.

I've seen Cindy in pictures on the Southern Charms Web site, but I really didn't know what to expect in person. Whenever I meet people or see rock stars in concert, I always expect them to be tall, svelte, and glamorous, especially if they are model types. Not so for Cindy, who is short and very petite — size three tiny. Her flaming red hair, more red than nature allows thanks to a bottle, is a tad messy after a long day. She wears frameless glasses on her face, but they don't take away from her magical feline blue-green eyes. On her small frame, she wears a spaghetti-strap black velvet minidress with pleats of chiffon at its bottom. Ostrich feathers accent the bustline. Clearly, Cindy does not frequent the Gap.

"Do you want something to drink?" she asks.

"No, no," I say. I'm tired, it's late, and I'm thinking that clearheadedness is probably a good idea tonight.

"Okay, round of introductions, this is my husband, Steve; these are our friends who are photographers, Rick and Marshall."

The three men are hovering near Steve's laptop, talking about computer programs and technological matters that sound Greek to me. Cindy sits on one bed; I sit on the other. As I look around the hotel room, it's clear that Cindy has packed and brought everything but small household appliances. A huge opened suitcase, looking as if it has exploded, sits on a built-in shelf. Panty hose, panties, and skirts pop out of it like girly shrapnel. Underneath the suitcase, a mysterious plastic bag of what looks to be cigars lies on the floor. Tote bags crammed with shoes litter the floor next to the wall. A case of bottled water is near the cigars. On top of the refrigerator, a bottle of Crown Royal sits. On the desk, computer equipment and cameras take up an entire corner of the room. There's more gadgets here than at a spy convention, and tidiness is apparently not one of Cindy's hang-ups.

"Let me show you what I bought today," Cindy says, bouncing up and off the bed and heading toward the large suitcase.

She pulls out a Jackrabbit vibrator, a double dildo, a Texas flag–patterned bikini, and some garter belts.

"You can't get this one in Texas," she says, holding up the flesh–colored double dildo that has a head at each end. "They are illegal."

In fact, in Texas, most dildos are illegal. State law says "a person commits an offense if, knowing its content and character, he wholesale promotes or possesses with intent to wholesale promote any obscene material or obscene device. 'Obscene device' means a device including a dildo or artificial vagina, designed or marketed as useful primarily for the stimulation of human genital organs."

Strangely enough, and with as much irony as the Bible Belt can yield, Alabama isn't exactly an open haven for such muff massagers. In fact, the legality of sex toys in Alabama has a complicated history. A 1998 obscenity law outlawed the sale of "any device designed or marketed as useful primarily for the stimulation of human genital organs." The penalty for selling a sex toy in Alabama was a maximum $10,000 fine and up to a year of hard labor. An overwhelmingly male Alabama legislature passed the law, which was primarily aimed at banning topless dancing, but the American Civil Liberties Union represented six women who either needed the devices for sexual therapy or sold them and challenged the ban's constitutionality.

A year later, a U.S. district judge ruled in their favor, describing the law as "overly broad" and saying that people would be "denied therapy, for, among other things, sexual dysfunction."

In 2000, the state sought to overturn the judge's ruling in the 11th Circuit Court of Appeals, where Alabama's attorney general argued that "a ban on the sale of sexual devices and related orgasm-stimulating paraphernalia is rationally related to a legitimate legislative interest in discouraging prurient interests in autonomous sex." Translation: The state has an interest in masturbation. Quick, call Joycelyn Elders.

The appellate court unanimously upheld the law, saying, in effect, that Alabama's "interest in public morality is a legitimate interest rationally served by the statute." On remand, though, the law was overturned again.

In early 2003, the state House of Representatives voted down a bill that would have removed the ban on sexual devices from the state's twenty-or-so-page obscenity law. The sponsor of the bill, Democratic Representative John Rogers of Birmingham, said that because of the court ruling, the obscenity law is unenforceable as long as it contains the ban on sex toys. Alas, because of the way the legislature voted, sex toys are once again illegal in Alabama but the state's obscenity law was deemed unconstitutional. That's the kind of crazy stuff that happens in Southern state legislatures. Meanwhile, as Dixie politicians battle, all sorts of wild sex antics are occurring in the South's small towns.

"Feel this," Ms. Cindy Charms says, handing me the flesh-colored dildo.

I've never touched a sex toy that felt so real. No wonder politicians are worried. If these catch on, pleasuring oneself may overtake NASCAR and fishing as the most popular hobbies down here.

"Wanna see some pictures tonight of what you missed at the bash?" asks Steve, distracting me from the toy.

I reluctantly drop the new toy and walk over to the laptop computer to see the slide show. Initially, there are several group shots of women — old, young, thin, fat — drinking and socializing. It doesn't take but a few clicks of the mouse for the pics to start sizzling. Various Southern Charms begin to reveal their tits. Some, even those pushing fifty, have pierced nipples. Others have rolls of fat. The pictures get a tad hotter with one of the women — a blonde in her late forties or early fifties — sucking the nipples of some of the

Southern Charms. Another picture shows the blonde with her dress pulled up, touching herself. Just when I am adjusting my eyeglasses to make sure I am seeing what I am seeing, the same blonde is featured giving a blow job to one of the male guests.

"That's me," says Steve, matter-of-factly.

Oh, my. Now that has left me speechless, and the weekend has just begun.

Cindy may be an amateur porn star, but she's also just a regular girl who likes the occasional shot of expensive tequila, the Powerpuff Girls, her gun, and eight good hours of sleep. She's been married for fifteen years to the same man, and together as a couple, they decided that Cindy could be a porn star.

Cindy had her first and only child, a daughter, at forty, and her porn career began when she was forty-two. Steve and Cindy met a man who asked if they would be interested in doing some photo shoots and having their own Web site. Cindy wasn't sure.

"I felt fat, ugly, old, a walking zombie. The baby didn't sleep at night, but after I lost that baby weight, I just thought it would be fun," she says. So she went for it.

The Web site was up for only two weeks and then it went down, but Cindy had met another woman who was on Southern Charms. Secretly, Cindy loved the rush that such racy modeling gave her, plus she figured the income might work for a stay-at-home mom. It had been a harsh adjustment for the couple to go from a two-income family to a single income when the baby was born. But Cindy never considered putting her baby in daycare, so she and Steve adjusted. In late 2001, they decided to try Southern Charms.

"It has just been so fun," she says. "It's something we get to do together, and it makes me take time for myself. I don't feel old anymore. I get e-mail from young guys, old guys, couples. When you are having a bad day, it's nice to read an e-mail from someone who is a little taken with you. It puts that sunshine in your dark clouds. I haven't regretted it once."

If Cindy sounds smitten with Southern Charms, that's because she is. She loves the Web site, creating a fan base, corresponding with her fans, and being a minicelebrity in the universe of the Southern Charms — or SC as it is lovingly called among the girls. There's no faking that kind of enthusiasm. She loves every bit of this life, even though it's a secret one. Her in-laws know about her modeling, but her family doesn't. Neither do a lot of her neighbors or Steve's coworkers.

The adult entertainment business was no foreign land for Cindy. The last job she had before the birth of her daughter was at a strip club. She worked as a cocktail waitress, and even had her baby shower at the club, which her in-laws attended. Before that job, Cindy worked in the corporate world, but she detested the day-in, day-out bureaucratic crap. These days, her work with Southern Charms suits her just fine. She can't imagine doing anything else.

The next morning, I venture to the lobby for some coffee. A group of goth kids dressed in black leather and spikes sit at one table, reading *USA Today* and watching Fox News. At another table, two all-American suburban couples chat over muffins and juice. I know their secret: The suburbanites are Southern Charms. The SC T-shirt gives it away. They look askance at the goth kids who are bemoaning the fact that they got stuck in Pell City when their car broke down. A large woman in a white tank top with fringe on its bottom, strategically ripped jeans, and brown sandals plops down at the table with a cup of coffee. It's not the kind of music video vixen look this particular woman should be wearing.

The kids look at each other and roll their eyes. They really can't believe what they are seeing. Neither can I. If only those goth kids knew what I knew — that the woman in the white tube top likes to strip down and get photographed like a *Penthouse* goddess. And she even has fans!

Up in Cindy's room, she's busy packing costumes, shoes, bottled water, makeup, stiletto heels, liquor, computer equipment, batteries, cameras, and an array of other paraphernalia so we can head to the lake house where the social was held the previous night. At a bash, the Charms gather to meet one another, greet fans, and indulge in photo shoots: individually, with each other, and with the fans. I'm not sure what to expect. I half expect Larry Flynt to show up; part of me figures that these women like to think they are wild but they probably aren't that uninhibited. Okay, maybe the one from last night who enjoyed Steve's hardness in her mouth. But the others may be all talk.

"There was a fight last night at the bash," Steve says.

He's unsure of the details but a tale of two Southern Charms getting into a catfight has the group spinning this morning. There are rumors about one SC husband punching another SC husband, but it's all very sketchy. Nonetheless, the show will go on, says Cindy, who didn't drive eight hours not to shoot photos for her fans.

Another photographer from a local newspaper, Jim, a friend of Cindy and Steve's, shows up, camera in tow, ready to shoot Cindy in all of her naked resplendence. Finally, with all the luggage and bags loaded into the car, we venture out of the motel and into the Alabama boondocks. Destination: somewhere in the woods between Pell City and Anniston, known infamously as the most toxic city in the United States, according to Jim, who is driving Cindy and me to the bash. He follows Steve who knows — we hope — where he's going.

One of the back roads we find ourselves driving down is notorious in this part of the state. It's where murderers brought dead bodies from Birmingham and Atlanta for years. Another rumor is that the Ku Klux Klan still haunts these parts. Conservative, right-wing: These terms don't begin to describe the residents who live in this area. Everywhere I look I see an American flag. As we roll to a stop sign, I spot a bumper sticker on it: IF OSAMA WAS A PIECE OF ASS, CLINTON WOULD HAVE NAILED HIM. There's no escaping Arkansas, no matter how far from home I get.

Cindy talks about NASCAR and football and cracks jokes.

"Why don't Junior Leaguers like orgies?"

"No idea," Jim and I say.

"Because there are too many thank-you notes to write."

Following a series of hot pink posters with SC on them, we turn down a dirt road, then another dirt road, and finally arrive at a three-story lake house. The woman who serviced Steve for the camera the night before greets us. She looks like her picture — platinum hair, tanning-bed skin, and heavy makeup along with long, coral-hued talons. A black stretchy minidress with a gold lamé design on it accentuates her long legs. She's holding a pair of black strappy high heels and is clearly aggravated by something.

"Don't bother getting your stuff out. They won't let us shoot in the house. It's muddy down there by the lake so you girls may ruin those expensive shoes," she says, not looking particularly happy.

"Why won't they let us go in?" Cindy asks.

"They don't want us to get mud on the carpet or some shit like that," she says. "I think it's got everything to do with that fight from last night."

Cindy is not happy at all. Her emotions range from pissed off to totally disappointed. She tells Steve to just leave the suitcases in the car. I don't think I'm going to see Cindy transform into sex goddess. Traipsing through the saturated ground, I dodge mud puddles to reach a gazebo where the party seems to be happening.

Scene: a wooden gazebo that looks like it came from a redneck *Gilligan's Island*, complete with Auburn and Alabama flags behind the bar and taped dollar bills hanging from the wooden rafters. Two sideways American flags festoon on one side of the gazebo, fluttering in the humid breeze and pots and pans hang from the other side of the shack. A deejay stands at a table spinning tunes like Nelly's "It's Getting Hot in Here," Prince's "Pussy Control," and Sir Mix-A-Lot's "Baby Got Back." I'll never be able to hear these songs again without a flashback.

A picnic table with two sleeping hound dogs underneath it sits in front of the gazebo, along with a rusted swing set and a riding lawnmower. Lawn chairs dot the sand near the lake's edge, and an RV camper rests in the far corner of the large backyard. To the right of the gazebo, a decrepit houseboat is docked in the water. A beagle on a leather leash tied to an oak tree barks loudly. Let's see: We've got dawgs, rusty furniture, toys, lawn equipment, transportation, and another dawg. Perfect.

Surreal hardly describes the scene, but it all becomes a helluva lot stranger when an overweight woman on the houseboat removes her shirt and a photographer begins shooting. Suddenly, like a tidal wave of debauchery washing over the women, naked and often flabby tits pop out everywhere. Soon, more women are naked or walking around topless with skimpy thongs on, dancing around on the houseboat, leaning against trees, swinging on the swing set — all posing for photos as if they are supermodels making five thousand dollars an hour. All naked hell has broken loose, and I'm smack-dab in the middle of it.

Jim wanders around with his camera like he is dazed and confused. He told me earlier he had never been to anything like this, and by his wide-eyed appearance, I'm thinking he was telling the truth.

"There's some sort of sex act going on in there," he says, pointing toward the gazebo. Alert!

Without wasting a moment, I dash from the picnic table to the gazebo. Sure enough, the woman who gave Steve his BJ is at it again, except this time two men — obviously fans — have stripped out of their khaki Gap shorts and boxers. Erect and ready, they lean against two bar stools while Miss BJ pleasures them one at a time. At one point she stands up and caresses each of their faces with her delicate tanned hand, the bright coral nails gleaming. She kisses them, all tongues flaming with passion. She leans back, putting her arms around each of their necks. As if on command, the two men simultaneously lean in to suck on her nipples. For a brief second, I gasp. One of the men looks exactly like a congressional aide that I know in Arkansas who has a love for strip clubs. I stare but realize that it's not him. Man, that would have been strange, especially since I know his wife.

Five or six photographers stand around the trio snapping pictures like porno paparazzi. This is as close to a bacchanalian buck wildness I have ever witnessed firsthand. Before either of the men have a chance to share their love juices with Miss BJ, she quickly stops, gets dressed, and goes about her business. The abruptness of the conclusion puzzles me, but the men seem fine with it, so why should I let it worry me? But it does. I hate when sex ends before everybody gets their cookies.

Dixie Photog — the gentlemanly founder of Southern Charms — is no Hugh Hefner. Or Bob Guccione. Or even Larry Flynt.

He's more like the crazy uncle who tells off-the-wall stories at the family reunion with a camera dangling around his neck. And he likes it this way. Dixie Photog craves anonymity, because he doesn't want anyone to know about this secret life. He and his wife, who knows about Southern Charms, live in a small Alabama community where she is active in their church. If it leaked that this sixtyish man shot photos of naked women doing all sorts of things most churches deem sinful, he'd be banished from his community. Nobody wants that, right?

"We have a 'don't ask, don't tell' relationship about Southern

Charms," he says, about his wife. "I go away on the weekends to shoot the charms, and when I come back we just don't talk about it."

Wowsers.

You cannot get more Southern than this. I flashback to a scene in *Gone with the Wind* when Ashley Wilkes, Rhett, and Dr. Meade visited Belle Watling's establishment, which was an Atlanta saloon. When they returned, Mrs. Meade asked her husband about mirrors on the ceiling and the saloon's decadent appearance.

"Good God! How can you ask such immodest questions?" Dr. Meade asks his wife.

That's how I imagine Sunday night in Dixie Photog's house.

Dixie Photog tries to attend every bash the Charms throw, even if they are as far away as Texas or New England. This time, he didn't have to come far, just up the road a piece, to meet some of his girls, who have made him a rich man over the last nine years.

In 1994 Dixie Photog, a computer geek who saw the potential riches in the Internet before most, started a BBS, a computer or an application dedicated to the sharing or exchange of messages or other files on a network. The BBS was used to post simple messages between users, much like the type of bulletin board found on the wall in many homes and offices. The BBS was the primary kind of online community through the 1980s and early 1990s, before the World Wide Web arrived.

Dixie Photog began charging for access to his BBS and paying Southern models by the photo shoot. The BBS was a long-distance dial-up, but it didn't matter to fans from places like Canada, the West Coast, England, and even South

America who paid to see the naked women. An early customer accumulated a three-hundred-dollar phone bill in one month, evidence that folks liked what they were seeing. Soon, as popularity increased, Dixie Photog needed a name for his project, and his wife came up with Southern Charms.

"All the girls were from the South at the time so she just thought that was a good name, and it was," he says.

In 1996, the BBS transferred to the World Wide Web and began exploding with members. Dixie Photog sold out in 1998, but he still has a finger in Southern Charms' sweet pie, so to speak, as its technological guru and liaison to the girls. He's traveled to England and Sweden to photograph Charms for the Web site. He's attended bashes in Texas, Pennsylvania, Florida, and Tennessee. The one this weekend is a first for Alabama. Dixie Photog has never missed one.

Like a superhero who retains his public identity, Dixie Photog is the "caped crusader" driving force behind the Charms, although he remains anonymous. Tricky to do in the small-town South, but he succeeds beautifully.

The bash is a bust.

Cindy doesn't like the down-home flavor of this bash. The sandy beach by the lake or the RV as a backdrop is simply not conducive to the image Cindy wants to portray. For her, it's all about fantasy and glamour, and this setting isn't that. Not by a long shot.

The mission for the weekend is for Charms to shoot as many pictures as possible for their pages. A good Charm, who wants to keep fans happy and make money, needs to update her Web site two times a week, the maximum allowed.

The Charms always shoot soft-core pictures for the free area to lure in new fans, a constant project for Charms. Some of the women have as many as six hundred to a thousand fans. Others, like Cindy, have about 150 fans. Still others have only about 25 fans signed up. Some Charms do it for the money, some for the sheer thrill of showing off their bodies. But there's no thrill for Cindy at today's shoot site.

"Let's get out of here and go back to the hotel," she says.

In addition to the rustic nature of the setting, the fact that just across the lake some young teenagers are fishing on the banks is troublesome to Cindy. She says that the event's location was promoted as secluded and isolated. This is not that.

"I want to shoot where I am not in the line of vision of people," she says. "I can just see us all getting arrested for lewd behavior down here."

Frankly, that's the last thing any of us need, but disappointment rains down on me. Like a horny adolescent, I wanted to see more. Now it looks like I'll be stuck in a hotel all afternoon with Cindy Charms bitching about the bash.

One. Two. Three. Four. Five.

Somewhere along the way during the bash, our foursome — me, Jim the photographer, Steve, and Cindy — became a fivesome.

"Who's the man with Steve?" I ask, as we drive back to the motel.

"Someone he met at the bash, a fan. He's coming back to the motel with us, I guess," Cindy says.

Fans at the bashes get full access to the Charms so that they can shoot photos with them, or of them, in exchange for the $35 registration fee. The Charms will also undress in private photo shoots for a price, as well as shoot custom-made videos for fans during nonbash times. This weekend, Cindy Charms and Miss BJ are scheduled to shoot a video together where they will French kiss for a marathon thirty minutes. The video will show only the two women from the neck up because it's for a Japanese client. In Japan, porn isn't as explicit as in the United States.

Cindy has shot some bizarre videos in her time. Southern Charms take special requests from customers for videos or photos, and the requests are often unusual.

Once, she endured getting hit in the face with thirty or forty cream pies for someone's wet and messy fetish. Another time, she dressed up like a hit woman, pretended to shoot a guy, and then sat parked in a car looking through mother-of-pearl binoculars and talking into a tape recorder while smoking nonfiltered cigarettes. There was no nudity or sex in either one of those videos, but someone somewhere got off on them.

One fan, Dann, flew from Scotland to Texas to photograph Cindy. He wrote to Cindy, asking her whether she would meet him if he came to Texas.

"I replied that if he came all the way to Dallas, of course I would meet him. I didn't really expect anything to come of it and was quite surprised when my next e-mail from him included dates for a potential meeting. Next thing I knew we had a private custom photo shoot planned during his visit."

Dann even brought her a Wedgwood china tea set as a gift. Originally from Japan, Dann was a perfect gentleman and extremely polite. "Honestly, I think he was more nervous than I was. I'll admit to a certain amount of anxiety — not really knowing how things would go or whether he was expecting more than a photo shoot. I had some concerns that we would have a language barrier, but we managed quite well, and it was a good time," Cindy recalls.

Steve took photos using Dann's camera and videocam, and Dann even shot some photos himself to get the ones he particularly wanted. After all, he had purchased a new digital camera for the occasion.

"Things going so well with Dann went a long way toward helping me feel more comfortable with meeting other fans and members who either just want to meet me or to pay for a custom, private photo shoot. Of course, Steve always accompanies me to such things. I do not meet anyone alone," she says.

Fans send Cindy lingerie, cigars, and props to use in photo shoots or videos. One man likes just armpit shots. Another one just likes to look at her toes. Some want to order her panties. Others send her shoes to wear around and then want the shoes sent back to them.

"The fetishes are the strangest things. You never know what someone is going to want," she says. Thinking back on my travels to date, I couldn't agree more.

Now that we have returned to the motel room, I study Kendall, the fifty-something fan who has tagged along this afternoon. Dressed in an olive-green T-shirt and black pants, Kendall holds a digital camera in his hand and sits on the edge of the bed. On his hip is perched a fancy silver pager, the kind like many doctors carry. He looks antsy, shy, and unsure of what he is doing here at this very moment. I get the feeling that he is being a very bad boy. I especially get that impression when I spot the gold wedding band on his hand.

Without a grain of modesty, Cindy strips out of her pink capri pants and matching blouse and begins searching through her suitcase. Jim, Steve, and I are somewhat oblivious to her nudity, but not Kendall, who looks as if he hasn't seen a naked woman in twenty years. Cindy bounces all over the room, grabbing this bag, that bag, a bottle of water, some high heels, moving about like a crazed roadrunner.

"So, does this turn you on?" Kendall asks me. His eyes follow Cindy around the room.

I have to be honest and tell this man the truth.

"Not really," I say.

He looks shocked, but of course, all I have seen are naked women and if I took off my clothes and looked in the mirror, I'd see the same thing. For some reason, men always feel the need to confess their marital problems to me, especially those that are set in the bedroom. Perhaps I look like an understanding woman; maybe it's because I'm not afraid to talk about sex. Who knows? But it's happening again.

Kendall begins to tell me his story. He's been married since the 1980s. At some point, his wife developed cancer, and since then she hasn't been at all interested in sex. He loves her very much, says he would never cheat on her, but they haven't had sex in five years. No doubt, a man has to have some sort of release, so he indulges in porn. Southern Charms lets him partake in porn in a whole new manner: going to a model's motel room and seeing real-time action.

"Does your wife know you are here today?" I ask, already guessing the answer.

"No, no, she's on the other side of the state, doing her thing with a friend," he says.

For a moment, I figure he means shopping, and I am sure

he does, but I can't help but wonder if maybe she, too, has concocted some lie and is at this very moment entangled with a George Clooney look-alike. While he talks to me, Kendall eyeballs a naked Cindy. Of course, why look at me when I am fully clothed?

"She has the best tits," he says, almost drooling. Clearly star-struck.

Cindy disappears for a second and reemerges in a long red gown. Her makeup is perfect.

"Let's do it," she says, downing a shot of tequila and revving up a Stevie Ray Vaughan compact disc.

What we are about to do, I have no idea. But earlier, I heard rumblings about Cindy's ability to "squirt." Yes, squirt. Doctors call it female ejaculation. I've seen a lot of things, and there are lot of things I want to see in life, but this isn't one of them.

"I'll let you shoot with my camera," Jim says to me. "You need to experience the shoot."

Well, okay. I can pretend I am Annie Leibowitz.

"No, here, you keep your camera and I'll give her this one," Steve says to Jim.

Steve hands me a small digital camera. Everyone is ready. Cindy lounges back in the desk chair, leaning her neck back, and opening her mouth ever so slightly. She caresses her breasts through the red gown as the four of us circle around her for the best shot. After about ten photos of Cindy in seductive clothed positions, she stops.

"Got enough?" she asks.

"Think so," Steve says.

These tame shots work for the free area of the Southern

Charms Web site, to coax men into the paid membership area, which offers more explicit, hard-core pictures. The free area has a list of rules as long as the Mississippi River. Charms cannot use these words: fuck, piss, pussy, dick. Keep vulgar language down to a minimum. Pictures cannot have real or simulated drug use, incest-themed photos (Cindy tells me there are pictures of two sisters getting it on somewhere on the site.) No children, animals, guns pointing at anyone, including yourself, penis shots, pubic hair, lips around the edge of panties, anuses, simulated sex, stuffed animals, or children's toys. Whew! The list keeps going: no see-through panties, bondage, U.S. flags displayed in anyway other than the correct way, or lactating or breast milk of any kind.

In a poontang flash, Ms. Cindy raises her long gown and spreads her legs. She wastes no time beginning to finger herself. There are moments in life when you wonder how in the hell you ended up somewhere. That's where my mind is at this very moment. It's not on this woman in front of me arousing herself, but more on how did I end up watching this in Pell City, Alabama, while clicking away on a digital camera?

I can't let my mind roam about this for too long, because Cindy is moaning me back to the present.

"Get ready, here it comes," she gasps. She's not kidding.

In the time it takes to sneeze, Cindy has squirted a two-foot arc of her love potion all over Jim and me. I'm in shock, and I'm drenched. Jim looks bewildered. Kendall appears aroused. Steve, well, it's old hat to him.

Cindy wastes no time in going again. She inserts her hot pink Jackrabbit and starts working it. I move back further on the bed and away from the dangerous squirter, trying to stay out of artillery range.

"Take the photos on the out stroke," she says, pulling the Jackrabbit out of her. "Looks better."

Kendall looks so red and turned on that I am amazed he can even take a picture.

In less than two minutes, she's moaning again and splat! She's projecting her juices again, but this time not as far and not near me. Thank goodnesss! Her red gown is drenched.

"Anyone need an umbrella?" Steve asks, laughing. "I told you she could do it. She once squirted eighteen feet in our pool."

Hello! Get me Guinness! That could be a world record. Eighteen feet! At this point, I believe it.

I move back to my original spot on the bed with my camera, but just when I think I'm safe, Cindy starts again. Less than thirty seconds pass, and she spews again like Old Faithful. I run for it this time and barely escape. Kendall is drenched. Steve hands him a towel, and Jim, who I have concluded isn't just a newspaper photographer but also a huge fan, shakes his head and looks at me with amazement.

While Kendall basks in his fantasy-cum-to-life, Cindy is more concerned with how the shots turned out. Like a couple at Olan Mills, Cindy and Steve examine the digital shots carefully.

"Those are some big drops. I like the shadows of the droplets in this one. Look, this looks like it is going all over the computer," she says, laughing with just a hint of pride.

Steve moves the wet chair into the bathroom and blow-dries it.

Reminder to self: Always put a towel down on a hotel chair.

Cindy is not one to dillydally when there is work to be done. In a jiffy, she's out of the red gown, naked as the day she was born, dumping out cigars — all shapes and sizes — onto the bed.

"What's this reminiscent of?" asks Kendall. I feel a Clinton jab coming on.

He must know this about Arkansans but whenever we see a cigar, there's only one thing we think of: Monica Lewinsky.

"Yeah, that's what I was thinking," he says.

Obviously, most Americans have the same thought.

"Hey, Suzi, you know that saying, kid in a candy shop, that's me right now," Kendall says, as excited as a cartoon puppy.

"Yep."

"That's me right now. I've never been to anything like this but I won't forget it," he says.

A knock on the door interrupts his verbal daydreaming. A couple I'd seen at the lake bash walks in and Cindy hugs them. The woman carries a couple of bags. Obviously, if you are a Southern Charm, you gotta have a bag with you at all times. Never know when a shoot might break out.

"You guys missed it by just a few minutes. Cindy squirted," Steve says to the newcomers.

"And squirted and squirted," Cindy giggles.

The two women start whispering and searching through the suitcases and bags. Kendall sits in a trance while Jim and I talk about toxic water in nearby Anniston. Steve and the new man on the scene chat about — what else — cameras and computer equipment. Everyone acts like this is what we do every Saturday afternoon. Maybe it is for some of us in this room, but not me.

Cindy, on the edge of the bed, seductively slides into ivory stockings and heads into the bathroom. A few minutes later, she emerges in an ivory lace teddy with satin bows. The newcomer woman, whose name is Devlynn, wears black panties, black stockings, and a turquoise tank top with sequins. Together, they pick out cigars.

"I'm, um, going," says Kendall. "Need to go connect with . . ."

He mumbles someone's name, but I think he more than likely needs to go hook up with Mr. Happy before more orgasmic nuttiness breaks out — Cindy's squirts clearly pushed him to the limit. He exits, and Dixie Photog enters.

"You missed the squirting," Steve says, proud of his wife.

"I've heard you are a squirter. You've tried to submit those photos," he says, ever the businessman.

"You won't let me because you think it's peeing," Cindy retorts. "Did that look like pee to you guys?"

Jim and I both shake our heads. "No way," I say. I'm not sure what it was, but I've got some DNA on my clothes for later analysis.

While Steve shows Dixie Photog the pictures from the last shoot, Cindy and Devlynn begin their next photo shoot by smoking cigars on the bed. Devlynn chokes and coughs, exposing her inexperience, but Cindy could puff Jackie Gleason under the table. After a few humdrum shots, the two women begin to undress each other, sucking on each other's nipples and teasing each other with their tongues. Cindy licks Devlynn's rose tattoo while Jim and Devlynn's husband shoot pictures.

Cindy goes down on Devlynn, and gasps and moans float from across the room. Strangely, Steve and Dixie Photog are engaged in a conversation about strange objects people stick up their butts, and don't really pay attention to Cindy and Devlynn's erotic adventure on the motel bed. Devlynn goes down on Cindy and doesn't stop, licking and flicking her tongue between Cindy's legs. She moans as Devlynn laps at her, then another switcheroo, and Cindy is enjoying Devlynn again. As Devlynn and Cindy dance the motel room tango, I notice Devlynn's love button is pierced with a ring. My anthropological thoughts are broken when Cindy keeps groping Devlynn but asks Jim, "How many shots do we have?"

"Eighty-five or so," he replies.

"We've got enough," Cindy says. "Rock and roll!"

Without a blink, the women hop off the bed. So much for coming. Don't these people ever get each other off?

"You've got my ring sticking straight out!" Devlynn says, looking down between her legs at her erect love button. The women giggle and hug. "Let's change clothes!"

Who has time to come, when there are more make-believe lesbian games to play?

It's a party now!

Another knock on the door, and about six more people pour into the room. One of the women, also called Dixie, who is fifty-two with gray hair, is an original Southern Charm from 1994. She could be anyone's mother dressed in shorts and a sleeveless blouse for a Wal-Mart outing. If someone told me this woman was an amateur porn star and men paid to see her, I'd say no way. But she is; you never know what kind of women flick a man's switch.

The room is abuzz with several separate conversations, and no one pays much attention to the naked Cindy, who is walking around smoking a cigar and wearing her glasses that she takes off during shoots. Meanwhile, Dixie Photog is a tad paranoid that it might leak out in the local community that he is involved in Southern Charms, especially with a local photographer in the room with us.

"My fear is churches, that the stupid Bible-thumping fanatics would go apeshit on us," he says.

Everyone reassures him that no one will tell on him; still, he doesn't look too convinced. He has a healthy distrust of the press. Dixie Photog's cell phone rings. Like an EMT receiving an emergency call, he springs into action.

"Gotta go. There's a three-way going on downstairs. Need to go shoot it," he says.

Devlynn looks like a powerful advertising exec I know in Little Rock. Her brown hair with frosted highlights doesn't move when she walks. She has a toned and tanned sexy body, and it's hard to believe that Devlynn is a grandmother. She has two daughters, two stepchildren, and two grandchildren. She is also a swinger. She's been married eight years to Hampton, who she met at a swinger club.

"That issue was already out there on the table so we didn't have to deal with it," she says.

She was a Southern Charm for about six months but decided to forgo the project because one of her daughters still lived at home. When the daughter left for college, Devlynn decided to return to the site. She also lost thirty pounds, which boosted her self-confidence.

The couple still swings, and she says it's a nice feeling to explore sexuality together without inhibitions or boundaries. She said because their relationship is so open and honest they really don't swing as much as some couples.

Like most of the Southern Charms and their spouses, they run their Web site as a couple. Devlynn's husband likes the electronics part of the site. She prefers photo editing.

"I'm definitely more outgoing. He tempers me, and I make his life more exciting," Devlynn says.

She says one of her daughters kind of guesses that her mother may be a swinger, but doesn't seem to mind. The other daughter doesn't want to know.

So far, they haven't found their mom's nudie pics on the Web. Maybe.

If the Old West was still filled with rough-and-ready cowgirls, Cindy would fit right in. There isn't one thing that this woman would decline to try at least once. If she liked it, then twice. She's petite but dangerous, funny and gracious, a people person who chats with strangers as if they are family and calls everyone sweetie or darling. Devlynn was a stranger to Cindy until they met the previous night at the meet and greet.

Less than twenty-fours later, the two charms were licking it up for the camera like reconnected lovers.

Costume changes keep Devlynn and Cindy busy. When they emerge, they look ready for a day at the office — well, sorta. Devlynn wears a lacy white bustier, a conservative red skirt, and white thigh-highs with red patent leather shoes. Through her stockings, I spy an ankle bracelet. Cindy wears a lacy black bodysuit, a brown floral miniskirt, and black leather high heels. Not exactly what I would wear to a business meeting, but hey, we all have our own style, and after all, this is about selling sex and fantasy.

On another motel chair with an ottoman, the dynamic duo initiate another photo shoot, but this time they focus a lot on choreography to make sure the shots are just right. When their legs get tangled, the floral ottoman starts to roll and take Cindy with it.

"Ack, I'm falling, stop the shoot! Will one of you guys help?" she asks while everyone stands around gabbing. Porno bloopers — gotta love that.

Twelve photos later, Devlynn starts caressing Cindy in an erotic way, signaling the start of the more hard-core action for the membership section. Cindy starts nibbling Devlynn's nipples.

"Damn, she's good at that," Devlynn gasps.

In a Houdini move, Devlynn puts her foot on Cindy's back as the women lick each other for pleasure.

"I'm about to come," Devlynn says. Cindy doesn't give up. She's going for the gold star.

The women flip positions, mastering a tricky sixty-nine that looks complicated. After a few seconds, Devlynn, says, "Stop, stop, my knees are going to give out."

The women laugh. Devlynn, out of breath, says, "We should have enough by now."

"Oh, yeah," Cindy says.

End of scene. Once again, no orgasm. I'm sensing a theme here. The break doesn't last long. Devlynn lies down on the chair and puts her head on the ottoman. Cindy, skirt raised uncovering an easy-access body stocking, stands over Devlynn.

"Warn me if I'm going to get wet," Devlynn says.

"I'll say duck, but I don't know where you'll go," Cindy says. "This isn't that comfortable so I don't expect that."

After a few minutes of tantalizing tonguing, Cindy seems close to the orgasmic brink. "Ooh, oooooh," she says. This could be it!

Then, just as quickly. It's over, and Devlynn and Cindy help each other out of their odd positions.

"God, I am so hot," Devlynn says, standing over the air conditioner.

"I know, it's hot in here," Cindy says.

I'm freezing, but obviously I'm not performing tricky sexual stunts.

It ain't over till the Southern Charms come. By their own hand, it seems.

In the chair, Cindy is masturbating like a crazy woman, and the room has now focused its collective attention on her. As I learned earlier it doesn't take her long to let go. Sure enough, she spurts. Devlynn, a brave soul, joins in the action. Within seconds — literally, the time it takes to say hello — Cindy fires off another round.

"I need a towel. There's standing water over here," Dev-lynn says, laughing.

"Told ya," Cindy says, chuckling. She's proud of her special talent, like the double jointed kid in elementary school or maybe the one who could burp the alphabet.

Cindy is all business. There's no postcoital kickback with a cigarette. For her, it's shoot, shoot, shoot. Absolutely no pun intended.

"How many photos we got?" she asks, drying off.

"Seventy," Jim says.

"We can work with that. Let's move on."

"I'll try to stay out of the wet spots," Devlynn says.

"Once we had two squirters going at a photo shoot, and the carpet squished when it was over."

Memo to self: If I'm ever invited to one of these bashes again, pack galoshes and goggles.

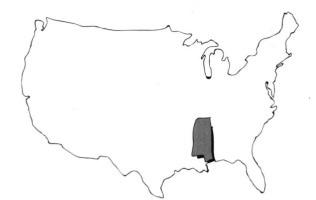

mississippi

tennessee williams
lives

Big Nelly Bottoms and Magnolia Blossoms

NATCHEZ, MISSISSIPPI — Angelo Dixon looks like a contestant on *American Idol*.

He has a dazzling smile and large cocoa eyes, and his personality radiates around him like a spinning planet. With well-starched blue jeans and a denim patchwork shirt, Angelo is very put together as we sit in Natchez's city park under ancient oak trees dripping Spanish moss. Thunder rolls in the distance and the first few drops of an incoming rainstorm create the sultriness for which this town is notorious.

St. Mary's Cathedral looms behind the park bench. This is the oldest Catholic building in continuous use in Mississippi. Built in the elaborate and vast Gothic Revival style, the cathedral, one of the most beautiful churches in the South, dates back to 1840. Its ornate interior possesses incredibly stunning stained glass, which creates amazing rainbow patterns on the marble floor. Appropriately, Angelo has chosen this spot in Natchez to confess some secrets to me about himself and his town.

Natchez has around nineteen thousand people, and the population hasn't waned much over the years. This is a place fluttering in a time warp circa 1864. Natchez still holds its annual pilgrimage in the spring when the fuchsia azaleas burst with color. The pilgrimage draws tourists from around the globe, especially Yankees and Brits, who travel hundreds of miles to tour the antebellum plantations and historic homes in this Mississippi River city. Natchez thrives on this event and banks its local economy on it, perhaps more than it should in the twenty-first century. Angelo knows this firsthand considering he works at a historic hotel here and sees the tourist-filled buses roll into the town every time the azaleas bloom.

This river city, like Memphis, holds a classic Southern gothic reputation well-endowed by history and lore. Tales of brothels and madams, Southern belles and gents, slaves and masters swirl in Natchez among the magnolias, oaks, and ghosts of long ago. The past haunts this town, and it's that glorious history that makes present-day Natchez appear so prim and proper, genteel and gracious.

"There are two sides to this town, the pretty side and all, the old homes and the flowers, but there is some ugly stuff that happens, some dark stuff," Angelo says. "What you see isn't what you get here."

Natchez has always fascinated me. No other place on earth in the modern age evokes the presence of Old South more than this river hamlet. At the Carriage House, a popular restaurant behind the stately Stanton Hall, which looks like an antebellum white wedding cake, volunteers for the garden club greet tourists. The majority of waitresses and waiters are black, dressed in white uniforms, a throwback to the days of segregation. It's a place where girls and gents still wear hoop skirts and Confederate uniforms for social occasions during the pilgrimage, and china and silver patterns are as important as one's place in the social register.

While buses dump tourists at the town's numerous historic stops, the busy, big-city life of buzzing cell phones and beepers hasn't really invaded Natchez. Life is unhurried down here, and even the Northerners who visit are quickly forced to adapt to the town's slower pace. While city girls like myself might find the slow life with a mint julep in hand refreshing, many who live here, like Angelo, find it frightfully dull. Angelo Dixon is a gay black man trapped in a small Southern town that still revels in a 1950s *Pleasantville*-type of world.

Angelo works the night shift at the Eola, Natchez's most historic hotel and — at seven stories — downtown's tallest building. He toils around as the Eola's night auditor, balancing books while the rest of Natchez snoozes away. Because of his work schedule, Angelo often can't sleep the nights he doesn't have to work at the hotel. Insomnia gives him a lot of time to pursue his passions: writing and men. It also affords him the chance to gather secrets about this river hamlet.

And boy howdy, does he have a few.

A black man in the South is raised to be tough, macho — the big daddy who gets the girl (or girls) he wants. Queer is not cool, especially in a town the size of Natchez. Even if a man believes that he is gay, he certainly doesn't come out of the closet unless he plans to head to New York or Los Angeles. Then it's okay, because he must be in theater or art. But otherwise, gay men stay in the closet in the small-town South, and that kind of repression festers into a world of duality. Guys can't help but be "down-lo" in a society that still thinks black men aren't gay, Angelo says.

Angelo isn't the first person to tell me about so-called

straight men who live gay lives. In Little Rock, rumors circulate about politicians who are gay. Some are rumored to have been found in bed with their male lovers by their social-climbing wives.

But, frankly, I've never heard of black men living this down-lo life in Dixie. Sitting on the park bench, Angelo lets the stories fall where they may.

"Okay, you got a single guy, black, unmarried, basically straight, no feminine qualities, who has a girlfriend. He's got the straight public life. Then, some of these guys have relationships, sex and all, with men just like themselves," Angelo says, matter-of-factly. "Some of them, though, have sex with men who they would never talk to in another situation."

These men don't act particularly feminine, they don't have the stereotypical gay attributes that people who have "gaydar" can detect. In fact, they are the poster boys of masculinity: the big burly man who looks like Shaft and has a get-all-the-ladies attitude. The sleek mack daddy in a three-piece suit; the good-looking college basketball star who will nail the ladies and move on to a multimillion dollar NBA contract; the thugged-out dealer who makes his living selling hard drugs.

Angelo has been involved with his share of married black men who have the 2.1 kids, the mortgage, and the suburban life. A couple of years ago, Angelo was working at the hotel one night when a local business held a function at the Eola. A man who attended the party struck up a conversation with Angelo.

"I had seen him before but I didn't know him personally," he says.

The pair's conversation was hardly sexual in nature. More

chitchat about life in Natchez, the weather, and the hors d'oeuvres than about blow jobs and bad marriages. A few weeks later, though, the man called Angelo late at night. Suddenly, the man is confessing about his relationship with his wife and explaining that the only reason he is still in the marriage is because of the kids.

"Why are you telling me this?" Angelo asked.

The man didn't give him an answer, but rather kept talking about his life. Angelo just listened and responded in different ways. For three months, late at night, the man called Angelo periodically. He often wanted Angelo to read excerpts from the stories Angelo writes. Angelo obliged, reading him erotic passages from several of his books. He told Angelo that he had been living a secret life, commuting from Natchez to his male lover's place in New Orleans, a two-hour drive, but his illicit relationship crumbled when his lover wanted him to make a choice between a gay and straight lifestyle. He couldn't do it, and the lovers parted ways. The man's wife never knew.

Sexual tension brewed between Angelo and his late-night caller. Eventually, they connected, having wild sex any chance they got and talking long hours on the telephone. Natchez is a small town, and there aren't that many places to go — whether you are gay or straight — to conduct an affair. Angelo says that people pull down their pants wherever they can to get it on: apartments, motels on the outskirts of town, parked cars. They do the nasty and then return to their normal lives. The straight men, diving temporarily into the gay world, go home to their wives, who are none the wiser about where their husbands' tallywackers have been.

Angelo's relationship became stormy and dark, and guilt clouded the frivolous fun of noncommittal sex. The break-up was nasty, mean, and confusing. The man repeatedly told Angelo that a woman, not a man, knew how to melt his butter. He told Angelo that women in panty hose were sexy and that women have that touch of seduction that men don't have. Angelo's reaction: Whatever.

"He was trying to prove all of this to himself. He was in denial about it, and his marriage is not going to last. He's going to have to be with a man. He is a bisexual man, but he has to make a choice at some point."

You said it, Angelo. Wishy-washy ain't my bag, either.

People in Natchez often end up in bed with each other. But they don't talk about it. Because the town is so small, and there's not much to do but screw, people have a tendency to just go in a circle. That's why, Angelo says, AIDS is spreading more rampantly in Natchez than anyone realizes, especially among black women. Their husbands and boyfriends live secret lives of denial, and because they have the urge to be with other men, they indulge in risky behavior and usually don't wear condoms.

"There are more bisexual people here than out-of-the-closet gay people, for sure," he says. But that's not the biggest secret in Natchez.

"Females are aware that men get down with other men and it wouldn't be that big of a surprise to find out that a homeboy is bumping his best buddy or the 'big nelly queen' in the hood," he says.

I'm not so sure. I'd be pretty shocked if one of my straight guy friends in Arkansas told me about getting it on with a big nelly queen. Damn shocked.

This is the big secret: Cliques. Cliques? Here's how it works: Everybody has their group of friends or their "clique" that they hang with to smoke dope or have group sex.

"Many people — those outside of the clique — might be surprised to find out just what goes on behind closed doors when a group of friends, usually all male or all female, get together," Angelo says.

He doesn't have a clique right now, but he has in the past.

"We would have mad drinking sessions or wild orgies that included gay and straight people. I can honestly say that the most exciting times I've had in my clique was to get a so-called straight guy to do it with another man. And believe it or not, it's not that hard to get a brother to carry on. With enough dope or enough liquor, most brothers will try anything at least once. I've also found that men love oral sex, and whether it comes from a female or a male really doesn't matter," he says.

Another big secret Angelo whispers in the park behind the church is that most people would be surprised to find out the number of men around here who portray themselves in the public as beefy brutal tops, but in bed are nothing more than big nelly bottoms. Translation please.

"In other words . . . instead of being the dominant one in bed, they prefer being the submissive partner. There are a lot of guys around here who — pardon my French — like to take it up the ass. Some of them can't even get an erection unless they get some anal stimulation first," he says, grinning.

So is there some secret handshake that lets gay men know straight men want a piece of them?

"If there is a secret handshake, I wish I knew what it was!" Angelo laughs. "The only password I know of is eye contact and gaydar. All it takes is a look or two and it's on, baby!"

One thing for sure, Angelo calls it like he sees it.

A few years ago, Angelo decided he had some stories to tell, and they weren't exactly the typical romances and mysteries you'd find on the shelves of the Natchez city library. He writes naughty erotica stories, the kind that might make even the most horny Southerner blush. His characters are fictional, the dialogue and situations real. Either he has experienced what he writes or other people have, and they've told him their stories.

Angelo self-publishes his stories; he even makes the books. No joke. I kid you not. He makes the books like they did in ancient times, one page at a time.

"Once I decided to self-publish my works, I knew I had a monumental task before me," he says. "I would not have the luxury of a printing press or bookbinder to get the job done quick, fast, and in a hurry. I would only have my own two hands to get the job done. Believe me, it's hard work and sometimes I feel like pulling my hair out."

He literally copies the pages, folds, staples, and glues them together before binding them into a book. Angelo says the final step is all about the book's cosmetics, which consists of printing out labels with the name of the book and his name. He uses a battery-operated label-making machine to create the labels and then wraps each book in plastic. Voila! An Angelo Dixon original.

He's tried to get his work accepted by publishing houses

but has received only rejection letters. To that he says, "You know that there is a market out there for your work, then by all means do what you've gotta do, my brothers and sisters; make your dream become a reality and do the damn thing yourself — show them who's bad!"

Angelo's gumption in exploring the black gay life hasn't rattled too many people in Natchez. His coworkers know he writes the books, but they don't say anything. He figures most people haven't read his books. Too bad. Angelo's stories make me raise my eyebrows in a wicked naughty arch and cause an evil grin to roll over my lips.

In my nice comfy room at the Eola, I read some excerpts from Angelo's collection of stories. He's most proud of *DL Brothaz — Double Life*, which he wrote a few years ago. The story is about how down-lo men act and live. It may be his ability to reveal such secrets that attract female black readers to Angelo. They read his books much more frequently than black men. I can see why.

> *With their eyes locked on each other, they sipped their wine. They placed their glasses on the table before them. They relaxed and sat back on the sofa. Jeff stared into Sam's eyes. Sam stared into his eyes. Sam reached over and trailed his fingers up and down Jeff's leg. The sensation began to stir him. Sam went for it and began to stroke Jeff's manhood, which was getting harder and harder by the second. Jeff closed his eyes. Sam unzipped Jeff's pants, reached into the fly, pulled Jeff's tool out, smiled in delight that the brotha was packin' dick*

fo' days, leaned over and went to town downtown. Jeff gasped from the feeling of being engulfed for the very first time in his life. He'd experienced sex before, but this was the first time that anyone (male or female) had given him head, but it was pure instinct, which led him to reach down, unbutton his pants and push them halfway to his thighs. It was also instinct, which drove him to lift Sam up off his tool for a second for him to get out of his boxers. He swiftly pushed his pants and boxers down to his ankles and just as quickly he grabbed Sam's head and pushed him back down on his tool. Like a sex starved maniac, Jeff tightly held Sam's head down on his tool, as he hunched up into his mouth and throat with vigorous jabs. "Yeah, suck it! Suck that dick," he said in short breaths. This was the most glorious feeling that Jeff had ever experienced in his life.

That's enough of that for the evening. Say good-night Angelo.

In the South, it's not easy to even talk about sex, much less come out of the closet at age fourteen. But that's when Angelo knew. He had just had his first sexual experience with a boy he had a mad crush on in band.

"He was my first boyfriend and my first love. He came to my house one day after school and we had sex in my room before my mother came home. I have to admit that I tricked the boy there, but I think he knew all along what was up. He didn't fight the feelings, if you know what I mean. He was my boyfriend the whole ninth-grade year."

Angelo says he still sees his first love from time to time, but the love is married now and has a daughter. A few years ago, they reconnected and had a brief loving relationship, but the man opted to get married and live the straight life.

"I still consider him as someone special in my life," Angelo says. "How could I not? He was the first boy I allowed to enter my body and fulfill my dreams. No matter who I get with or have a relationship with from now on . . . none of them can top my first love."

So young Angelo came out to his parents. His dad was understanding, his mother a little less so. In a short time, she came around and supported him. His most ardent supporter is his grandmother, who worries that her grandson may be getting mixed up with trashy folk. She always wants to make sure he isn't, and like a good Southern grandson, he always reassures her.

Like a lot of gays in the South, Angelo doesn't go to church.

"It's not that I don't believe in God. I just don't like institutionalized church. I carry God in my heart. I try to treat people with respect and live my life in an honest way," he says.

A quick look in his eyes shows that this man, on the brink of turning forty, is sincere and honest in his life and his writing. Angelo likes to make people think, and his stories do that. One reader posted a letter to Angelo on a Web site saying more than likely she contracted HIV from a down-lo brother. She asked if a man isn't honest with a woman about sleeping with other women, why should anyone be surprised if they aren't honest about sleeping with other men. She's got a point there. Angelo says that is the very reason every woman should insist her man wear a condom. That's not to say that Angelo is always the cautious guy in the bedroom, but he's tried.

When he talks about AIDS in Mississippi, Angelo is brutally honest.

"I'm sorry to say, but condoms are not common in Natchez. The gay community is much wiser about using condoms, but the straight people seem to still have blinders on. Take the recent situation here for instance. There's this guy, whom everyone believed to be one hundred percent straight, who is an AIDS carrier. His girlfriend died this past weekend. He infected her. He has also infected other females here in Natchez. One of his victims is a gay guy from the coast. He called up here to Natchez and informed the Health Department that he was dying from AIDS because of this guy and that he's still infecting others. I also heard that one of his victims is still in high school. That's so sad. So yes, the attitude is still it can't happen here."

Yikes.

I ask him how many lovers he has had over the years.

"Oh, honey! I wish I could tell you, but I don't even know. I guess it's a shame to admit such a thing, but I've been honest till now, so I guess I have to keep being honest. I've been quite the whore in my day. Now, if you had asked how many partners I've loved, I would say five."

Wow. I don't think I've been in love five times. Unless I count all the way back to first or second grade.

I tell Angelo I've always wondered if gay men ever had sex with women or if they find it repulsive, much like straight men think having sex with other men is just not cool.

Angelo says he's only been with a woman in the company of another man. Huh?

"What I mean by that is I've shared men with women. I've had a few best friends who are girls who liked to get off that way. Believe it or not, there are bisexual men who have sex with men and women at the same time in the bed together. It's a hot situation and you have to be there to get the real feel of it all. As a matter of fact, that's how I got my last boyfriend. It started out as a three-way with him, my friend, who is female, and me and ended up as a two-way relationship between him and me that lasted for three years."

Tennessee Williams never wrote this kind of story!

Angelo knows all the crazy scoop in Natchez, which is its own version of a Southern gothic Peyton Place.

He tells me about the only gay black man in the town who is bold enough to dress up in women's clothing and strut around town. A tall Amazon, this man's trademark is blonde wigs that glow like the desert sand on top of his dark brown head. Josie the Transvestite Prostitute likes to say that he prefers white johns to black ones, but Angelo says even Josie has a secret. He uses the "white johns" line just to lure white men, because they have more money. But Josie keeps a young black man at his house as a secret love slave. The young man doesn't work; he doesn't lift his finger to do one thing, even take out the trash. He's a kept man.

Mind-boggling. One hundred thirty-eight years after the Civil War, and slavery in Mississippi has changed a bit.

A lot of the down-lo guys like only oral sex, Angelo dishes.

He says maybe men don't get it at home. Maybe they don't think blow jobs are cheating. Sometimes, they'll pretend they don't like it to their wives or honies, but they're lying.

"I know straight-laced men in their marriage and then they are out in the streets doing everything, oral sex to anal sex," Angelo says.

Here's the twist to all of this. Angelo explains that a lot of married men didn't ever have or consider a homosexual relationship until they got married. If they did have latent tendencies, they didn't act on them. Then, once the wedding band was slipped on their finger, they went hog-wild. Maybe, Angelo reasons, they suddenly had confidence to go for the dick because they had a safety net and an excuse: "No, man I don't do that kind of stuff, I'm married." Maybe they felt like they showed all their manliness when they walked down the aisle and then a few months later knocked up their wives. Spewing seed can give a man the confidence he needs to get the sex he wants — even if it's with another man.

"Those are the strange ones. The ones who never had tendencies and then all of a sudden . . ." Angelo trails off.

No wonder women don't trust their husbands.

My mind is blown after I catch myself reading another excerpt from an Angelo story. In this one, one gay friend asks the other for a favor. The favor: to see what kind of underwear this masculine hunk of man is wearing. Harmless enough, I guess. But dig what kind he is wearing: a pair of pink panties with white lace trimmed around the waistband and the legs.

Heavens to Betsy. Is this what Michael Jordan has under

his gym shorts? Soon, I'm wondering about every African-American male icon that I know. Jesse Jackson — thong or no thong? Taye Diggs — a big nelly bottom? Morgan Freeman — would he have actually preferred to drive Mister Daisy? As I sit in the courtyard of the Eola, inhaling the mixed scent of magnolia and my own sweat, I know one thing for sure — I'll never look at Spike Lee the same way again.

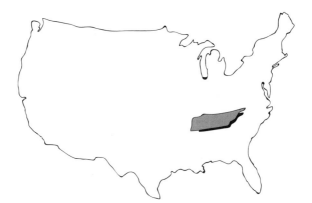

tennessee

la, la lap dances

Hoochie Coo and Lollipops

MEMPHIS, TENNESSEE — My home state of Arkansas is known for many things: Bill Clinton, the Little Rock Central High crisis of 1957, Wal-Mart. But the Natural State is not known for her strip clubs, and for good reason.

Arkansas strip joints — or "gentleman's clubs" as they're sometimes known — are best described by noting what they don't have. Disco balls? No. Laser-light shows? No way. Flashy, pulsating runway stages? Forget about it. Guys playing pool? You betcha!

And the women? Well, they're lacking a little oomph and a whole lot of vamp. Arkansas strippers often seem unsure whether they should be bumping or grinding. But, certain they are supposed to be shaking something, they sorta wiggle or sway. Judging from these uninspired routines, it's clear that much of Arkansas is still waiting on the arrival of MTV.

Exhibit A: After a few drinks one summer Friday night, a group of us decide to go to Miss Kitty's, a small strip club in the middle of some dense pine woods on the outskirts of Little Rock. I'm thinking there's a better chance of spotting road kill on the way to this place than of seeing a sexy babe once you arrive.

Bill, a divorced thirty-something guy, spearheads this

stripping, gyrating adventure. He thinks Miss Kitty's will shock little old me, the solo chick on this adventure. After all, it's my first excursion to such an establishment.

He invites Dylan, also divorced and more recently than Bill, and Stan, (yes, divorced but for longer than Bill or Dylan). Stan lives in the remote Ozark hills of Arkansas where New Age hippies and mystics mix freely with conservative gun nuts and Ku Klux Klan members. Stan is neither. He has a respectable nine-to-five job, is the epitome of normal, and is a huge fan of nudie bars. But don't think he brags about his obsession all over the state.

"I really need to keep up my image as a fine upstanding member of the community," he says.

Two swinging vivid purple doors greet us as we step inside Miss Kitty's. The only thing separating us from babelicious heaven on the other side is the formality of joining the private club. For five dollars, you can be an official member and get a hot pink membership card with the cute Miss Kitty logo printed on it. At least I think it's cute. The guys don't even notice.

We dole out the fivers and a burly grunt scrawls our names in a thick membership ledger with a black cover. Stan, our resident pro on the strip-club scene, comes prepared with a horse-choking wad of one-dollar bills to tuck inside the girls' G-strings. I have, maybe, two dollars with me. Dylan and Bill have fives and twenties. Call them the big spenders, or more likely, the unprepared.

We pass through the swinging doors to erotic city. Smoke and loud rap music engulf us, and I can't believe what I see. I'm not really sure what I was expecting — maybe glitzy Hollywood sets from *Flashdance* or *Chicago*. Certainly something more than two small stages edged in cheap Christmas lights with two girls sullenly meandering around the illuminated squares. One stage has a pole, the other some sort of brass handle that looks as if were discarded from a playground monkey-bar set. The two featured performers are decidedly unglamourous — one is ultrathin, the other just a tad more curvy and sexy. Bottom line: If I were a lesbian, I wouldn't take either home.

I'm no dancer, but I can get my swerve on. I know what turns a man on and swaying like a tranquilized grizzly ain't it. But that's how these two topless strippers are dancing when we first arrive. Well, Arkansas topless, that is. In the land of Bill Clinton, a dancer is not allowed to be completely naked. Would-be strippers must wear a thong or G-string bikini on the bottom and flesh-hued pasties on their nipples, giving the illusion of toplessness anyway. I guess if men see too many nipples they go blind? Blindness must be in abundance here, I reason. Why else would men pack into a room to see women in bikinis?

Stan ushers me to a front row seat near the stage and stuffs five one-dollar bills in my hand. Bill, as usual, looks skittish and heads to the bar. Dylan looks embarrassed yet intrigued. About twenty men sit at small tables watching the girls caress their covered breasts. A few other strippers sit in skimpy outfits and flirt with the men.

"It's all about the girl getting the guy to buy her a drink," explains Stan. "And who wouldn't want to buy a pretty girl a drink?"

A deejay hovers in a tiny booth, smaller than my apartment's pantry, and spins an array of bizarre tunes. I've never imagined women dancing seductively to the Christian band Creed but here it is in front of me — her hips moving to the wailing as her hands run through her long sandy-blonde hair.

"If every woman would come to strip joints, there'd be less divorces and more happy men," Stan says in my ear. "They could pick up a few tips and do that in the bedroom."

Truthfully: Most women wiggle more than that just to get out of a pair of tight panty hose.

Even in daily life, Bill stalks around as if he were a spy or being followed by KGB agents. At a strip joint, this pose stands out more than at your average coffee shop or bookstore. It appears that he might be either about to arrest a stripper or stalk her. Hard to tell. On the flip side, Dylan's always searching for adventure, so he inspects the joint from back to front, including the pool tables in a room to the side of the strippers. There's something not the least bit sexy, and mostly sleazy, about motorcycle dudes and hicks clacking balls while a girl gyrates to bad arena rock.

Dylan takes a liking to a new girl on the other stage, curvy with short red hair and a wicked booty wiggle. As Bill lurks around the strippers, I sit in front of the stage, mentally pretending to be a celebrity judge at the Miss America pageant. Then something strange happens: the more money Stan throws on the stage, the more the woman looks at me. She winks.

"Ah, she likes you. A little girl-girl action," Stan laughs slyly.

I suddenly realize what should have been obvious from the instant I stepped into Miss Kitty's — I am the only woman in the joint beside the strippers. Most women, of course, don't support other women taking off their clothes and letting men get their jollies. It's just the way it is, especially in the South, where girls are raised to be good girls, marry rich, and join the Junior League. Certainly, you don't shake your hoochie-coo in public for money.

Indulging the women, I throw Stan's one-dollar bills on the stage. More money, more winks. After each dance number, the strippers walk up and kiss me on the cheek or just say thank you. Over the next hour, few men get the consistent attention I do. Of course, few men give the women the respect that I do.

By the time I'm beginning to get into the three-minute strip-a-thons, the men, especially Dylan and Bill, are ready to blow the joint. I leave somewhat reluctantly. Even though it wasn't the most shocking show I had ever seen, it was enlightening.

Leaving Miss Kitty's for the bright city lights, Stan harps on the girl-girl vibe I was attracting. Bill says he didn't get anything from Miss Kitty's, not even a tingle in his loins. Dylan admits that strip joints just make him feel sleazy, much more than our whip-cracking adventure in Alabama. Stan says he couldn't wait to go to another one. Boys aren't all the same.

A week later Stan acquires a membership card to another strip joint in Missouri.

"Some folks go to sports bars. I hate televised sports. If the choice was between watching a bunch of sweaty guys beating each other up and watching pretty girls strut around, I will choose the pretty girls every time," says Stan.

Dylan tossed his Miss Kitty's pink membership card in the trash can. Bill isn't sure where he placed his.

"I may have taken it out of my wallet. Who knows?" he says unconcerned.

But I know exactly where my pink card is, hidden away in a blue box on my antique bookcase.

For years, all I have heard, is this: Platinum Plus in Memphis is the place to go in the mid-South for stripping entertainment.

Arkansas strip joints are said to be nothing compared to the upscale shows available in Memphis. Even my friend Julie once told me she experienced an unforgettable grinding lap dance at Platinum Plus. This I've got to see.

Memphis sits on the edge of the muddy Mississippi River, and like many river cities, an undescribable seediness looms over it even on sunny days. Its historic art deco buildings fuse with dilapidated and abandoned housing projects creating a meld of the past and present that isn't all that inviting. Mississippi River port cities all have this bawdy grittiness, a result of riverboats, carrying hundreds of cotton bales, docking for decades and men indulging in too many late nights of blues, booze, and brothels. This is the town where Elvis and Martin Luther King Jr. died, and their ghosts haunt the place just enough to keep hordes of tourists visiting Graceland and the Civil Rights Museum.

In the last decade, casinos in nearby Tunica, Mississippi, have put cotton on the area's economic back burner and slot machines on the front one. An influx of tourists seeking blues, Elvis, and gambling riches have poured into the mid-South. Those visitors mixed with the residents of the tri-state area — Tennessee, Mississippi, and Arkansas — provide places like Platinum Plus with a fresh clientele. Case in point: Vince Jenkins.

At twenty-six, Vince Jenkins loves the blackjack table. He loves smoking Marlboro cigs. He loves naked women. Since he turned twenty-one, he's visited the Double P, as he calls Platinum Plus, at least fifteen times with his gambling buddies. For Vince, who works in an entry-level job at a large Little Rock advertising agency, the Double P is a wonderland of tits and ass. So enamored of the place is he that once, when Vince had to deliver some business documents to Memphis from Little Rock, he had lunch at the gentleman's club before heading back to the office. He says he paid for the excursion on the company's credit card without any retribution from his bosses.

"The girls are incredible," Vince says, taking a deep drag off his cigarette. "It's the place for sure. Vegas isn't this good. You don't even see this in Vegas. It's like putting a kid in a candy store. The girls are hot. It's an adrenaline rush and you bond with your buddies."

On a Sunday afternoon, Vince sits in Pizza D'Action — a popular hangout for artsy types and musicians — drinking a Bud Heavy, as he calls the beer, and wearing a Grand Casino baseball cap, a symbol of his dedication to gambling. This haunt is more my scene than his. Vince says he prefers the River Market area of Little Rock, which attracts frat boys with pagers, cell phones, and office badges dangling from their belts.

A stripper named Pocahontas granted Vince his first Double P experience. A half-black, half-white goddess, Vince says that Pocahontas wooed Vince like no other woman ever has.

"When they give you the dance, they are, well for the lack of a better word, trying to get you hard. Those girls are masters at accomplishing that mission. You are totally a different person afterward. That's why you have to pay up-front."

The cost: $40. Vince says for $500, some girls will "go around the world." Translation: They'll do anything. She says once when he won big in Tunica, he spent about $400 on lap dances and drinks for his pals.

Vince weaves salacious stories about the wild women of Platinum Plus. One night he and his buddies invited one of the Double P girls back to Tunica. While some of the guys gambled, Vince's friend and the girl enjoyed themselves in one of the casino's hotel rooms.

"She didn't charge him," Vince explains.

Very kind of her, but hard to believe, I say, that a woman who flaunts her body for dollar bills would give it away for free. But maybe it was love at first sight.

Vince may say he's a good Methodist boy who attended private Christian schools, but he's a wild child at heart. He recalls another time when he and his buddies were staying at one of the larger Tunica hotels and they called the concierge to find a girl for them.

"She was a hooker, an 'escort' you'd call them. There were six of us in the room and she shows up. She wasn't all that hot. We were just looking at her and no one wanted to do her. Two of my buddies who were drunk finally said, 'Screw it, I'll do it.' "

Vince says he felt sorry for the girl. He even feels bad about going to Platinum Plus when his Southern Christian guilt gnaws at him. His parents know he's been once, for his twenty-first birthday, but they don't know he frequents the club as often as he does. They'd flip. A wild night for Mom and Dad Jenkins is going out to dinner and his dad indulging in a beer, his mom a frozen margarita.

"I feel guilty for going, yeah, but there's guilt in everything that's fun. I just block out everything I've learned. I say just give me two hours to do something dirty."

It's no secret to Vince that I want to visit Platinum Plus. I've got to see what the fuss is. On his second beer, he offers me tips as if he is a member of the nouveau Rat Pack of the mid-South. According to Vince, I'm to arrive at the Double P before nine so I can get a prime seat. By ten, the joint is packed. The guy friend I choose to drag along should wear a suit.

"That makes you look like you have money and you get more attention," he advises.

Vince tells me to have plenty of ones, but if I don't I can get change at the club. The girls like girls so they'll be on me like white on rice, he tells me. Because it's nice to have other women in the room besides the strippers, women don't pay covers at the Double P, unlike at Miss Kitty's.

Oh, and one last thing: "Watch out for the smell of rubbing alcohol."

"Why?" I ask.

"Some girlfriends of mine who went with us once said that the girls reek of that stuff. I guess they rub themselves after the lap dances."

Surely, I wouldn't get that close to the women. What if I did?

"When I'm in there my sense of smell is deactivated. It's all about the eyes. Just walk in and keep your eyes open," Vince advises.

Dylan, who is my partner for misadventures, is my chosen beau for the Double P escapade. He loathes strip joints and continues to say, "Miss Kitty's was enough to last a lifetime."

"I don't think we've seen anything yet," I say with a wink.

Every trip to Memphis requires a visit to the historic Peabody Hotel to see the ducks that, every morning, march out from their rooftop penthouse to a waiting elevator that whisks them to the hotel lobby. Tourists, cameras in tow, flock to see the ducks strut down a red carpet rolled out just for them. The ducks spend the day splashing about in a marble fountain until the duck master escorts them back to their suite at five every afternoon.

"Let's watch the ducks," Dylan says before we sit down in the spacious art deco lobby.

We walk over to the fountain where five tourists with a couple of cameras loll about watching the ducks. Then, we see something amazing. The king mallard duck jumps on the back of one of the wood ducks and goes after it. The mallard forces the duck-of-his-choice's head underwater and keeps at her for at least two minutes as we stand, mouths agape.

"Nothing like some ducks getting some sweet lovin' to get the party started," Dylan says, as we sit down for some coffee to rev up for our evening at the Double P.

Dylan and I spot the purple neon-light glowing the words "Platinum Plus" before we actually see the white stucco building. On a Saturday night, cars from around the South, especially Arkansas and Mississippi, pack the two large parking lots with iron fences around them. Burly guys wearing STAFF T-shirts are scattered in the parking lots, directing traffic and eyeing customers.

"Who knew this many people came here?" I say, genuinely shocked by the volume of cars.

"Let's hope a fire doesn't break out while we are in there," says Dylan. These are the kind of thoughts Dylan has, always looking for a way out.

"We'll stand next to the EXIT signs," I say.

Platinum Plus sits on a corner of busy Mt. Moriah, a wide

avenue that has as many car dealerships as fast-food joints. Behind the plain white building that houses unbridled ecstasy for men, there's a two-story office plaza with law offices, a travel agency, and insurance companies.

In 1992, when the gentleman's club was opened, area businesses protested with picketers walking around with signs. In Memphis, the 1990s were a rocky decade for clubs like Platinum Plus. They were often busted by vice squads and padlocked for days because of violations. In the twenty-first century, though, morality watchers and the police have tended to pay less attention to what they often call a public nuisance.

As we walk toward the front doors, a good hunch tells me that, unlike at Miss Kitty's, I won't be the only girl at this party. Two more burly staff members guard the doors and tell the masses of horny men and women what to do. Curiosity, not horniness, has brought me here, and I can't wait to see what awaits me on the other side of these doors. Dylan doesn't seem as thrilled. Vince told me that any man who said he doesn't like a strip joint was lying. Honestly, though, I can tell that Dylan hates this place already. He gets his kicks some other way.

"You'll go in and pay at the counter inside. Cover is six dollars," says one of the bouncers. "Ladies free. I need to look in your bag, miss."

I open my purse as if going through airport security to show the guy a black leather organizer, some lipstick, and a bunch of receipts.

"Go in," he commands.

Once inside a small, surprisingly quiet foyer that could be the entrance to any suburban home, a twenty-something woman in a black velvet tank top smiles invitingly. Behind her, an array of Platinum Plus souvenir T-shirts embossed with a 1980s Nagel-looking babe are for sale. A tip jar sits on the wooden counter. I'm not sure what she does to deserve a tip and I'm not really sure I want to know. Dylan shells out six dollars to her and she launches into the house rules.

"Ladies free. You need to buy your first drinks before entering the club," she explains.

She stops our rules tutorial for a second to address a trio of men at the bar next to her counter. One Hispanic man is having problems understanding the female blonde bartender. In a flash, the brunette in front of us whips into rapid-fire Spanish, straightening out the man's confusion.

"Thank you, enjoy your visit. Buy your first drinks at the bar," she says, dismissing us to the bartender.

Vince had told me that Platinum Plus was a BYOB joint, and he was right. But before you can swig on your own Jim Beam, you have to buy a drink. Dylan's beer costs $4.75, and there's no discount for my soda. Same price. Before we've even entered the main area, Dylan's dropped nearly sixteen dollars — all in the name of pleasure. Behind the bartender, a frosted glass window etched with an outline of a curvaceous woman allows us to peer into the club. It's dark with flashing laser lights.

With our drinks in hand, we open the entry door to the club and an outrageously loud wall of pulsating techno sound blasts through us. Men, young and old, are everywhere, sitting in chairs, skulking in corners. As my eyes adjust to the strange dark room with the lime-green beams of light bouncing around, I begin to see things. Shocking things.

To the left, a woman in an über-short gray pleated skirt straddles a man in a club chair. To the right, a woman in a teal

G-string and nothing else cozies up to another man. Then, with Dylan elbowing my ribs, I look and see two blonde women — not strippers — sitting in front of the stage. Their tongues probe each other's mouths more than Lewis and Clark explored the Louisiana Purchase. Call it energetic tonsil hockey. Dylan and I stare at the women and then at each other.

The round stage in the middle of the room soon commands our attention. The three sets of steps leading up to it are crawling with men. An Amazon-sized black woman arrives in a skimpy black bikini. Within ten seconds, she's out of the getup and naked, completely nude except for six-inch stiletto heels. She walks around, strutting on the stage, showing her doo-lolly to the crowd. I'm in honest-to-goodness speechless mode. I look at Dylan, who seems unable to close his mouth.

Before I finish taking in the black beauty on the stage, the deejay starts playing "Family Tradition" by Hank Williams Jr., a surefire way to bring out the redneck in any Southern male. As the men scream the lyrics to the song, a buxom blonde wearing pale pink chaps, a bikini top, and a G-string whips off the chaps, magically sheds the rest of the costume, and begins strutting around in her white patent leather stilettos that should come with some sort of warning label for the wearer.

She rolls around the floor, the sharp weaponlike heels flying in the air as she spreads her vaginal wares for all to see. Men throw dollar bills onto the stage as she touches herself. They whoop and holler as all around them cocktail waitresses take their orders and nude girls who have already danced strut around inviting men to the VIP room. "You ready for that dance yet?" is a common question around the Double P.

On a smaller cagelike dance floor encircled with brass

bars, a curvy chick who looks like the one Dylan took a liking to at Miss Kitty's strips down and moves her legs in the air, drawing figure eights in the sky. As a man approaches the steps leading up to the stage, the young girl gets up and walks over, buck-ass naked. With the agility of a gymnast, she vaults onto the bars. In a swift, take-no-prisoners ninja-style move, she wraps her legs around the man, rubbing her doo-lolly in his face. He basks in the moment and gives her a dollar for her trouble. Leaving the stage naked later, she carries off about seventy dollars.

"I've never seen anything like this," Dylan says.

"Me either," I say. "Never, not even at Mardi Gras or in Alabama. Not anywhere."

The night moves like a John Woo movie, sometimes too fast-paced to keep track of what's going on. Quickly, a succession of girls take the stage, wiggling, stripping, and then wrapping their legs around customers's faces, some of whom, no doubt, take a lick or two at the goodies. I wonder if these girls buy their G-strings in bulk at a stripper's discount mart.

"I can't believe for one dollar you can get your face buried in tits, muff, even ass," Dylan says.

What can I say: Me, either.

"What happened to the days when strippers wrapped themselves around poles? Now they wrap themselves around your head," Dylan says.

We move through the club like aliens making a maiden voyage to Planet Earth. Dylan and I say nothing to each other for two reasons: One, the noise level cancels out thoughts in the brain. Two, Vince was right. The senses are so overloaded that the brain doesn't seem to connect in a manner that allows any words to emerge — like some sort of strange

drug trip. It's all just pussy, tits, and ass in a sea of men rang-
ing from wealthy Brooks Brothers–clothed businessmen to
middle-of-the-road nine-to-fivers bold enough to wear their
company logo jackets. QualChoice and Coca-Cola Quality
Systems are two popular ones. Cigar-smoking, beer-swigging
fraternity boys mix with *Deliverance*-type rednecks in overalls.
Who knew that strip clubs were the great equalizers?

"Holy shit," says Dylan, emerging from his pussy-induced
coma. "That's my insurance agent."

I look over toward a corner near one of the smaller stages.
A man holding a beer with a blank stare — a cunt zombie,
I call them — zones in on the strippers.

"That's him, all right," Dylan says.

"You going to say hello?" I ask.

"Hell, no. This is like when you are in the men's room and
you don't acknowledge other men. I don't think you are supposed to go up to someone here and say howdy."

I shrug. Who knew such rules existed among men?

Then, just when I think am incapable of more shock, I spot
one of the dancers escorting a woman in her sixties, surely a
grandmother, into the VIP room. Dylan and I look at each
other in utter fright.

"Is she going back for a lap dance?" I ask.

"Um, I think so," Dylan says. The look on his face reveals
the grind-on granny scene taking place in his brain.

"Holy shit," I say, wondering if a senior citizens discount is
honored in the VIP room.

The VIP room is a sunken den near the back of the club. Dylan and I venture to the edge of the steps that lead down into

the pleasure pit. Through the red-light darkness, a mass of writhing arms and legs sway in the air as men lounge on one suburban love seat after the other. There are at least two and a half dozen sofas crowded in the room. The women move in a hypnotic hover over the men, and some women. Hands roam all over the women, cupping and massaging breasts, thighs, hips. The smoky room possesses an *Arabian Nights* air, a consequence-free harem room in the Middle Eastern desert.

In one corner near where I stand, a completely nude woman grinds herself backward into the lap of an overweight plaid-shirted man. He could be anyone's father, son, husband, or brother. The stripper works the man into a hard-on frenzy for more than ten minutes. I recall Stan telling me at Miss Kitty's that a really great lap dancer can make a guy lose control without actual contact. Just a rub through the jeans and he needs a moist towelette to clean up his mess.

"Can any poor male stand a pretty gal burying her head, boobs, and bottom in your lap?" asked Stan after our Miss Kitty's experience. "Hell no. Poor old Mr. Stiffy will dang near grow legs and follow a gal back to the dressing room. The best girls will give you a little peck on the cheek, a big hug, and a great smile. Usually more than a fellow is getting at home."

Judging by the men in the VIP room, there are a lot of husbands not getting anything in suburbia. The women here have all the control and it's apparent that the men lost theirs as soon as they paid the cover charge. Platinum Plus is a sea of men with open wallets, and the women are picking off victims left and right.

Turning away for a second, I watch another woman work a man standing against the wall outside the VIP room. She presses hard against him, looking into his eyes, massaging his cock, trying a seduction plan that goes awry when a cocktail waitress passes.

"Hey, I need another beer," he says, totally interrupting the mood. Oof. No wonder he has to pay for it.

One of the French-kissing women from earlier in the evening keeps smiling at me. I'm not one to exaggerate but both Dylan and I think she's flirting with me. Obviously, by the empty bottle of liquor on the low bar around the stage, she's also smashed. When she and her posse get ready to leave, she offers the empty chairs around the stage to Dylan and me.

And perfect timing.

On the main stage, the other tonsil-hockey blonde woman has gone wild. A stripper lies on her back and the woman dances over her with a dollar bill in her mouth. The stripper spreads her legs, and the woman dances her way down to her shaved mound. The woman teases the stripper with the money. The crowd of men goes wild. Another stripper walks up on the stage and begins to pull the woman's pants down but she balks, backing off. As she exits the stage, the PA booms.

"We have a bachelor party in the house. Come on up, Win. Get on up on that stage," says the deejay, who hides in a glass room above the stage and over the bar.

A statuesque woman with two brown pigtails and a very pointed nose moves one of the club's chairs onto the stage. She wears an oriental black satin strapless dress with splits on the sides and black leather boots. Two other strippers — a blonde and brunette in skimpy gear — join her. Win, the twenty-something bachelor, finally emerges from the crowd.

"Come on up," says the leather-boot chick.

He smiles sheepishly but once on the stage, in the glare of the spotlight, a male cockiness emerges, but not for long. The tall stripper grabs him by his jeans' belt and yanks it off. She's taller than he is, and in an aggressive nanosecond she pulls his yellow boxers above his jeans waistband and even faster she has ripped out the elastic. With that move, she pushes him into the chair and gags him with the elastic. The other strippers join in the fun, but when she starts to whip him with his leather belt, Win bolts.

A series of women prance around the stage. Montana, Rosie, and Tyson all show their goods to us, up close and personal. After about ten doo-lollies in my face, I feel like a gynecologist after a long day. Next!

Let's get rrrrrreadddddyyyy to rummmmbbbllleeeee!!!

The words reverberate throughout Platinum Plus like at a San Antonio Spurs game. Suddenly the deejay bellows, "Are you ready for the Pussy-Eating Championship of the World?"

Dylan looks at me, eyebrow cocked. "What did he say? Bush-eating what?"

"I think he said pussy-eating championship," I say, but really doubting that disembodied stentorian voice from above said such a thing. Surely, he jests.

It is soon apparent that my ears are in working order.

Two topless blondes, one of whom had been wearing the pastel pink chaps earlier in the evening, appear on the stage. In one corner they place a silver bucket and they prance to the center like a pair of prizefighters. The throbbing beats kick in and the two topless women arrange themselves strategically on the floor. Prizefighter Number One spreads her legs and her opponent — sporting a self-portrait tattoo on the arch of her back — dips her head between the tanned thighs. She pushes back the skimpy panel of the flesh-colored G-string and begins to caress the clit of the moment. A-whooga! Is this legal? Some of the men around the floor literally appear to be drooling. Others sport the cunt-zombie look. Crumpled dollar bills fly through the air and land on the stage.

"The more money they see, the wilder and nastier they are going to get," the deejay's voice echoes.

More money — all Washingtons, no Lincolns, certainly no Hamiltons — arc toward the stage. The girls receive the message and suddenly, they transform into every guy's dream position — sixty-nine — licking and sucking as if they both were delicious ice cream cones. I've seen girl-girl sixty-nine in porn magazines but I've never seen it in live action. At this moment, I wonder: What's a good Methodist girl like me doing in a place like this? The girls never seem to climax, but rather just keep kissing and licking for the cash until the deejay tells them to stop after about five minutes. I can't help but try to count in my head how many erections are in the room at this very moment. Too many, I conclude. Is that possible?

Sensing the crowd needs a break from round one of the pussy-eating tournament, more girls emerge onstage, wiggling out of their G-strings. Each one seems to target the man to my left. An older man in his sixties with gray hair peeking through his baseball cap, he looks like he enjoys a good stiff gin, a round of golf, and the occasional romp with a pretty young thing in an expensive hotel room. He watches the dancers with great discretion, occasionally placing a dollar between their breasts when they give him a rolling good show with lots of spread eagles.

A super sexy model-type with a black Chelsea Girl cut hits the stage, her black chauffeur's cap to one side and large silver hoops on her ears. She immediately takes a liking to me. All night, I have refrained from giving a dollar to anyone, but what the hell? I hold one of the dollars Dylan handed me earlier in the evening. She presses her breasts together and urges me to put the dollar between them. I do. As the music blares, she attempts to lure me on the stage but I shake my head. No way, José. I'm a risk taker but it's good to say no sometimes. This is one of those times. Chelsea Girl looks disappointed but quickly moves on to Dylan, who nestles a dollar in betwixt her tits, too. She then wows us more with a trick I have never seen anywhere. She takes hold of her vagina's lips and pulls them over each other in a crisscross applesauce Jacob's ladder manner. Then with a flick or two, she turns it inside out and back, all while gyrating to the funky groove of "Double Dutch Bus." Whoa. Did she learn this on this playground as a kid? The last time I heard this song I was at the roller rink in elementary school. Thanks, Chelsea Girl. My childhood soundtrack will never be the same.

Dylan looks at his watch. We've been at the Double P for nearly two hours, although in strange ways it seems much longer.

"Are you ready to go?" Dylan asks. He clearly is. No doubt he has had enough Triple X fun for one Saturday night.

The voyeur in me cannot leave just yet because I crave one more peek into the VIP room. I tell Dylan this.

"I'm going to the bathroom," he says.

"Don't leave me out here," I squeal.

"You'll be fine," he assures me.

While he makes his temporary exit, I stand once again on the edge of the den of sin and peer in like a little girl looking in a pet shop for the first time. A Pamela Anderson dead ringer leads the old man who has been sitting by me at the stage to a sofa in the back. She's the lucky winner who finally convinced Daddy Warbucks to open the wallet.

Dylan emerges unscathed from the bathroom so I figure I'll go, too.

"Bathroom," I say, heading toward the dark hallway.

The women's rest room is at the end of a small hall, next to the men's. Opening the door, I see strippers cramming the small area, piles of one dollar bills covering the counters. There are only three stalls.

"I am so fucked up," says one lap dancer-stripper as she stumbles into the last stall.

The middle stall, which I choose, is out of paper. A dirty plunger is lodged between the toilet and stall wall. I decide to go for the first stall, which has paper. That, and it's a better place to hear the shoptalk.

"Fuck, I'm ten dollars short. I knew I needed to work it harder the last hour," says one stripper. "I need to make that ten dollars."

Leaving the stall, I walk over to the sink. A washed-up cocktail waitress sits on the vanity counting money.

"Don't mind if you wash your hands, dear, but don't get any water in my drink."

I smile and notice an orange juice concoction next to the sink on a tray.

"I'll make sure I don't," I say, quickly exiting the depressing bathroom. Far from glam, the dancers could have been three pizza delivery guys in the break room.

We head toward the door. Before we can escape the wicked carnival, the deejay announces round two of the pussy-eating contest. Immediate change of plans. It's like a train wreck. Who can refuse the chance to see round two? Dylan and I almost decide to forgo it, but like curious on-lookers staring at a dead body in a ditch, we have to stay and watch more.

Shimmery silver pale lights bathe the stage, and the men jockey for prime position. The girls, look-alikes from Nash-ville, have wild half-braided hair in minuscule corn rows that flare in the middle to create manes. A silver stud accents one of the tanned babes' chin, and she sucks a round red lol-lipop. At the deejay's cue, the girls tear into each other like delirious dogs. Oblivious to the men around the stage, they go after each other full force. Then to my surprise, the lollipop steals the show. The lollipop-wielding twin pops the candy out of her mouth and teases her partner's pussy with the sticky sweetness. Rolling around on the stage in playful romps, the women are out-of-control in their lesbian-induced haze.

"Look over there," Dylan says.

A girl from the audience walks up the steps to the stage to get in on the action. The twins attack her. One takes off the girl's shirt and begins to suck on her nipples. The other one goes after the jeans. She buries her head into the girl's panties. The crowd screams with excited hysteria and throws more money.

"Don't throw quarters, men," the deejay admonishes the cheapskates as coins bounce across the stage. "Throw some real money. The more money they see the wilder and nastier they are going to get."

To me, the entire scene teeters on rape. But before I can even say this to Dylan, a chubby college girl wants in on the action. She holds money, and she wants the girls to take it from her. The college girl lies down on her back and puts the cash in her mouth. One of the strippers straddles her face and grabs the money with her down-under lips. Talk about pussy control. Kegel City. The irony about all of this is when men attempt to get on the stage, the strippers flatly refuse them. But the more girls the merrier.

The lollipop strumpet continues her dual licking, holding the sucker in her mouth while pleasuring her partner. The strippers moved from sixty-nine to yoga-like positions. One guy stands by the stage, an eye on the action, an ear to his cell phone giving his phone partner a play-by-play description. Alexander Graham Bell must be very proud. By the end of their act, the cunnilingus dream duo have rolled around the entire stage, not missing one spot on the floor. They end up in front of a young black man, handing him the lollipop. He stares at the sucker, thinks for a minute, and then puts it in his mouth.

Shudder. Bad decision. Never a good idea to eat the stripper's doo-lolly-pop.

"I've got to get out of here," Dylan says, not enjoying the room with a thousand views.

"I've seen enough," I say.

In the car, we stare at each other trying to decipher what the hell we've just seen in there, hoping we will be the same again, but knowing we might not.

"I may never be able to hear AC/DC again," I say.

Dylan just shakes his head like a disoriented shock victim. As we pull out of the parking lot, a random woman in a yellow sweater flashes me. Dylan's face is ashen, and I know he's reached his limit.

"You go to a strip joint and everyone thinks they are a stripper when they leave," I say.

"I don't see us going back there anytime soon," Dylan says, looking straight ahead and obviously trying to fill his mind with thoughts of puppy dogs and ice cream.

"I don't see it either, I can't believe it," I say, the images still burning in my mind as we crossed the darkness of Memphis at midnight.

"I need some Disney, some innocence, some antidote," Dylan says.

He's not joking, and I know exactly what he means. As I lay down all snug in my bed, visions of pussy plums dance in my head.

giddy up, trigger!

Sugar Cubes and Shoulder Rides

NASHVILLE, TENNESSEE — I've done a lot of things, but I've never met a horse at a hotel.

Trigger the Human Equine is hanging his tail for the week-end at the Club House Inn and Suites near the Grand Ole Opry. It's a big deal for Trigger to appear for a pony-play demonstration in Nashville because in his universe, he's as famous as Gene Autry or Roy Rogers. Or maybe Seabiscuit. Needless to say, the Nashville Leather Association is psyched with anticipation about Trigger's lecture this afternoon.

So am I. My lust for learning, always begging to be fed with more crazy tidbits, can barely wait to feast on Trigger, who possesses a most curious fetish: He likes to pretend he is a horse. In every detail. It's called pony play. One person takes the role of the pony and another one is the trainer, rider, or groomer. Honestly, I'm not sure what to expect. A man who needs medication? A centaur? Someone who is more normal than most of my friends? The voyeur in me tingles.

Walking into the lobby of the small hotel, I spot a she-male with a sweet smile. Bingo.

"Hi, I'm looking for Trigger," I say. Most people would have giggled at hearing themselves say such a thing, but not me. These days, asking a she-male how to find a man-horse is par for the course.

"You can find him setting up in there," the she-male in the black wig and makeup says, motioning toward a room. On the way, I wonder: What is the proper etiquette for meeting a horse? Do I stroke his mane? Offer a sugar cube?

Sure enough, Trigger, a short, stocky, balding fifty-something Alabama native who lives in Washington D.C., is setting up shop in a small banquet room. On a long table, Trigger straightens up magazines — *Equus Eroticus,* which is Latin for "Erotic Horse" — and some videos that feature him in pony-play mode. Some horse gear — a bit, some fancy two-sided tape — is also on the table. On a coat hanger, off to the side, a leather harness hangs on a doorknob. It looks like a complicated outfit to slip into in a hurry.

Trigger introduces himself as various workshop attendees float in and out to catch a glimpse. I cannot wait to hear his story. How does a man become a horse? The answer: Elvis Presley, of course.

Around the time that Elvis died, Trigger was working Sundays at a small Alabama radio station. On his way to work, Trigger stopped at a convenience store and picked up a magazine with a cover shot of Elvis. Settled in at the station spinning tunes and reading, Trigger came across an article about clothed women sitting on men's faces.

" 'Wow, what magazine is this?' I asked myself," recalls Trigger, his blue eyes twinkling.

The magazine was *Forum Variations* and in between the covers, Trigger discovered another story about human ponies that raced, were swapped between owners, and auctioned off. His fate was settled. He wanted to be ridden like a pony, but Trigger found it wasn't so easy to explain what he wanted in the 1970s, an era of uninhibited crazed sex. He spent a lot of his free time in those days playing in a band. You'd think that going to nightclub after nightclub would afford Trigger the perfect opportunity to find what he wanted. But even after a woman nicknamed him Trigger, he still couldn't get his point across.

"I'd ask women if they wanted to ride, and they'd say sure. We'd go to the woods, and they would think we would be having sex in the woods. No, I meant really 'Ride me.' There was a communication problem, obviously," he says smiling.

At the time Trigger left the gate, he was married. He gradually became less inhibited about expressing his interest in pony play but life in the Bible Belt kept most people, including his soon-to-be ex-wife, from joining in. Like so many people with fetishes in the early days of the Internet, Trigger used the computer to find other people with the same kinds of kinks. He became hooked on a BBS and remembers his first CompuServe bill being over three hundred dollars.

"In those days, they had human sexuality forums (much like chat rooms) and I was hooked on talking to other people with an open mind. I even met a guy from Wisconsin who had a saddle and had been a pony for his girlfriend and her lesbian lover," he recalls.

Trigger was open minded but much of the rest of the world wasn't. He tried swinging, but being a single male barred the doors of Swingingville. He created his own BBS and met some free-thinkers but still didn't find any interested in being a horse.

Fortunately, by the time the Internet was really kicking up,

Trigger had found fetish conventions where he quickly learned he wasn't alone in exploring his noble-beast side. In fact, exploring one's "inner pony" is becoming one of the hottest and fastest-growing trends in BDSM and fetish groups. Many ponies credit Anne Rice's *Beauty* trilogy with inspiring ponies everywhere to indulge in their fantasies.

Sure, the whole thing is a little kinky, and Trigger knows that his lifestyle might wig out some of his vanilla friends.

"For some people, kinky is smoking a cigarette before you have sex," he says, chuckling.

"Ride me, think of me as a horse, treat me as your horse." That's the message Trigger wants to convey to me about his fascination with pony play. It's hard for me to get there mentally. I'm a city girl who has never ridden, or even been close to, a real horse in her life. But I'm trying to get into that mindset. Trigger is a horse. Repeat. Trigger is a horse. Even though he wears purple sweatpants and a blue race-car T-shirt. Stop. He really is a horse.

Trigger's message has earned him quite a celebrity profile among fetish groups. He has appeared in videos, television sex specials, fetish magazines, and even in advertisements for pony camp. Some people spend their summers at the beach reading trashy novels, some learn how to be a better pony at an undisclosed location.

Pony camp is where ponies learn the art of becoming a horse, and riders learn the finer points of equestrianism. On the first night of pony camp, ponies and riders attend a Padlock Preview, a social to get to know each other. The next day, workshops galore. Courses include "The Psychology of the Human Horse," "Discipline of Lunging," "Proper Fittings: How to Select and Care for Tack," "Two-Legged Riding," "Four-Legged Riding," "Haute Ecole or Showpony Training," "Cart Training," and "Violet Wand Branding."

Quite a full day for a pony. For those who don't want to spend all day in school, they can head to the Kinky Karnival pony-centered events, which include the human animal/pony carousel, free pony and cart rides, and a petting zoo. On Sunday, pony camp resembles the National Horse Show with its parade of ponies and an equestrian show where ponies have a chance to strut their stuff and win ribbons.

Pony camp also features amenities like grooming and bathing facilities with a cold-water hose. Ponies like cold water. Single ponies at camps shouldn't worry about finding a rider, and vice versa. Both get hands-on, or hoofs-on, attention. At some camps, the curriculum includes puppy and kitty training. Now we're talking. Who wouldn't want the life of a house cat?

For Trigger, it's all about pony space. He has to get his mind into a certain place where he transforms mentally into a horse. From there, the physical follows. He can act just like a horse.

"If the rider can project and see me as a horse, if she has balance, she can get me to pony space pretty quick. I have no sense of time when that happens. A good rider can put me into a deep pony space," he says.

One of Trigger's fondest pony-space memories is when he became pony spaced-out at his first camp in 1998. There, Trigger was so entranced by his pony feelings, that he fell into deep pony space for seven days. Yet, he was very con-scious of life around him, which isn't always the case when pony space takes over. Many people came up to Trigger but he couldn't talk to them. He went a week without speaking a word. His second foray into pony camp, in 2000, he spent nine days with a mistress named Lalique and another pony named Onyx. Trigger was in and out of pony play be-cause he helped Lalique with the other pony. But in the end, Trigger met a tall, beautiful woman from Connecticut named Marie who rode him in a competition.

"She was fantastic! That was a great experience," he says of the happy times. "I don't think I've had any really bad pony experiences."

Question: What does a horse think about while standing around nibbling on a sugar cube?

Answer from Trigger: "I may have light thoughts about var-ious things like people around, et cetera, but they usually fade and I go into a zonelike state. I'm aware of some of my physical feelings, but just lightly. I've actually had people tell me they came up and petted me as a horse and I don't ever remember seeing them. It's a very deep, peaceful mind-set for me and I think there is a part of me that also thinks like a horse, doing anything to please my rider."

Trigger likes when a rider says, "You are the horse, you don't have a choice in the matter." "Do as you are told." "Okay, stop." Doesn't this sound like some sort of BDSM sub-missive lingo? Yes, it does, says Trigger, but he's not about being a submissive like a slave. He likes being a horse with a rider.

"Do with me what you do with a horse. You wouldn't use

anal plugs on a horse. You wouldn't use clothespins on a pony's nipples." I'll take his word for that.

Trigger recounts a story about a couple who once used him as foreplay. They had no interest in riding him, but rather just wanted to watch him in pony play action. Another couple who was initially just curious about pony play asked Trigger if they could watch him. The woman decided to ride him but only stayed on for fifteen seconds. The next time Trigger saw the woman, she had transformed from a shy rider who was shaking in her boots to a progressive confident equestrian.

The entire concept of pony play blows my mind. It has nothing to do with bestiality or anything to do with animals except being one. It's all about a mind-set in which those with this fantasy want to be a horse. Trigger isn't alone in his horse universe, but he is in a minority because there are more mares than female trainers. Yes, more women like to be ponies than to ride ponies. Plus, it's easier for girl ponies to find trainers and riders because women are more open to either men or women training them. Most boy ponies prefer female trainers. In the world of human ponies, just like with real horses, various kinds of equine exist: work ponies, show ponies, mules, cart ponies. But unlike real horses, some human ponies like to be on all-fours, and some prefer standing up with a rider on their shoulders. One woman in the pony scene even likes to pretend she's Pegasus, the flying horse. Edith Hamilton didn't prepare me for this.

Some riders and horses will pretend to be a cowboy and an untamed mustang in the wild, wild West. Others lean toward medieval times as warrior and warhorse. Still, some prefer the genteel country life as squire and riding horse in merry olde England, a country where pony play apparently gallops rampantly as a fetish.

Speaking of ancient times, Trigger tells me Aristotle liked being a pony to his mistress. Rumors also bubble that Queen Elizabeth I liked to ride on the shoulders of men. In the pony-play community, reference is always made to sixteenth century lore, when many young women around the ages of fourteen to eighteen who lived in boarding schools were forced to become pony girls by men who ran the institutions. According to pony-play scholars, this apparently peaked between 1880 and 1930 when the word whinnied out and erupted into scandal. The schools were closed. Needless to say, these were dark days in pony-play history.

People pack in for Trigger's Saturday afternoon demonstration. When the leader of the leather association tries to call the forty or so people to order, he says, "Hey, hey." That leaves the door open for Trigger to say, "When you say hey, I think it's time to eat." The crowd laughs as they hold cups of Diet Coke and munch on fresh baked-cake and chips. This could be a meeting of the Young Democrats. Except, of course, the main speaker is a man-horse instead of a state legislator.

The first thing we learn is that Trigger doesn't like rubber bits. To him, it's like moving his head with a gag in his mouth. That creates a problem because when the rider controls the reins, Trigger can't feel the commands. He wasn't really aware of this problem until an expert pony player, who also owns a real horse farm, was trying to train Trigger in nonverbal commands.

"Wait a minute," the trainer said.

She tied Trigger up and walked back to her house. She returned with some two-sided adhesive gauze that she wrapped around the bit. Magically, Trigger knew exactly what his rider wanted. With the reins, she gave seventeen commands, and he missed only one. Trigger passes around the adhesive for us to see.

Sitting here, I have to wonder how Trigger's obsession really began. As if he can read my mind, he addresses that very issue. It began, like so many attractions and fetishes do, when he was a boy. In the summer, he loved swimming up to a girl, scooping her up, and putting her on his shoulders.

"It just felt good," he remembers wistfully.

I'm distracted by Trigger's childhood memories when the woman beside me hands the tape to me. I examine the double adhesive — as if I'll ever need any of it for myself — and hand it off to the woman on the other side of me.

"No, thanks, I have some at home," she says.

Well, okeydokee.

If a horse has ever had capers, it's Trigger. Once in a rather liberal town on the Massachusetts coast, Trigger, donning his horse tack, was traveling with a mistress, her slave, and another "horse." Whenever the mistress wanted to smoke, her slave would bend on one knee to light the cigarette. Not something you see every day.

The mistress decided that she needed to visit a local pet store and get a water bowl for her submissive, who preferred to act like a cat. She left Trigger and the other horse tethered to a pole in front of the store. A policeman walked by and saw Trigger. Trouble right here in River City.

"Tone it down," the female cop warned Trigger and the mistress.

So they did. Sort of. Off they went to a local restaurant, where the mistress again tied up the horses outside the joint. As the mistress sipped on her happy-hour wine, Trigger munched on sugar cubes that the restaurant's waiters slipped him through the back door. Soon, the townsfolk had gathered to snap pictures of the human ponies.

"I bet I had over three hundred and fifty photos taken that day," Trigger says with a chuckle.

The cop returned soon. "The chief says you've got to leave town. You aren't doing anything wrong, but you've got to leave town," she said.

The mistress confronted her in true domination style. "Why?" she demanded.

"If you don't leave I'll have to arrest you," the cop said again.

The mistress decided to visit the police chief and see what the problem was with their behavior, especially since the cop repeatedly said the group wasn't doing anything wrong. What was the problem exactly? Money. Too many people were looking at the ponies, not buying souvenirs in the touristy stores, and business owners were complaining. Plus, the spectacle created traffic jams in the town from people who wanted to see the human ponies. Damn cop, I think, seething about past traffic tickets.

The adventures really don't stop for Trigger. He has been ridden in city parks, in parades, and in woods all over the country. One time, in a San Francisco city park, Trigger was ridden by a six-foot-two Amazon. Again, the police appeared.

"We've seen some unique things in this park . . . have a nice day," they said. Okay, now that's a cop!

Trigger gives a word of advice to the group about where to practice riding: "I wouldn't do it in the parking lot of the First Baptist Church," he says. Good advice, I reason, imagining how pony play would go over with some of the pastors I know.

This lifestyle isn't perceived initially as a sexually oriented activity. It's more like adults who like piggyback or shoulder rides. Trigger even confesses that he doesn't like sex as much as most guys, so for him being a horse is more erotic than it is out-and-out sexual. Sometimes, Trigger gets an erection when a woman rides him, but more times than not Trigger just feels pleasure and a sensual vibe.

"It's erotic but I don't have a sexual focus to it," he says.

Some of the women who ride Trigger find the experience orgasmic. Trigger says that he can tell that some women have orgasms while they are on his shoulders. It's no secret that some women like to ride real horses for the vibrations between their legs. I've never ridden a horse, but I remember a group of girlfriends from ten years ago who always took to riding horses in between boyfriends. If only they had known Trigger.

He isn't currently in a relationship but is seeking riders. (Personal ad: "Man-horse seeks jockey.") One day, he hopes to ride in all fifty states. So far, he's trotted through nineteen of them. He also hopes to find someone to own him so he can be a horse twenty-four seven. He wants to live like a horse, and pony play with a good owner will afford him the luxury of living in a stable.

Would he get bored?

"Maybe. It depends on the owner and routines. The owner may ride each day for several hours or have friends that ride.

I might look forward to the 'boring' times. The few times I've been twenty-four though, the boring times were not so much boring but actually just peaceful. Keep in mind it's not just doing nothing, but there are no thoughts or worries, no concerns, no time or delays. It's very peaceful!"

Whoa, Trigger!

We took a break and have returned to see Trigger in a getup that almost defies words. Beginning at the feet, er, hooves. Okay, he doesn't really have hooves. He simply wears black socks and tennis shoes like someone's dad at the beach. Moving up bare hairy legs, I spy black nylon swim trunks, a tad on the baggy side. And then . . . a leather harness with complicated straps and real stirrups on each side of Trigger's waist. On Trigger's head is a leather bridle, reins, and, in his mouth, a metal bit wrapped in tape. I never thought I would see a hairy middle-aged man standing in a hotel conference room decked out like a horse. Never say never. He's here, in full equine glory.

A woman across the room gets the party started with a question. "How do you deal with spurs?" No joke, this is a serious question. Yeowch!

"I'm not a stupid pony. This belt is where the spurs would be," he says, showing us his gear.

When Trigger turns around, a black horse tail flounces around to greet us. The tale of the tail is that initially Trigger didn't have a tail to go with his homemade modified tack. Soon after getting into pony play, Trigger traveled to a pony convention in California and met a pony boy named Boots who asked, "Well, where's your tail?" Being a nice pony,

Boots made him a black tail from horse hair, which Trigger still wears.

Some tails are equipped with butt plugs, adding a BDSM touch to a pony. These devices are mostly used with cart ponies or those who like all fours. For the rider who wants something extra, there are saddles with dildos in them. Trigger isn't into the saddles or the butt plugs, which he has never used so it's hard for him to address the next question: Do butt plugs rub you raw? Trigger's not sure. I'm guessing yes.

Trigger holds up some gold Christmas bells that a friend gave him last year as a present. "Every horse needs bells," the friend told him.

"Yeah, but I've yet to figure out where to attach the darn things," he says. I'm thinking he should maybe ask a Clydesdale.

Martha Stewart has nothing on these industrious pony players. While those in the scene can buy leather pseudo-hooves from companies in England and Connecticut, one attendee explains that ponies or their riders can make homemade hooves by sawing concentric circles, if someone has the time or inclination to do so. Some ponies take their hooves to blacksmiths to have horseshoes put on them. If a pony wants hooves, that's fine. But remember: Metal hooves don't work well on concrete. They can make a pony slide like he's ice skating, and who wants to endanger a pony with such risky action.

The antics of ponies never cease to amaze me. Trigger has a friend in Washington D.C., who pulls a cart while in-line skating. Another friend in the state of Washington obtained a permit from his city to go around town with his girl pony pulling a cart while he rides in it. I'm trying to imagine how any of this would play in Little Rock. Once, the famed groupie Connie Hamzy — known as Sweet Sweet Connie from the Grand Funk Railroad song "We're an American Band" — generated a miniscandal when she donned in-line skates and a thong swimsuit and went skating in downtown Little Rock's River Front Park. In-line skating as a pony, I imagine, would force the city board to call a special meeting.

Trigger struts around in front of us in his leather gear, cracking jokes and answering questions. If he was at pony camp, however, chances are he would not be wearing the black swim trunks. Horses like to feel a little more free and easy in the privacy of pony camp. The woman beside me quizzes Trigger about pony life, and, spotting the leather rodeo boots on her feet, I know that somewhere her pony awaits her return. She even tells Trigger that some of the best carts for ponies are beautiful aluminum ones from the Amish communities. Bet that's news to Eli and Amos up in Dutch country.

Before too long, everyone becomes antsy wanting to see Trigger in action. Does he really live up to his legend? Should we believe the hype? One of Trigger's friends who is in the BDSM community in Washington, D.C., is coincidentally in Nashville the same weekend as Trigger. She's popped in to see her friend demonstrate and to give him a pony workout. She likes riding with spurs but for this weekend, she's left them in the nation's capital.

It's been awhile since the fortyish petite woman with black curly hair has been on Trigger. Wearing blue leggings and a sweater, she's ready to mount, which can be a tricky task. A chair is pulled up next to Trigger and she stands up on it. Two women help her mount from the left just like in real riding. First, the left foot in the stirrup, and then a big heave-ho, as she slings the other foot over Trigger's back and into the right stirrup. Hi ho Silver and away they go!

The D.C. woman sits on Trigger's shoulders, and her head almost touches the ceiling tiles. She holds on to the reins and when she lightly taps Trigger in the sides, he takes off, trotting. As she taps again, he runs faster. She pulls on the reins and he slows to a leisurely gait. Strangely, even to me, Trigger has become a horse. It's hard to imagine him as anything else like, say, a man.

The conference room is small so Trigger and friend don't have a lot of space. She rides him for a minute or so before dismounting, which is far more tricky than mounting. Feet have to come out of the stirrups and there's no chair to help this time, because the logistics don't make sense. The only way off of Trigger is to just take both feet out at the same time and slide down his back. She does so with an uneven grace.

Before Trigger appeared here in Nashville, he had visited Kentucky and was ridden outdoors, which he prefers. Two women from the Kentucky adventure have joined Trigger in Nashville. Man-horses have groupies, apparently. While Trigger demonstrated riding, they sat in a corner, one in the other's lap, while one stroked the other's long brown hair. Rather large women, they wear riding pants and leather boots, and hold crops. They look like they mean business and have experience riding.

Well, not exactly. They know how to ride real horses but not a man-horse like Trigger. The day before, they ran into trouble mounting, dismounting, and keeping their balance.

"When someone is new and has balance issues, I keep my hands out to spot," Trigger explains.

The woman in her twenties in tan riding pants, black blouse, and a black satin bustier unsteadily mounts Trigger. She's on, and off they go! Trigger seems to have a little trouble balancing her but he does his best to give her a good ride. She, too, finds it difficult to dismount, saying she feels like she will just fall forward. The stirrups are used to adjust and center balance but they don't seem to help that much.

She eventually slides off.

Next!

Soon women are lining up to ride Trigger. Before another rider gets on, the woman who has just had problems getting off Trigger's back walks up and gives him some sugar cubes. He licks them out of her hand, just like a real horse. He nuzzles her neck.

Then another question from the woman beside me. She is curious about drooling ponies and what kind of bits make a pony slobber. We learn that some trainers like for their ponies to drool, but Trigger doesn't drool. Sweat and saliva can create mouth irritations, in part because there is a metal bit in the pony's mouth. Trigger says he finds a bigger problem with sweat getting into his eyes. Once someone sprayed bug spray on Trigger and while his rider was on him, he began to sweat. Soon, he had sweat and bug spray running into his eyes, blinding him. Not good for a pony or a human. Occupational hazard, I guess. Some bit equipment, Trigger informs us, can be bought at everyone's favorite bondage store: "Dom Depot," or as it's called in the vanilla world, Home Depot. Plastic tubing also works well for a bit.

The woman beside me explains she has been doing bit training at night, leaving the bit in her husband's mouth while he sleeps.

"What have you and John been up to?" jokes a woman in front of her with an incredulous look. "I want to come to your house!"

The crowd laughs. She later confesses to me that she and her husband have been trying to attempt pony play but they live at and run a twenty-four hour ministorage facility. They are worried that while pony playing someone might drive in and need to retrieve something from storage.

Trigger adjusts the stirrups so that they are longer for the other Kentucky girl. She mounts Trigger but she, too, seems to have a hard time getting balanced on his shoulders. The shape of a person's body can make a difference in gravity and balance. Finally, she succeeds in getting on Trigger's shoulders. With riding crop in hand, Kentucky girl takes her stroll around the room for a few minutes. Because she isn't as short as the previous rider, she has a slightly easier time dismounting.

"You've got to ride Trigger," says a woman in a black silvery shirt.

"No, no, I don't know," I say, suddenly feeling very strange.

"Oh, go ahead," says another. "You should do it. You only live once."

Well, okay, I guess. Maybe. I'm a city girl, I've never been on a bio-horse, as they call them, but I guess my first adventure in equine enjoyment can come from a man who people say has the soul of a horse.

I approach Trigger with trepidation like he may be about to bite my hand or nuzzle my neck. I'm just not sure which one.

"Do I need to take my shoes off or leave them on?"

"Whichever way you want," Trigger says.

Opting to leave them on, I climb up on the chair and with a thrust I put my foot in the silver stirrup. The Kentucky girl helps me swing my leg over Trigger's back and into the other stirrup. My feet hang in the stirrups at the front of his waist-line. It seems a tad odd but also a bit — no pun intended — normal, as if I am the cheerleader I never was who will flip off his shoulders and say "Go team!"

I make Trigger turn to the right by lightly tapping my foot on the side of his waist. Then, I try it with the left. He does as he's prodded. Good boy, Trigger. Riding around the room, a strange, but not erotic, sense of power overtakes me, but it's quickly overshadowed by the fear I might fall off of him. I am not that fond of heights, and on his shoulders my head almost grazes the ceiling tiles. Again, no pun.

After about two minutes of riding Trigger in circles in the conference room, I'm ready to get off — not sexually, you dirty minded people — but back down with both feet firmly on the carpeted floor. I'm worried I might rip his chest hair off if I grab the bridle too hard as I take my feet out of the stir-rups. If I grab on to his neck, I might choke my horse. Finally, there's no way to do it but slide down his back. Whew! Off the horse, I say thank you and Trigger smiles. Then . . . gasp! I see what I have done. There on the floor beside his tennis shoes is his tail! Oh, my God, I've ripped off a man-horse's tail.

"Um, I think I took your tail with me," I say, reaching down to pick up the tail.

"It's okay," Trigger says, holding it in his hand continuing his chatfest with a smitten fan.

I smile, not knowing what to say to Trigger. "Happy Trails,"

I say, walking out of the room. He laughs, but I'm not sure if he heard me or not, since maybe he was still in pony space.

A few days later, Trigger e-mails. He thanks me for the ride, although it was way too short, he says.

"You have a natural feel for riding . . . maybe someday you'll decide you want me to come visit you as your horse for a day or weekend and enjoy some nice all-day trail riding! I've never been ridden in Arkansas!" he writes.

Who knew Trigger would say such sweet things after I ripped his tail off?

He signs the e-mail: "Your horse at heart, Trigger."

One day, maybe Trigger *will* visit me in the Natural State and we'll journey through the Ozark Mountains, pretending I am Dale Evans who stole away on a horse named Trigger.

naked mermaids
do porn

Fins and Fetishes

SOMEWHERE, TENNESSEE — In the back room of what looks to be your ordinary film company in this rural Tennessee hamlet, a lot of fishy stuff goes on.

At first glance, Ken Gentry is an average businessman with a day job that includes shooting commercials and public service announcements. He's tall. He wears a pager. He could be the guy who sits next to me in church on Sunday. Ken's family is aware of his penchant for films, cameras, and other digital gadgets. What they don't know is that Ken also does something else. He films and edits underwater porn videos, known in the fetish world as aqua porn.

"I had a little fetish about this, just a little bit, that's how I found it," he explains. "A lot of things we make is because it turns a buck. I have an interest in making films, but we run a regular production house. The reason we do aqua porn is because it is quite lucrative, and making these videos pays for other things we want to do."

Aqua porn is all about women underwater wearing bikinis, sexy lingerie, or the clothing God gave them. While immersed, the water goddesses perform all sorts of acts — everything from underwater striptease to scuba diving to masturbation and sex to bondage and drowning. Yes, there are people out there who like the thrill of watching a drowning woman struggle unsuccessfully to survive. Others enjoy watching a near-drowning and then witnessing a rescue.

"These videos break out into two or three major subcategories: erotic, drowning, and breath holding. Drowning videos are the most popular, then the erotic, and then breath holding," he says.

The drowning and breath-holding videos are artistically challenging, echoing the work that goes into filming a horror video. I don't understand the drowning fetish considering I almost drowned once myself, and it scared the hell out of me. Of course, if I had known about this fetish then I might have taped myself and sold the video on the Internet for big bucks. It was the creation of the World Wide Web that opened people up to an array of fetishes — like aqua porn — that previously lay buried in the psyche. Once people could explore fetishes in the privacy of their own homes, a lot of people realized that they were not freaks alone with their fetishes. There were other people out there just like them. Before the global access for porn, men and women with obscure fetishes had to collect magazines, books, and videos in adult video stores or catalogs. Or fantasize without the aid of visual materials.

Ken's aqua porn business began in 1996, the year the Internet exploded, and it continues to be the largest producer of such flicks. But the number of customers who like to view mermaid muff is only about two thousand, a very small niche. I wonder about this number. I've never met a man who didn't want to see a girl naked in a bathtub. Maybe they just haven't discovered their lust for water babes is a kink.

When Ken began in the aqua porn film business, he

would go out and rent locations in other states, particularly Florida, and film in the properties' swimming pools. A rented house in Destin served as a popular locale and was the setting for many films. Finally, over the years, Ken decided the best thing to do was buy a house with a very large pool in a remote area of Tennessee.

"We can do things in the privacy of our own backyard and no one knows. Of course, nudity is the worst thing we are doing. Everything we shoot is soft porn, if you could even call it that," he says.

At the start of the Internet boom, everyone with an H_2O kink was at their computers searching to buy something that would get them off, especially a video or several of them. Initially, Ken was taking home $250,000 to $300,000 a year selling aqua porn. Now, he says he is lucky to earn $50,000. That's because the market has become saturated and, he says, kinky folk have become overfed on their fetishes. Now a general drowning video or erotic underwater video of two women kissing among the bubbles just won't do. Customers now request specific types of scenes, and if a video doesn't have it, they aren't shelling out the bucks. One customer might want to watch a black-bikinied woman drown for the camera. Another might request that a woman wear va-va-voom red lipstick while a killer ties rope around her neck. Another may want their babe on film to look like a Bond girl, nude with scuba gear on her back and completely shaved in her nether regions.

"We've been doing custom work for three years. Unfortunately the demographic is skewed toward the low end of the earned-income spectrum, and people are reluctant to pay for what they want," he says.

Enter Ms. Cindy Charms. She's back! Yes, that very one from the Alabama bash who practically lives in her backyard Texas pool during the summer. Cindy is an underwater goddess, known on aqua-porn sites as a bubblicious babe who rules the pool. She has created a niche for herself that attracts certain fans to her Southern Charms Web site who like only her water photos. Forget about the squirt shots or the girl-girl action. Always eager to please, Cindy is all about turning on men who like water.

"Everyone has this fear deep down that their fetish makes them weird," Cindy says.

The sub-fetishes in the water genre are as multifaceted as in any other fetish. Some men, and women, like underwater bondage with ropes, scarves, and chains wrapped around wrists and ankles. Complete scuba gear — without showing a square patch of skin — gets some men all wet. An ultimate fantasy for others is basic scuba gear with a bikini. Goggles and swim masks get some engines revved up. And some guys are into only bubbles. Bubbles?

"If I could fart on cue, I'd make some guys very happy," Cindy says.

She's not joking. Somewhere, my cotillion teacher is rolling over in her grave.

Men often send Cindy bathing caps to wear in the pool. There's a lack of bathing cap videos on the market so Cindy has seized the opportunity to be the Esther Williams of the Internet porn generation. She has gussied up for underwater bondage shoots with seventy-five pounds of chains wrapped around her and donned sexy swimsuits — one- and two-piece — while swimming around in the water. She has shot in the bathtub and in hotel pools, where she has to be careful in case children come around. There are no professional underwater lights or lighted studio tanks. Cindy and her photographer husband, Steve, have learned that the best time to shoot underwater is from about eleven in the morning until three in the afternoon. When clouds get in the way, the photo shoot pauses until the clouds pass. Naturally shadowed pools are a no-no because the lighting is horrible. But if the light is good and there's clear water with a camera available, Cindy's there.

The most frequent requests she receives are for water and smoking pictures.

"If I were tough enough I could take a puff and blow it out underwater," she says. As if she was a mermaid in a seagreen foam, Cindy, with her piercing blue eyes and crimson lips, finds a certain thrill in the water. It started when she was a kid and her mother would get annoyed with her sister and her because they would play underwater all the time in the pool. She would get paranoid that her children were drowning and beg them to stay up for just a little while so her nerves could calm. After she married, Cindy would float around at the pool on a raft and Steve would splash her. She hated it.

Back then, she couldn't imagine doing some of the things she's done underwater and being paid to do them on film. Cindy's frolicked underwater in swimsuits, teddies, garters, stockings, and even dresses, including one long evening dress complete with red panties, red garter belt, red stockings, and red high heels. She's worn goggles, swim masks, and a snorkel. Her sexual underwater antics include cunnilingus, sixty-nines, wrestling, intercourse, and fellatio. She's says that she has performed fellatio while spinning three hundred and sixty degrees without breaking contact.

"Try that on dry land," she says, chuckling at her weightless feat.

To accommodate Cindy's fans addicted to underwater scenes, Cindy and Steve purchased a fancy digital video camera. In past summers, she turned down lots of photo requests because they didn't have underwater housing for the digital video camera. They do now, so watch out.

Being an aqua goddess is hard work.

Cindy doesn't slack off when it comes to an underwater shoot. In fact, she may invest more time getting ready for them than for other shoots. First, there's the mascara issue, making sure it's waterproof. To set her makeup for water, she uses setting powder and a semipermanent lipstick and moisturizer. She always lines her lips with a red pencil before applying the lipstick. That's important for maintaining color underwater. She's learned that her eyes feel better if one day she does full eye makeup and the next day of underwater work she'll place more emphasis on eyeliner and forgo mascara.

"Water can be very drying to the eyes," she advises.

Cindy thinks hard about the image she wants to portray. Sometimes, she has a plan, a theme — like a 1940s bathing beauty — that she's initiating on film. Other times, she just lets things flow in the water. She loves experimenting with various looks, especially dresses that can move like shimmery tails in the water while creating a draping effect across her svelte body, or sparkling earrings that attract the golden rays of the sunlight. Flowing, dreamy lingerie also shimmies well underwater.

Making sure everyone is on the same page, Cindy, just like a lot of high-dollar models, discusses with her photographer, usually her husband, what shots will be best for a photo set. The photographer submerges first and gets into position. Cindy counts to three and submerges into the pool. Sometimes, the photographer tells her just to swim. Other times, Cindy has to swim over to him. It all depends on the focus of the shoot — feet, face, hands, legs — or a particular look, which could mean lying on the bottom, body arched gracefully, floating, stretching, rolling, swimming. When the photographer rises, Cindy does the same.

"I also rise whenever I feel like it," she says with a diva grin.

She adds that Steve, or the photographer du jour, is usually naked in the pool, too, when they are working. That gives her a great barometer — I bet it does! — to show her if the shots are working.

"If I can get a rise out of him, I am doing it right," she says, laughing. "He's always hoping I'll want to practice that three-hundred-sixty-degree rotating blow job."

Water shoots last about thirty minutes and yield about a hundred photos. After that, everyone goes into the house and takes a break to download the new shots and then it's back to work. Cindy always wears her long, thick, deep-blue terry bathrobe on the side of the pool and during the breaks.

"It has nothing to do with modesty; the AC is cold in the house when you've been under so long," she explains.

Some people call the video I'm about to watch smut.

Fiddlesticks! I've been watching aqua porn since I was fourteen. Okay, it was a music video by Duran Duran called "Girls on Film." That controversial video was banned by MTV for its pornlike qualities and extreme raciness. Natch, that made me want to watch and analyze it more than ever. The video still burns in my mind: A sexy woman attempts to give mouth-to-mouth to a drowning man in an inflatable swimming pool. He wears goggles and a bathing cap and the more the video babe kisses him, the more alive he becomes. Erotic stuff for a teenager.

Flash forward to the present. Like so many people in suburbia, I'm secretly watching some porn on my computer on a Monday night. I feel naughty when I click "play" and an athletic-built man wearing black swimming trunks and black goggles swims across the screen. Quickly, a woman appears in a black athletic swimsuit, black swimming cap, and goggles. Her red lips create a stark contrast to the chlorine-blue ripples. She chases the man, who swims faster. The woman proves too quick for him, and in a split second, she climbs on his back, grabs a handful of hair, and yanks it back.

She wrestles him and keeps him underwater, holding on to his hair and staying on his back for a few seconds. With her strong legs wrapped around him, she rides him like an amusement park pony. In one quick swoop, she flips him over and he rests on the bottom of the pool. I can't tell if he is dead or not, but I hear gurgling bubbles on the soundtrack. The swim babe makes sure he stays down by circling her red lips into a perfect O and performing a wicked blow job. The water allows her to float about, but the curious thing is this: If she has a dick in her mouth, how is she not getting a lot of water down her throat? Why doesn't she look like she is choking? She must be Aquaman's daughter because she doesn't seem to be experiencing any breathing problems. At all. (Cindy tells me the secret to such aqua feats is good editing.)

After the water vixen tortures the poor guy with all the fellatio he can handle, she removes his swimming trunks and then positions herself on top of him. She slides the crotch of her swimsuit aside and slips him into her. Neptuna Chick rides the man as if he were a bucking bronco at the rodeo, her hand waving in the air to maintain her balance.

Esther Williams never did this in a mermaid movie.

Don't touch that dial! Up next — drowning.

Sitting on my living room couch, I'm ready to see some smut. Many people believe that the drowning videos are horrific, signaling some sort of sadistic behavior toward women. These types of videos often spark massive debates on aqua-porn Web sites. My theory is the one I adopted from the Alabama bondage workshop: "Your kink isn't my kink, but your kink is okay." On with the show!

I've selected a video with several short flicks hosted by a female Grim Reaper. I figure if I'm going to see the real deal I might as well have the old Reaper on hand to walk me through the ghastly scenes. The first video is about two water spirits who grab and hold a strawberry-blonde chick underwater. The point: to fill her lungs with water so that she can become one of them. Munching on my popcorn, I critique the film as if I am Leonard Maltin on *Entertainment Tonight* — the whole concept seems contrived. The women are sort of sexy, though: curvy, tortured underwater souls with long hair and 1980s New Wave makeup. Kind of cool to look at, but not particularly erotic.

When that segment is over, another one rolls onto the screen. A large wooden tub — the kind gardeners use for planting flowers in the South — sits on the concrete edge of a swimming pool. A wooden fence — the kind any of my neighbors have around their backyards — serves as the backdrop. This video may have been filmed anywhere in Little Rock or Nashville or Birmingham. Who knows what happens in backyards on sunny days?

A blonde woman in a long black dress appears on the screen, taking a drag off of her cigarette. She decides — for some goofy reason — to hop into the tub in the dress, stockings, and a sexy garter. This feeds someone's fetish somewhere, guaranteed. Dum, dum, dum! Here comes trouble! Another woman, a brunette, appears in the same outfit, and she doesn't have friendship written across her face. The blonde tries to escape but she's no match for the evil brunette. Dunk after dunk, the brunette pushes the blonde down into the water. She gasps, she fights. Water splashes. Her black dress comes off at one point. Finally, the blonde succumbs and floats to the top of the tub like Sparkles, the goldfish I had in sixth grade.

The next clip focuses on a girl's best friend who suddenly decides to tie her feet while she's swimming. The end result? You got it. She drowns her. Not hard for me to imagine, considering some of the friends I've had.

Next, two girls lounge by the pool on a cloudless summer day — a scene I've witnessed a hundred times at the country club and neighborhood pools. Ms. Amber decides to plunge into the pool in a red bikini. She swims along as happy as Ariel in *The Little Mermaid*. Like all things in this video, the skies turn dark as soon as the dreadlocked Miss Thang enters the pool.

Summoning all the strength of an underwater Iron Belle, Miss Thang wrestles with Ms. Amber and then ties her ankles. The drowning continues until, well, Ms. Amber just doesn't have an ounce of strength left in her. Poor thing. Drowning does not become her.

None of this freaks me out, I guess, because I can't swim and, like a cat, I'm seldom in water for long periods of time. Certainly, it doesn't get me aroused in the least. In fact, I'm sitting on the couch, still munching on popcorn and polishing my toenails in pink glitter. Nick, my friend who has the foot fetish and desires a life as a servant, should be here to help.

The next aqua victim swims along for a while in the pool when suddenly a garden hose from the side of the pool falls in. The green hose comes alive, encircling the naked girl and holding her down until . . . you guessed it . . . she drowns. Not a lot of suspense or plot here. In fact, it's downright hokey. The end result is: The girl is gonna drown.

I can only stand the Grim Reaper in my living room for so long before I turn it off and watch some Powerpuff Girls. Curiosity has clawed its nails into me, though, and I can't properly focus on Blossom and Buttercup while wondering what's next on the video. This time, voyeurism beats out cartoons. I return to the Grim Reaper of Atlantis.

Girl A needs help with her lifeguard skills. Girl B — what a good friend she is — decides to assist her. After a few seconds, Girl B decides that Girl A needs some heavy weights around her, and where else would this occur: the deep end. That way, Girl B can show her how a rescue is really done. Big mistake. Girl A panics and freaks out; the expression on her face says it all. She's one scared aqua bunny. In her fear-driven state, she drags in Girl B. Double whammy: they both drown. This is disturbing, and I don't see how anyone could properly be aroused at watching a double death. Even if it is fake.

While most people who watch these videos are all about the girls, I notice other things like the fact that all of these minimovies were shot in the same pool. The ceramic tile around the pool's edge gives it away.

The phone rings as the next short film starts. It's my AARP-aged mom.

"Whatcha doing?" she asks.

"Watching aqua porn," I say.

"What's that?" she asks, never too shocked at what I could be doing.

"Videos where girls drown, sometimes people have sex underwater. It's all about the H_2O."

"Oh. I've never heard of such a thing," she says.

"Niche fetish," I say, as if I am discussing a new emo band.

"Gotcha," she says, like she got her degree in kink studies.

I chat with her for a few seconds while a girl trapped in a cement tank drowns on my screen. Next.

Oooh. Change of scenery. The producers have decided to take us to the beach with girls in scuba equipment. An exotic woman — who could have easily been the chick in the Duran Duran "Rio" video — with curly black hair, wearing a sexy black bikini, does not look happy. At all. Come to find out, the woman beside her on the beach who wears the same bikini has been boinking her husband. Bad, bad girl. Sexy exotic woman ties and gags her competition. Soon, the women, complete with air tanks and goggles, are on the bottom of the ocean's floor. The exotic woman punishes the bad girl, and, do I need to say it? She drowns.

I'm slightly appalled. But I'm more fascinated with these homegrown actresses' ability to swim underwater, hold their breath, pretend they are dead, and float endlessly.

Back to the pool, probably because it costs money to film on location. This time, a young girl, posing as a model, floats about the pool on an inflatable raft. She wears nothing but shiny gold hoop earrings. A video guy shoots her; just like in real life.

"Turn over," the photographer says.

Oops. She does so, but not gracefully. Splunk. She's in the water. Trouble. She can't swim. Help. Help. The photo guy sets up his equipment to film the drowning and dashes. Those photographers — always about making a buck and never wanting to dirty their hands with a dead body. Okay, that one was a little sick and weird.

Thankfully, the last clip pops onto the screen. A pretty woman with long bleached-blonde hair prances about the pool in a chartreuse bikini top and matching hot pants. Oh, no, something is wrong with the swimming pool drain. The woman sticks her hand in to fix it. No, no, tell me it's not so, she can't get her hand out. She falls into the pool. Yep, she drowns.

Okay, I feel a little disgusted now. Flipping the television channels, I stop on a rerun of *Gilligan's Island*. Oh wait, that has water. Click. *Jetsons!* I'll watch something space-age instead.

Not everyone who considers themselves an aquaphile gets excited about women drowning. Some men, or women, just like the way a person looks underwater. It is curious to watch, especially that first video with the underwater BJ. Cindy says that in her work, she has found that men who order custom water shoots are highly intelligent, discriminating, and have a great appreciation for the beauty of the female form.

After my foray into aqua porn, I join an Internet chat board for others who are fascinated with such underwater activities. It doesn't take long for people to ask me if I'm a model, do I swim in the nude, and if I don't, could I? Eh, no.

One man on the board decides to confess to me he and his wife's secret. Tee-hee-hee, a secret. He'll only tell me he is from the South and I can't help but wonder if it's someone in Little Rock that I know. He tells me his name is Krogard, as if that were a birth name. He tells me that he and his wife love underwater movies, especially if the guy is giving the woman as much pleasure as he is receiving. They call that sixty-nine, I tell him. The couple also basks in underwater frolicking, with Krogard taking photographs of his wife underwater while she is in various outfits.

"These photo shoots always end up in some pretty hot sex," he tells me.

He says the couple has taken great pains to shield their

eighteen-by-thirty-six-foot home pool from the snoopy neighbors with plants and walls. So that's what all those people are doing on the weekends: buying tall palm trees and ferns at the nursery. One suburban mystery solved.

By far the most interesting man I meet is Dr. Sebastian Gomez (naturally not his real name); he lets me call him Gomez. My new friend Gomez lives on the coast of Texas, where he and his woman friend enjoy aqua pleasures. He's in his sixties and he loves watching women swim. I know what you are thinking. If you saw this man at the pool you'd think he is a dirty old man checking out the young hotties. But even old folks still like taut bodies.

"I like pretty ladies in the surf," he says. "Water is the first thing I consider when I think about sexual fun. When I see a pretty lady I always imagine her in a sexy swim suit or lingerie in the water."

Gomez and his "much-younger lady," as he calls her, enjoy cuddling, feeling, fondling, licking, sucking, and every imaginable type of oral sex in their inflatable pool o' fun. He tells me point-blank that they very seldom have intercourse, because she is a very tight fit and more into clitoral stimulation.

Damn, Gomez. Maybe I didn't need to know that much.

The couple also has a water hose that they use to stimulate each other.

"Try it sometime!" he urges me. "Put on a brief bottom and let your partner stimulate you with the strong stream of water . . . or do it alone. Feels good from both front and rear. Nipples appreciate it as well," he says slyly.

Thanks, Dr. Ruth Gomez, for that tip! Who knew I could still blush?

Maybe I should have been a psychologist but it always amazes me as to what jump-starts a fetish that lasts a lifetime. Gomez isn't shy about telling me. He began having sexual feelings at twelve just like most boys. The difference was that Gomez was small for his age and that allowed him lots of room in the bathtub. He liked holding his breath underwater and fondling himself, letting his cock slide along the bath-tub's bottom. That was just the start.

"I wasn't at all athletic or interested in games so I spent lots of time at the pool swimming and admiring the girls from un-derwater," he says. "I also found that the water jets that shoot from the sides of the pool were very stimulating. Some of the girls found them as well, and I occasionally had a chance to watch them as the water massaged their breasts and stimulated them to climaxes."

I can't help but wonder if such antics were going on at Eden Park Country Club, where I spent many a summer at-tempting to swim but never mastering even how to float.

When Gomez turned sixteen, he got a job working at a small private swim club for kids. A mysterious olive-skinned older Greek woman in her forties owned the pool. She had very long black hair and dark piercing eyes that looked as if she had seen the devil up close. No one could pronounce her last name, so everyone called her "Miss A." She was svelte with curves in just the right places like a movie star siren. Against her dark skin, she always wore white swim-suits at the pool, and she didn't have a preference with re-gard to one- or two-pieces — she alternated, Gomez told me dreamily. Unlike the girls at the pool who wore bulky padded swimsuits, Miss A wore thin ones with no padding.

"There were even occasional hints of nipples, which were just not seen in those days," he says wistfully.

Several other boys and girls worked at the pool. Miss A wanted her staff to look good so she furnished them with matching swimsuits. The boys wore snug black briefs with flesh-tone side panels. The girls wore sexy two pieces.

One day, Gomez helped Miss A tighten some bolts that held the ladder. He swam about three feet underwater to twist on the wrench. He came up for a breath of air, while Miss A stood on the bottom step and held on to the top of the ladder. Gomez was between her and the ladder, and he could almost sit on her legs and lean back against her for balance and leverage. He finished tightening the last bolt, and the wrench slipped. She grabbed him around his waist to steady the young teenager.

Miss A slipped her hand down to Gomez's crotch and held it there for a long pause as she fondled him. When the ladder was repaired, Miss A suggested she and Gomez swim to the shallow end to rest. Gomez followed her. They sprawled back on the concrete steps and Miss A told Gomez he had done a wonderful job and she called him a pretty boy. The straps on Miss A's top were loose, and her breasts undulated beneath the tight white fabric. Miss A asked if she could do something for Gomez, call it a bonus for his work. Gomez, having no idea what it could be, agreed.

Rolling over to face Gomez, Miss A hovered between his legs. Her breasts looked as if they were about to burst from the suit. She looked down at her breasts, and Gomez followed her stare. He felt as if he were having an out-of-body experience, warm and tingling in the cool water. Miss A took a deep breath and dove underwater. She pulled Gomez's thin swimsuit down and began to pleasure him. Only two or three more breaths, and Gomez exploded in her mouth. Miss A, ambitious, pursued his pleasure point again, sucking until he exploded again. She returned to the surface smiling. But her smile was no match for Gomez's.

That aqua temptress Mrs. Robinson started Gomez on his journey of water fascination. Gomez grew up to own a boat, surf, and scuba dive, beginning in 1958 when there were no rules or regulations. He also worked as a salvage diver for nearly ten years. Most of all: He never forgot Miss A. What young man would?

Much later, I sit out by the local swimming pool in Little Rock, my feet with the pink-glitter polish dancing in the cool water. My eyes, covered with dark vamp sunglasses, glance around the sides of the pool, the slide, the diving board. My mind floats into the world of aqua fantasies, imagining naked women and men frolicking around in the pool. The curvy slide, the erect diving board, the sparkling pool floor shimmers in the sun, looking innocent enough, but my mind is hardly that. I see good lighting from the afternoon sun, a perfect camera angle from the ladder. Lights, camera, action.

In one corner of the pool, a boy is trying to dunk another boy; a little girl in a green swimsuit looks at them. In the shallow end, a young couple snuggles, and I can't help but wonder if a drowning tragedy is about to strike. Are any of these people into aqua porn? Perhaps. And, hey, what about that older guy in his fifties on the deck chair peering at the water play from behind his *Wall Street Journal*? He looks as if his mind could be roaming to the same illicit place mine is at this very moment. There's a mom over in the shallow end showing her kids how long she can hold her breath. If I look hard enough on the Internet, will I be able to find a video of her doing the same thing?

Surely, naughty aqua no-no's haven't happened here. Right? Eyeing the crowd and the pool, I'm not so sure about that. This is, after all, Little Rock.

north carolina

love, north carolina style

Swinging, Swapping, and Switching

GREENVILLE, NORTH CAROLINA — I grew up on tales of toga parties.

In downtown Little Rock around 1980, a sordid raid at the legendary and cosmopolitan Sam Peck Hotel by a renegade sheriff yielded a hundred or so prominent residents swinging in the sheets. As the tale played out on the local television news, I remember thinking, even at that young age, how naughty these men and women were. Needless to say, I was intrigued, and the memory of sweaty, sex-starved, sheet-clad adults being busted stuck with me.

Even today, when I drive by the hotel, which sits across from the federal courthouse that saw many a Bill Clinton Whitewater trial play out and only a few blocks down the street from the state capitol, I can't help but think sex.

Little did I know, back on the cusp of the disco era, that swinging shenanigans had been occurring since the days of Julius Caesar or that they became more popular during the Second World War, when husbands who never returned from war asked their friends to take care of the needs — even the sexual ones — of their wives. By the 1950s, wife swapping was common in suburbia. At dinner parties, games were often played in which husbands would throw their house keys in a bowl and wives would draw out the keys of the men they would bed for the night. That, I hear, is still a common game played in suburbs around Arkansas. No surprise since swinging is a known hobby to many Arkansans. A bedroom community outside Little Rock could easily be called Swingingdale for all the antics that occur there between husbands and wives, especially at the local country club.

Swingers, especially closet ones, are prolific in the South with their decadent lifestyle of "indoor sports", as they call it. These men and women possess the desire, and subsequent ability, to live out their fantasies of getting it on with someone other than their spouses, who are usually doing the same thing in the same bed or at least nearby. Whether in official swingers clubs or in each other's homes, swingers live in a curious world where jealousy doesn't seem to exist and wanton lust for another couple reigns. And here's a note of interest: Swingers don't like single folk. Many clubs don't allow any singles. That's because swinging is viewed as a couple's lifestyle.

Like the world of whips and chains, swingers possess their own inside lingo. Care for a few definitions?

Closed swinging: Sexual interaction among couples using separate rooms in the same house. It also means that partners of a marriage or other intimate relationship do not visually observe each other's swinging.
English culture: Sexual activity with pain.
French culture: Oral-genital sexual activity.
Greek culture: Anal sex.
Roman culture: Sexual orgies.

Swedish culture: Use of the hands for petting to sexually stimulate another.

Group room: Room for group sex, furnished with wall-to-wall mattresses or pads. Popular only in the United States.

Triad: Three people, two of one sex and one of the other, in a continuing relationship of emotional and sexual involvement. Not the same as a threesome.

Whew! After all of that, I need a trip to the International House of Pancakes. Passport breakfast, please.

To infiltrate the world of swingers, it's good to have someone with a Ph.D. on board.

That's where Dr. Edward Fernandes, Dr. Eddie, for short, enters the picture. He's studied swingers in North Carolina for nearly a decade. As an academic, of course. He teaches at a North Carolina university, and he has written several research papers on swingers. He's really not into the swinger lifestyle. He wants me to believe that. And I do.

Dr. Eddie hails from the cold snowy tundra of Canada so it's no surprise, really, that the sultry, sexy South makes him giddy and more curious than a cat in a rubber mouse factory. The fascination of church and bedroom — a combination not often seen in the land of the Mounties — has made Dr. Eddie somewhat of an expert on the swinging lifestyle, which is apparently as prevalent in the South as fried chicken and crooked politics. That's because, according to Dr. Eddie, swinging provides an outlet for the repression that festers in this region that Jesse Helms calls home. In North Carolina, like many states in Dixie, swinging is incredibly common. From the top of the state near the Virginia border to the most Southern part that edges South Carolina, North Carolina is a hideaway for switching partners.

Through the years, Dr. Eddie has become friends with a lot of swingers, who are just like you and me except they like to switch sexual partners ever so often. They work in nine-to-five jobs, wear jeans and sweaters, and own standard pets like dogs and cats. Some of them drive Volkswagens, others prefer Harley-Davidsons. Some are twenty-somethings, many others are baby boomers or longtime card-carrying members of the AARP. In general, swingers are average Southerners who just like to fool around with people other than their spouses, usually while their partners are watching. And many times the swingers are a helluva lot happier than couples who are trapped in sexually strangled relationships, Dr. Eddie says.

"Swinging is all about the present relationship. They aren't trying to compensate for something that was lacking in another relationship; rather, they are adding something to the relationship because the level of trust has increased tremendously," Dr. Eddie says.

I'd say. It takes a lot of trust to watch a significant other get it on with someone else. It takes even more trust and confidence if that person is a fantastic lover or has a bigger and better package than you.

A lot of swingers don't have sex on the first date. Yes, swingers date — other couples.

Sara and Craig are a prime example of such a rule. Young

professionals who have been married less than five years, the couple lives in a bustling metropolitan area in North Carolina, where basketball is ingrained in everyone's life and technology accounts for a host of high-salaried jobs. Sara works as a public health researcher — emphasis on sexual education — with a master's degree from a prestigious medical school. Craig works as a high-tech computer guru. They are educated and successful. Looking at this happy couple, no one would suspect what they do on the weekends.

Sara, who is in her late twenties, brought Craig, who is in his early thirties, into the swinging lifestyle. She was introduced to swinging by an ex-boyfriend. When that relationship ended — for reasons unrelated to swinging — Sara began chatting online. That's where she met Craig, who contacted her through a swinger Web site. Craig had not "officially" been in the lifestyle prior to meeting Sara, but he certainly wasn't the Virgin Mary. He had led, shall we say, an adventurous sex life and was no stranger to threesomes.

"We developed a friendship online and on the phone before meeting in person," Sara says. "We did not develop our friendship or meet with the intention of becoming lovers, but after we met and became good friends, we quickly fell in love with each other," she says.

A match made in swinger heaven.

Sara says that they usually date another couple a few times before getting it on.

"We don't get intimate with a couple until we have built a significant comfort and chemistry level with them to the point that we want to take that step," she says. "The amount of time it can take to build up that comfort and chemistry level varies — sometimes it happens in a few hours, sometimes it happens over the course of days or weeks or months. We don't usually have sex with a couple on the first 'date' (more · likely the second or third, if all are amenable), but sometimes the chemistry between the four of us is almost instantaneous, and a few hours after meeting we find ourselves all going at it hot and heavy."

I wonder about all the couples I see having dinner at nice restaurants on Friday nights. Just friends? Or exploring other options? Sharing a bottle of wine takes on a whole new connotation in my mind.

Some couples set rules for each other. Sara and Craig don't.

"Craig and I don't have a lot of rules or boundaries that we need to discuss ahead of time with another couple. We don't have any 'You can't do X-Y-Z' or 'You can only go so far' types of rules. We have an always-use-condoms rule, but that's pretty much the default in this lifestyle and doesn't generally need to be mentioned ahead of time. If a partner tries to go for penetration without it, we simply stop and ask them to put one on. We're certainly open to discussing other couples' boundaries, since it's likely that their boundaries are going to be more restrictive than ours. With us, almost anything goes."

In a group-sex situation, activities tend to include oral sex, vaginal and anal penetration, sex toys, some light S&M — tying up of wrists, spanking, fairly tame things — and girl-girl play.

"Let's just say we're adventurous, try-just-about-anything-once kinds of people," Sara says. "We've played in groups of up to a dozen or more and done things in semipublic places. Heck we once got together with another couple, covered the bedroom — bed and floors — in plastic, slathered each other up in oil, and had a slippery-sliding orgy."

For Sara, little is off-limits with other partners. She enjoys pushing her boundaries because she finds it exciting and erotic.

"I don't know where my limits are — for example, how much pain I can take — until I reach them. Then I take a tiny step backward, and that's where I like to be," she explains.

Sara makes it clear that the couple aren't into anything involving animals, minors, or bodily waste. Good to know. They're also not into heavy BDSM, although they occasionally play with light bondage and some pain and domination.

"I could open up the Big Book of Fetishes and point out any number of crazy fetishes and bizarre sex acts that we're not into," she says. "But most of the books you can find in your local bookstore, or even your local porn shop, that aim to give ideas about new and exciting 'wild' things you can do to spice up your sex life haven't got a darned thing to teach us. Believe me, I've looked. I'm always looking for new ideas."

When Sara and Craig concoct a fantasy it doesn't stay mental for long. They try to make sure it becomes reality. Of course, sometimes the wildest fantasy has to remain just that: a fantasy. For example, it's probably impossible for Sara or Craig to have sex with some firm-bodied celebrity. And, if they fulfilled their fantasy of having sex in public like a restaurant or a park, the cops could arrest them. Then there's the whole superhero fantasy which melds with her Hollywood lust in a symbiotic dream. Sara would love to knock boots with Tom Welling, who plays Clark Kent on *Smallville*. To her, he is sexy as hell. She confesses that he's popped up in a few erotic dreams, but always as Clark, not as the actor Tom.

"Something about the innocent good-guyness of him is very appealing, but at the same time he's strong and sexy and, of course, full-o-superpowers," she says dreamily.

Her other fantasy? Stretch Armstrong.

"Just imagine the possibilities with a man with infinitely changeable and sizable body parts. Instead of thrusting his penis he could just make it grow and shrink and move about at will," she says.

Confession: That thought has never crossed my mind until now.

Sara's tried double penetration — a penis in both her anus and vagina — once, but she's always wanted to try triple penetration — anus, vagina, and mouth.

"I've just not gotten around to it yet. Nor have I gotten around to trying double penetration again, as much as I enjoyed it and would like to," she says. "While I've been in plenty of situations where there were enough willing players involved to make it happen, it's not a situation you just kind of 'fall into,' so to speak. It takes orchestration."

It's complicated. Sara explains that it takes someone, probably someone like herself, to stop in the middle of a romp and explain that she wants to do an X-Y-Z dance. That means a shift for everyone, who most of the time are caught up in the passion of the moment.

Sara and Craig certainly have lived the swinger lifestyle. Over the years they've been together, they've horizontally tangoed with at least thirty couples — a rough guess on

Sara's part, she confesses. With some of those couples, they've been intimate on many occasions.

"For about a year and a half, for instance, we were very close with one couple in particular and had sex with them frequently, often several times a week," she says.

Zoinks!

Doesn't the green-eyed monster play havoc with the purple-headed warrior?

Nope. Sara isn't jealous. Once, she was in a relationship with a jealous guy early in her love life. That was all it took for Sara to decide she didn't want that kind of worrisome negativity in her relationships. "The jealousy that most people would experience with regard to their partner's being intimate with another person stems from their fears that their partner will want to be with that new person more and will leave them. Craig and I love each other very much. We both trust each other to respect the boundaries that we set with regards to our intimacies with other people and have no fear that based solely on sexual intimacies one of us would want to leave the other," she explains.

Like most relationships, there's more to Sara and Craig's than sex. She doesn't worry if he finds another woman sexy or even if he has great sex with her. Awesome sex doesn't mean he will leave Sara. She knows that when the orgasms have come and gone, he's coming home to her.

"I know that she doesn't have much of a chance of being a better lover to him than I am. Because we know each other so well and are so well suited for each other sexually, no matter how sexy another woman is, I know she won't be hotter to him than I am between the sheets."

Swing out, sister!

Sara says that she may be wired a little differently than the "average" woman, too. I wouldn't disagree with her on that. Most women would erupt into a Glenn-Close-in-*Fatal-Attraction* rage if they knew their spouse was getting some sweet puddin' elsewhere. But not Sara. Her explanation?

"My husband is an amazing lover. One of the ways that I react to that is with the feeling that other women should be allowed to experience how great it feels to have sex with him, to feel all the wonderful sensations he can bring about in them. Knowing that many women will never experience such a skilled lover, I feel like I ought to 'share the wealth' and open these ladies' eyes to how good sex can be. Craig calls it our '*Sesame Street* upbringing' — that we were taught to share our toys when we were growing up."

I never learned that from watching Big Bird all those afternoons.

"When I've got a great toy, whether it is a 'mainstream' toy, a sex toy, or my husband, my reaction isn't to hoard it for myself, but rather to want to share it with my friends so they can experience how much fun it is, too. Sharing him with others does not diminish the pleasure I get from him, and it can bring others so much pleasure, so there's little reason not to."

Hello, Bert and Ernie!

Sharing a man can create a bond between two women. Sara says that when Craig makes love to another woman, she automatically has a connection with her that makes everything more beautiful, like a rose-colored-glasses romance for three.

"It is a turn-on. I know how good it feels when he does the

things to me that he is doing to the other woman, so I know how good she must be feeling. That is a turn-on, as is the small sense of pride I get from knowing how good he's making her feel. It is also a turn-on to see my love enjoying himself and being turned on."

I'm not sure I am grasping all of this, but I have understood some of what Sara means. Like any fetish, swinging is a way for people to explore fantasies and transform them into reality. In order to do this, a couple — regardless of their sexual adventures and games — must have a keen and undying sense of trust and confidence. Sharing their escapade brings them closer together while adding a constant element of newness to the relationship.

"We each [individually] get the excitement of having new partners. Being with someone for many years enables a deep kind of connection and passion that is truly wonderful and amazing, but you'll never have that same exact type of fire and passion that you experience with a new lover," explains Sara.

In turn, they socialize in a very relaxed, laid-back, friendly setting in which they can truly be themselves and not worry that they will be offending someone's sensibilities or incurring someone's jealous wrath. It sounds adventurous on paper, but so does being a pirate on the wild seas.

Adultery has nothing to do with swinging. Huh? 'Tis true. Who knew such a loophole in the Bible existed? Swingers do, that's who.

Dr. Eddie says he's learned from his years of research that many swingers are religious and attend church regularly. They attend the most typical churches that dot the South:

Southern Baptist, Presbyterian, and Methodist. He explains that like any group, some swingers aren't religious. Sara and Craig, for instance, aren't. But then Dr. Eddie says that he knows a Baptist preacher in Raleigh and another one in Wilmington who are avid swingers. That's all fine and dandy. Why? Because adultery is different than swinging. Adultery is cheating on someone behind their backs — in other words, taking someone's property away. Swinging is not that. It's consensual and fun. No one gets hurt. That's how Christians resolve this particular hairy question.

But even swingers who aren't holy rollers have to wonder if this is cheating. Sara says it is absolutely not.

"Adultery, to me, implies sneaking around, sleeping with other people without your spouse's knowledge or approval," she says. "The sexual dalliances we have with others are completely out in the open. We have a 'full disclosure policy'; we do these activities together, and with prior approval. If I were to find out that Craig had sex with another woman without my knowledge or approval, I would view it as cheating, the same as any other woman would. Well, no, probably not the same as other women. In this lifestyle, cheating is generally considered to be a greater offense than with nonlifestyle folks, because we give our partners so much freedom."

Makes sense. If freedom reigns in a relationship and anyone can boink anyone as long as permission is given first, then why would anyone cheat?

Dr. Eddie knows about adultery. He and his wife, Rita, founded the Intimacy Institute in Greenville, a town with about sixty thousand people and close to 150 churches.

They help couples with marital problems, and cheating is a common ailment. Surprisingly, they seldom see swingers. That's because swingers, unlike most couples, lay everything about a relationship out on the table. That's not to say that some swingers don't have problems, but chances are those problems have less to do with sex than a lot of other relationships.

At the institute, Eddie, a clinical sexologist and psychologist, and Rita, a psychiatric nurse, attempt to heal broken bonds, but sometimes, Eddie says, a marriage is over. No amount of counseling will help. If a couple thinks that adding spice — swinging — to their love life will help the marriage, forget about it.

"If one person doesn't want to stay in the marriage, then it's no secret the marriage is over," he says. "I don't try to make people stay together."

One thing Dr. Eddie has noticed recently is that the world, even in the South, is facing a paradigm shift about sex. The same thing happened in the 1960s as the country zoomed out of the calm 1950s. In the 1980s, according to Dr. Eddie, negativity festered about sex. "Sex Kills" was a common slogan because of the AIDS epidemic. In the 1990s, concepts about sex changed — especially when the country saw that even the president needed a release once in a while. Okay, maybe more than once in a while, but you know what I mean. Let's say, "Thank you, Mr. President."

"People are looking at sexual behavior in a more liberalized way," he says. "People are admitting to more bisexuality and they are having more sexual interactions. I see it at the university with students telling me things that are going on. It's all about emotion versus sex, and people are separating that a lot."

Dr. Eddie says people are realizing it's okay to have a relationship, but it's equally okay to have a one-night stand. But this philosophy, he says, is not progressing as fast in the Bible Belt. In the South, people do one thing but pretend to be doing something else. That's true. When I interviewed swingers, most were insistent on pseudonyms. Some, like the BDSM group in Tennessee, turned the tables and wanted to quiz me more than I wanted to question them. I found that those who were skittish were usually more worried about losing the image they have in their social circles than they were talking about sex.

"It's a facade down here, a polished view of society, a goodie-goodie attitude," says Dr. Eddie. "You see a lot of people who criticize other people's behavior, and that's because they are jealous or they have engaged in that behavior some way themselves. A lot of times people in the South have their heads up their asses and it's not sexual."

Guess Dr. Eddie's not shy about summing up what's wrong down in Dixie.

Martin and Mona call themselves "heteroflexible." That means they have both had bisexual experiences, and it's fine with them if they are in the mood and others are in the same headspace. They aren't into the domination or submissive scene. They just like sweet swinging loving.

The fiftyish couple live in Raleigh, a city that voted overwhelmingly for George W. Bush in the 2000 election. Some people would call this a conservative paradise where any of the newscasters from Fox News would feel right at home. After all, Raleigh's ties are to the Old South. But although it's very conservative on the exterior and controlled by right-wing elements, the city has been heavily influenced by new money from the technological and medical revolution from Research Triangle Park. That adds an educated population who like to try new things in the bedrooms. Like Martin and Mona, who have been together for nineteen years.

It's not, however, all about sex. Martin and Mona enjoy swinging more for the friendships they've developed than for the sex. The sex, if and when it happens, is a fringe benefit. Martin sees himself as bisexual. Therefore, Mona cannot give him everything he needs sexually, so swinging is an outlet for him. Mona admits she has a rampant desire for multiple male partners, so she doesn't have to sneak around either, like she had to do in previous marriages. With swinging, Mona has the opportunity to explore her bisexual side as well. No one feels repressed.

Martin and Mona know what they like in a couple. They prefer a pair usually about ten years younger than they are with good mental agility and a great sense of humor, who enjoy themselves and life. They will only date couples of their own race, and they are not into substantially overweight people. That said, Mona is quick to point out that they have several friends who are overweight. "We just don't sleep with them. This rule is actually changing a bit as time goes by," she adds.

Unlike Sara and Craig, Martin and Mona have several set rules. Rule 1: Never play on their own without permission and knowledge. Rule 2: What Mona says goes. Rule 3: Neither of them is required to "take one for the team." Finally, Rule 4: The code for escape.

"We have a preagreed subject. If either of us brings it up,

it's time to leave. No fuss or discussion about it, that comes later," Martin says.

Mona has used it twice; Martin hasn't used it at all that they can recall.

Martin and Mona are not particularly religious. She grew up Southern Baptist; he evolved from the environs of New England congregations. Between the two of them, they have three children — Martin has two, Mona one. All three children know about their lifestyle. Martin's son is a bisexual cross-dressing dom in the BDSM community, and the two girls in the family have a "to each his own" attitude but don't lean toward swinging.

Hmmm. Wonder what Christmas dinner is like at Martin and Mona's house? God bless us, everyone!

Alert. Interesting tidbit about swingers: They like to use swinger-friendly businesses especially for photo developing. Obviously, no respectable public photo processing business or the local Wal-Mart would develop personal photos of sexual activities that could be used in special advertisements for swinger sites. Some people have even been reported to the authorities for "indecency" violations because they liked to pose like porn stars in photos. So an underground cottage business began and people friendly to the lifestyle started developing film that could not be developed elsewhere. Digital cameras have hurt these businesses in recent years, but they helped swingers be more expressive on camera.

Many businesses benefit from alternative lifestyles. Some don't even know that they are. On weekends throughout the year, at many unsuspecting hotels throughout North Carolina, swingers abound. But more notable among swingers: At least eight major swingers clubs exist in Tar Heel country. That's not accounting for small clubs in rural areas with a local following or the ones that pop up in people's private homes.

Somewhere nestled in a remote area of North Carolina is a swinger bed-and-breakfast that caters to the lifestyle. Yes, guests are served breakfast just like in any other B&B in the country. But they get a bonus: Swinger parties on Saturday nights for only thirty dollars. Eat, drink, and play in the hot tub. Swingers can spend the night for sixty-five dollars and play until the sun rises. Sounds like a bargain to me.

The club situation in North Carolina has an interesting history. The largest swing club in the state is Carolina Friends. According to swingers in the area, this group has a clubhouse around Charlotte. This same group has parties at hotels in five or six cities around North Carolina, South Carolina, and Georgia. Carolina Friends also opened an inn in downtown Durham with a funky nightclub that caters just to swingers on the weekends.

A number of other smaller clubs — about a dozen or so — constellate the state. For many years, though, the only competition for Carolina Friends was Southern Exposures. They had parties once a month at a hotel in Raleigh. They would use the hotel's on-site nightclub and reserve several floors of the hotel. Sometimes the group would rent the entire hotel. But the hotel was sold and then closed. The group searched for another home but had trouble finding another location in Raleigh. During the following months, the group became nomads, moving around to various hotels before settling in Greensboro, which already had a couple of active swing clubs.

More bad news followed for Southern Exposures, according to legend. The couple who owned the club split up, and a core group of club members split off to start their own club, Magical Sinsations. Southern Exposures continued but without a permanent home. Hope bubbled that the group would eventually return to their original location in Raleigh when it reopened. Alas, it hasn't happened yet. Southern Exposures has faded, their parties more sporadic than in yesteryear.

If I check in to a Holiday Inn during a swingers weekend, I won't see a toga bonanza going on in the lobby. Hotel parties are usually held in a ballroom or nightclub and full nudity and sexual activity aren't allowed. But don't think sex isn't exuded. There are enough skimpy outfits and heavy petting to make someone look twice. An area in the hotel — usually referred to as the hospitality area — has rooms and suites reserved for play where revelers can get naked and have sex. Some groups, though, will reserve the entire hotel so that no prying eyes will snitch on anyone.

How does a party shake out in the end? Some people socialize and talk. Some dance erotically. Most everyone flirts. As the clock hits midnight, couples start moving off to other areas to hook up in hospitality rooms or hotel rooms. But not everyone connects. Some people dance until the deejay quits spinning records in the wee hours of the morning. Some go with their own partners, some hook up with one other person or a couple, and some get into big group gropes. Then, there's only the lonely who don't connect with anyone at all.

"The party is just as much about socializing and meeting people as it is about finding people to hook up with at the end of the night," Sara says.

The International Lifestyle Association, a nonprofit corporation registered in Nevada, provides some interesting statistics on their Web site:

- *Fifteen percent of couples in the United States have, at some point, incorporated swinging into their marriage.*

Hmmm. Chances are one or several of my friends like the swinging scene.

- *Swingers appear to be predominantly conservative to moderate in political orientation and to identify with the Republican Party.*

Quick! Get the shock paddles. Jesse Helms may need them.

- *Data gathered indicate that 90 percent of swingers identify a religious preference and 47 percent regularly attend religious services.*

Swingers dig the Bible.

- *Lifestyle couples are, however, more "middle-of-the-road" politically than other studies have found and, at least when it comes to attitudes about sex and marriage, may be less racist, less sexist, and less heterosexist than the general population.*

Guess they have to be.

- *Swingers do appear to lead happier and more excit-ing lives than nonswingers.*

No surprise there. It's not every weekend the average sub-urban male gets to have sex with his friend's wife.

Making my way across Tennessee on my way home from North Carolina, I consider what I know about swingers in my own backyard. I do know that a large group of swingers live in a bedroom community outside Little Rock. One cou-ple, Gwen and Lee, are very popular on the Internet and host many swinger events in my home state. When I get home, I check out upcoming events on their Web site. Camping! Fishing! It's all happening fairly soon in Hot Springs, a well-known resort area with blue lakes and moun-tains with secret nooks and crannies, the perfect spot for a meeting of swingers to roast weenies and play a mystery whodunit on a Saturday night.

I check my calendar. That weekend appears free. I rub my chin and feel a devious smile cross my lips. Surely, Dylan will go with me on this adventure. I see sweet-talk in my future. Fishing and swingers. One thing is for certain: Everyone at this retreat brings their own poles.

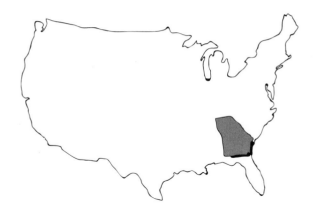

georgia

torchy taboo's
naked agenda

Virgil, Margaret Mitchell, and Bettie Page

ATLANTA, GEORGIA — Eva Wynne-Warren, also known as Torchy Taboo: the Human Heatwave, wants to get one thing straight. She's a burlesque dancer, not a stripper.

There is, indeed, a difference. Burlesque is about tease, anticipation, dramatics, leaving something to the imagination. Eva Wynne-Warren says imagination is dying in America these days. And that's a bad thing because imagination is needed to grow as a person, and if everything, including naked women, are served to men on dance stages like hamburgers on silver platters, well, then there's no hope for sexuality in the future. Eve likes to pontificate about such matters as if she's a professor lecturing to a college class about the decline of Western civilization. Oh, and if you aren't using her surnames, just call her Eve.

Eve lives in Atlanta, a city often touted as many things — capital of the New South, Finance and Transportation Hub of the South, even Gay Capital of the South, and Sex Capital of the South. The gay thing may be true. One of the first things I see upon arriving here is a huge billboard with three-dimensional closet doors advertising Absolut Vodka with the words "Absolut Out." I've never seen that billboard in any other Southern cities.

Right now, Eve wants to talk about where we are going for the night. She talks fast, but her Southern drawl slips through like honey through a tea strainer. The accent sucks you in like the sweet taste of a magical crème de menthe cocktail.

Eve suggested we meet at the Starbucks on the corner of Peachtree and Seventh just a few blocks down from Atlanta's equivalent to Mecca — the historic home of Margaret Mitchell. When I arrived, no one matched Eve's description. In other words, no one looked like the burlesque dancer I'd concocted in my mind. All I knew about Eve was this: Part of her hair was shocking azalea pink.

Since I had left Eve's phone number at the hotel room, I just had to hope that if she had waited for me and gotten bored, she would show up again. As I'm lamenting my stupidity for leaving her phone number by the bed, I spot a woman walking across the street with confidence and sassiness. Her short dark auburn bob is accented by bangs, à la Bettie Page or Mamie Eisenhower, depending on the decade. A floor-length vintage fur coat covers a long black satin skirt and an ice-pink bustier. Funky boots highlight the outfit. A row of fuchsia edges the back of the bob. Her makeup glistens electric bubblegum pink, too, with shimmers of lightning-bolt silver glitter sparkling on her eyes and cheeks. Deep cherry-plum lipstick glints on her kewpie lips, lips that curl up in a devilish smile when she approaches.

No doubt, she's Eve.

"Hi. Lord, I'm late. I was wondering if you would be here, and I left your number at the apartment," Eve says. She sticks out her tiny hand for me to shake.

"No, I was late, too," I say.

"Okay, here's the deal. The Clairmont, I really want you to see it, but . . ."

But the problem is the Clairmont Lounge, a legacy in Atlanta's sex-club world, has gone disco for the night. Occasionally, the seedy lounge brings in a deejay and the place transforms into a Studio 54 dance floor. The strippers become a backdrop as club kids crowd the joint to dance the night away. It's crowded, hot, and not at all fun, says Eve. The Clairmont is best known as the home of a stripper named Goldie, who crushes beer cans with her tits. The strippers hail from the "natural beauty" genre, meaning they prefer strutting around with what God gave them rather than what expensive plastic surgeons molded. It can also mean that they might be skanky, thin, washed-up, or drug addicts. But it doesn't matter. The Clairmont, after thirty years, still attracts a cross section of Atlanta's population — celebrities, CEOs, faded-out socialites, winos, bums, conventioneers, gangstas, and anyone in between.

"We need to go to Master's," Eve says.

That's settled. Off we go, driving past upscale men's clothing stores, the Atlanta Botanical Gardens, and from what I can tell in the street-lighted darkness, upscale condos. Eve tells me to turn down a street and soon, neon green and purple towers glow in the distance. That's it, says, Eve. That's the strip club? Hmmm. As we get closer, I see two life-size camouflage helicopters floating in each tower. I feel like I'm going to Universal Studios. Master's sits on a thoroughfare lined with adult entertainment venues on each side. It's perfect for the nudie connoisseur.

"I know some girls who work here. Well, I used to know some girls who work here," Eve says.

For eighteen years or so, Eve worked as a stripper. Her story is a curious one of old Atlanta meeting an edgier modern South that still isn't comfortable in its new skin. As we venture into Master's, I'm more curious about Eve than the naked women who will surely be flaunting their rude bits on an illuminated catwalk. Who is this four-foot-eleven pixie and how did she become Torchy Taboo?

Eve's life began in the most Southern place on Earth: Savannah, Georgia. To this day, she will still return to Savannah, on the eastern coast of Georgia about two hours from Atlanta, and stroll in the town's many beautiful squares. She'll wander to her favorite spot, Forsythe Square, where she will sit with her boom box listening to Eudora Welty spin stories while she eats tea sandwiches and dreams. Eve, like so many Southern girls, is a hopeless romantic conjuring up moonbeams, magnolias, and mint juleps in her mind while awaiting her one and only, her Rhett Butler, to arrive and sweep her off her feet with firebolt desire.

Baby Eve, who was teeny-weeny and named after the family's matriarch, didn't stay in Savannah for long. She grew up in Atlanta where she lived with her old — ancient, she says — overprotective grandparents in a part of town filled with massive oak trees. From those wise elders, Eve heard stories, tales about an Atlanta that no longer exists. Stories about Reconstruction and segregation — the days before Atlanta became a melting pot of foreigners and Yankees.

"I know more about the history of DeKalb County than any stripper should," she says.

Like many creative children, Eve found herself often bored, staring off into some far-away galaxy where she was the Supreme Goddess Ruler, the little pistol who could charm the Milky Way with a grin and a wink. Her earliest memory was seeing *Gone with the Wind* on television. The classic movie etched a strong memory in Eve's psyche.

One summer when her grandfather's illness was preoccupying the family, Eve escaped from the house and found a gnarled oak tree in which to hide away with a copy of *Gone with the Wind*. Like all good Southern belles, she devoured the novel, set practically in her very own backyard, and realized she was much more Scarlett than Melanie. From that point on, Eve's fate as a spitfire was sealed. Whatever it took to survive, Eve would do it. She had no choice. She came from the very rich soil of Tara. Plus she was Irish, just like Scarlett.

"I was absorbed in it so deeply, her survival instinct, and that's who I was in my youth to the nth degree. I was going to scrape and make it. Mores be damned, and to hell with what everyone was saying about what I was doing," she says, taking a sip of her Diet Coke.

Eve grew up a punk. She still lives the lifestyle, shunning nine-to-five jobs and early mornings, and listening to music from the likes of the Ramones, Circle Jerks, Dead Kennedys, New York Dolls, Iggy Pop, and her biggest influence — the Cramps. Being a punk was one thing. But Eve also grew up to be — much to the dismay of her Southern Baptist family — an exhibitionist who liked to shimmy and shake.

Her family freaked when they learned she was dancing. Southern Baptists don't dance. But Eve did, and she took it a step further: She did it in the nude.

"I said 'Watch all of me dance now,'" she says.

The rebellion of this modern Southern belle with an edge that could give the toughest Bubba a paper cut transformed Eve into the black sheep of the family. She didn't, and doesn't, care. But it was a long while before she admitted to her family that she was a stripper. Her path to the stage didn't begin like many little belles', as a beauty-pageant winner in a contest like Miss Black Eyed Pea or Miss Sugarloaf Mountain. No, a series of happenstances mixed with a childhood fantasy brought Eve to her career.

Eve always, always wanted to be a stripper. She grew up with a red-headed girl in elementary school who kids called Susie the Floosie because of her big breasts at an early age. While Susie was traumatized, Eve's brain ginned in overtime.

"The kids always said Susie the Floosie would be a stripper, and I thought, 'Now that sounds cool,'" she says, glowing.

A high school boyfriend told Eve that she was hardly vampy or sexy enough to be a stripper. Ha, Eve said, tossing the boy to the curb like a crumpled fast-food bag. Wanting to leave home and explore the world, Eve opted to show the boy he was wrong. She found a stripping gig in a gritty downtown dive with really good stages — large ones that let a stripper really perform, not just march around in high heels. At the same time, Eve straddled a fine line, attempting an engagement with conformity — majoring in art at a Georgia university and soaking in beauty and color around her. Her creativity extended from the canvas to the stage. Even in the world of flashing tits and ass, Eve was different, a pint-sized fireball of seduction. It wasn't about sex for Eve. It was all about the act.

"I didn't even lose my virginity until I had been a stripper for a couple of years," she says. "How crazy is that? I was the stripper who was still a virgin. No one would believe that shit."

I would. A common thread in the South is weaving public images of one thing while the flip side of the tapestry displays something of an entirely opposite nature. If a woman is outspoken and independent in Dixie, she couldn't possibly have a heart of gold. If a woman attends church regularly, surely she couldn't be the town slut. If a man is an upstanding elder in the Presbyterian church, there is no way he can be nailing the cute, bubbly college student. You get the picture.

In the 1980s, Eve worked in a nude world much different than the one that exists today. Girls didn't get onstage to show everything they had for a dollar. A held-over mentality from the days of burlesque still floated in the clubs, even the run-down sleazy ones. So conservative were the joints back then, that managers told the strippers to pretend they were holding a dime between their knees so as not to show too much of their goodies to the crowd. For Eve, the performance always mattered more than the final splash of nudity. In her spare time, she'd search out Atlanta's vintage clothes shops and thrift stores looking for costumes. She'd prance onstage wearing an old wedding gown or a Girl Scout uniform, seducing the crowd night after night as if they were watching an MTV video in real-time.

The crowd in Master's appears slim for a Saturday night, but Eve doesn't notice too much. Honestly, neither do I. Eve possesses a Tinkerbell aura that fuels the imagination like a colorama trip through a psychedelic amusement park. Surely, she lives in a low-rent flat but in my mind she lies her head down on a lush-green leaf pillow in a pink tulip bed when she comes in from a late night of clubbing. Enchanting, she is, and much more intriguing than the skinny girl in scuffed-up white go-go boots shaking her meatless rib cage in front of us.

"It's porn chic. That's the way it is now. All of these clubs are into porn chic, which is basically just having porn on-stage. There wasn't a lot of stripping when I started. We all had more layers of clothes. The reality is I don't make a lot of judgment because clubs everywhere are different," she says.

Recently, Eve said she ventured into the Cheetah, one of the city's more upscale clubs where she once worked.

"The girls looked better; they have gotten away from hiring phony Barbie dolls. There were some boob jobs but they had these beautiful ethnic girls. The Cheetah is like a clean corporate strip club, like Disneyland."

When Eve worked in strip clubs, she says if "seedy" was up someone's alley, it could be found. Some strippers had regular customers who tipped very well. Sugar daddies provided some girls with extra money if they gave a little hoochie-coo. Eve says she never played those games.

"With this porn-chic thing, strip clubs have feature dancers who travel the circuit and do nasty stuff on their third song, really explicit stuff. They can have contact with customers. That changed strip clubs, and it lowered the common denominator on what guys will pay for. They no longer have to offer a hundred dollars for tiny this and that. I'm a prig. I never took money for anything offstage, but some girls knew that if they took a hundred dollars to do one thing, the next girl who came along would do it for seventy-five, and eventually you'd make no money doing anything."

Exactly the thought I had when I visited Platinum Plus in Memphis.

Eve slips out of her fur coat to reveal three tattoos on her upper arms. Even something as ordinary as removing a coat has a certain slinky appeal when Eve does it. She knows how to draw attention to herself, like there is a movie director in her head giving stage directions for the most seductive angle. Strangely, few men in the place look at her, and this is what makes Eve the maddest. Not that she thinks she is the belle of the ball — okay, maybe she does — but if that's the case, why aren't men looking at her? Of course, she is clothed and most of the women around us are naked or have just one more thin layer between us and their booties. But there is something else at work here, and it's prevalent throughout the South.

Eve's complicated — multifaceted — and that doesn't always play well in Atlanta.

"People here want to think simple," she says. "That's why you see a lot of people moving from the North to Atlanta. They want everything in their little boxes, their little places, and this city gives it to them. Everything, everyone here has a place. If you are gay, you belong in one place. If you are a lesbian, you belong in another. If you are rich, it's a suburb."

But Eve defies easy categorization. She may be three-generations of old Atlanta, but she doesn't have the image to accompany it. She doesn't have the typical Dixie-fried look. Far from it. She's not superthin from too many diets. She doesn't have big, teased hair held in place by expensive salon hairspray. Her flawless porcelain complexion, which makes her look much younger than her forty years, is real, not propped up by BOTOX or face-lifts or highlighted by a fake tan glow. Strangely, if Eve's face resembles anyone Southern, it's Margaret Mitchell.

Part evanescent child, part gritty urban adult, part vanishing belle, Eve is a magical concoction of the unknown and the uninhibited. She's a walking Flannery O'Connor character who possesses an inside track to the gothic underbelly of this city. For instance, a recent adventure took Eve to a black strip club, where she worked one night as a cocktail waitress. While naked black beauties flounced about, the focus was on boxing.

"There was a boxing ring and you had these big black men just get in and beat the hell out of each other. Then, there were women, big women, who got in after they finished, and they fought each other," Eve explains. "It was too damn scary for me. I worked there one night and that was it."

Southern men, it can be easily concluded, would be afraid of someone like Eve, who could undoubtedly hold her own at the Junior League luncheon. That is, if she could get invited to attend one. But while the society mavens are lunching on iced tea and chicken salad sandwiches or playing tennis on a private court, Eve is going places that would raise their perfectly waxed highbrows an inch or two. For instance, the place she takes me next: the Chamber.

"The Chamber is the only bar in Atlanta that makes even the hardest club goer, even those with piercings and tattoos, go, 'You went where?'" Eve says. "Seriously, when I worked as a Camel representative, we'd have to go to all of these clubs for cigarette promotions, and only me and another girl would take the Chamber. It freaks people out."

The Chamber, a fetish bar, is located in an office complex just down the street from Master's and near an Asian massage parlor, also known as a Jack shack. Vince Jenkins, the strip club authority who likes Platinum Plus in Memphis, says that he and his buddies, on a wild trip to Atlanta, once visited a Jack shack. The little geisha hotties, according to him, do anything you want if you got the right amount of Ben Franklins in your pocket. Eve says she thought about working in one once, but passed on it for reasons of disgust.

It's a tad past midnight, and the Chamber crawls with nocturnal souls who look like they haven't seen daylight since Ronald Reagan lived in the White House. Inside the front door, a gigantic snake is coiled in a corner of a huge glass window. Snakes freak me out, so I don't get too close, but I suddenly recall Eve mentioning something about snake acts. Hopefully I won't see one tonight. In her confident way, Eve claims a table, lays down her satin purse shaped like a Chinese take-out box, and her silver glittered cigarette case. In this smoky dark Blade Runner universe of black latex, spiked collars, and body piercings, Eve looks like a neon-dream Powerpuff Girl ready to take on the world, as soon as she has one more drag off her cigarette.

One of the reasons we are here is because of a boy. Eve has a schoolgirl crush on a guy she has been dating who eats fire and performs at the Chamber. He just has something about him that makes Eve giddy. There is no doubt: Eve is Scarlett O'Hara incarnate. One minute, tough as nails with an agenda to make burlesque a popular artform. The next, a Southern belle giggling with delight about this boy who makes her as dizzy as an overproof whiskey cocktail.

Heavy, moody industrial music throbs in the Chamber. In a floor-to-ceiling glass case behind me, a woman in latex and leather flogs a man who is on all fours in a doggy-style position. A strobe light in the case shows the entire act in slow-motion. Frankly, after my Alabama experience, it's hard to get hypnotized by the act, which seems innocent and almost poser-like in comparison. In a larger room, latex babes who buy eyeliner wholesale by the box dance on two large stages with an iron cage perched on one. *City of Lost Children*, a surreal French film from the 1990s that is all about children's imaginations and dreams, flashes on panels of canvas hanging from the ceiling

"Ooh, I love that movie," Eve squeals.

The boy of the hour arrives. A surly dude in leather, he is the strong, silent type, the punk ying to Eve's glam-girl yang. He eats fire. He walks on stilts. He's a gothic clown. Really, he is. Basically, he's a circus freak, and that makes Eve's engine roar with unbridled passion.

"Clowns make me all sushy," Eve says of her clown fetish.

Sushy is her word for dreamy, aroused, loopy. And right now, Eve's in sideshow freak heaven at the fetish club of her choice.

"Jesters are all the better," she adds with a grin.

Eve's been down the aisle three times.

"The first time I married I, like Scarlett, was too young and impetuous," she says. "I married Mr. Butler (Yes, really, Michael S. Butler! Tall, blonde, with a deep, rich, velvety voice and a great sense of humor) because we had been living together for two years and we thought that getting married was what you did at that point. We were married for six weeks. I left him for number two."

Number two was a boy named Philip with whom Eve spent seven years. They were married for the last year of the seven.

"Short, Jewish, funny, and freakishly intelligent; a gifted writer. He wooed me with Shakespeare and Baudelaire. We traveled Europe for six months, drowning ourselves in poetry, mythology, and art. Perhaps my one true love. We split up because we were horribly sexually incompatible."

Number three was a boy named Tony. He came into Eve's life when she was going through "a real dark night of the soul" following Philip.

"He was like my Virgil. We drank — oh, how we drank. He was tall, dark, and almost Asian looking though he wasn't. Smart, funny, dark, and spiritual. A geek to end all geeks. A gifted chef. I left him ten years ago, when I finally found my way out of the valley of the shadow of death; we spent four years together. Sometimes I regret not sticking with him; we got along quite well. He's the one that never really forgave me for leaving him."

She falls in and out of love easily. So sue her. Boys are a hobby to her. And she likes that.

"Yeah," she sighs in a little girl yawn. "Boys. An expensive hobby."

So are her tattoos. The troika of flesh art symbolizes Eve's other passions. Two of the tattoos touch each other, but they are distinctly different pieces of art. The first tattoo Eve got was a locomotive.

"I wanted something bold and somewhat masculine to express my Southern roots and undying lifelong love and appreciation for my country music heroes Johnny Cash, Willie Nelson, Johnny Horton, Waylon Jennings, Merle Haggard, and, of course, Hank Williams Sr., to mention just a few. I'd lived alongside the railroad tracks since I grew up and left home, and many of my heroes' songs were about trains, so the flames around the train came about a year later when I first started performing with fire."

On the same arm, just above the train, a peacock feather floats. That symbol expresses Eve's dedication to burlesque. Many of Eve's costumes have feathers on them, creating a beautiful, glamorous look from days gone by. Peacock feathers also represent Hera, the Greek goddess and Zeus's wife.

"She reminds me that I am now a fully grown, powerful woman, not the wisp of a timid girl I once was . . . and that it's a good thing," Eve says.

On the other arm is a band with the Latin words *Divus Donum Animus Incindium* that loosely translated means, "Divine gift of spiritual fire." Above those words are blue flames and, hidden in the midst, a pair of piercing eyes; between them is the third eye.

"I had this tat done in Brooklyn while in New York City performing and healing from getting 'burned' by a man," she says. "It reminds me that the fire from within is just as great and terrible as the physical fire I use in some of my acts and from which I take my name. Tattoos are expensive; that's the only reason I don't already have a giant snake below the train (for my snake that I dance with, Usssila), and many more that are in the idea stages and will come to fruition when I'm cashy."

The surly boy and Eve often haunt the Chamber, which is called a "sexually extreme" dance club by its owners. Girls in latex shorts dance topless with only black electrical tape crosses covering their nipples. A man wearing a Nazi uniform prances around with fire and teases the girls on the stage. At one point one of the girls becomes chained in shackles to the ceiling. The Nazi guy then takes hypodermic needles and places them under the girl's flesh near her breasts.

Yawn, says Eve. I agree.

Off to the side of the main stage, nocturnal babes drift in and out of side rooms. One is a small store that sells fetish wear, fishnets in every color, skeleton jewelry, and an array of goods that every dark soul needs. A three-headed shower contraption sits in a corner in the room next to the boutique. A table with shackles makes me flashback to Alabama. Apparently, there are BDSM shows in these rooms, but not tonight.

On Eve's first date with the fire eater, the couple ventured into one of these secret side rooms. Eve says it was like some sort of *Rocky Horror* show with someone tied up getting a substantial spanking. The memory is fuzzy for Eve, who said she was pretty drunk at the time and bored.

"Any kind of sex show bores me because I am not participating. I never saw another one, probably because of the look I gave him, which was like 'Show me another sex show and I'll strike you down with lightning bolts from my fingers,'" she says. "I didn't really mean it that way but he has never taken me back."

Over a club-mix Depeche Mode song, I discover Eve's fascination with burlesque — the peekaboo theatrical strip-tease of legends like Gypsy Rose Lee with a hint of kick-ass chick Bettie Page. When Eve discovered burlesque, she was getting into rockabilly music and the retro fad of swing music and dance.

Concurrently, she was working at a strip joint that wasn't the most exciting place on earth, but it was next door to a lesbian club with fabulous drag shows. The fantasy enter-tainment captivated Eve. Realizing she already possessed a sense for stagecraft savvy, thanks to her time in the adult en-tertainment world, she decided to transform herself into a burlesque goddess.

"I thought I was too old to strip anymore, but that wasn't it; I was just bored. I was playing the goth girl in the strip clubs — at least it was sensual. That's pretty bad when you're playing the goth girl in a strip club to cheer yourself up," she says.

The time had arrived for her to be boopy — another word from Eve's personal lexicon — and she became so by dye-ing her hair flaming red, styling it in a Bettie Page 'do, and donning a red polka-dot dress with vibrant makeup. She re-alized this shtick was nothing new; she had always been do-ing it. From the time she began stripping she had been copying Bette Midler in her Divine Miss M days and David Bowie as Ziggy Stardust.

As she immersed herself into the world of smoky jazz music and Glenn Miller, she learned all about Bettie Page, the Tennessee girl who became known as the queen of bondage, and Tempest Storm, a Georgia burlesque dancer with measurements of 41DD-25-35.

I tell Eve that I grew up hearing a burlesque story from my mother. She wants to hear it. In the early 1950s, my mother traveled to New Orleans on her senior class trip. In the Big Easy, Mom attended a burlesque show — considered incredibly racy for a small-town Arkansas girl in the post–World War II decade — and saw a woman who could do unimaginable tricks with tassels. Tassels as pasties covered each of her nipples, and two more were placed on her hips. In time to swanky music, the dancer would make each tassel spin like an erotic kaleidoscope, twirling them in different directions at the same time. The glam girl on the stage mesmerized my mother, and as a child, her story entertained me.

"I know what you mean," Eve, who makes her own pasties, says. "Those women were amazing."

From the 1930s until the late 1950s, burlesque was one of the most popular forms of entertainment in American theater. During those twenty-plus years, the art form's true stars possessed curvy bodies, fanciful costumes, frolicsome choreography, humor, and usually an exceptional erotic gimmick. Evangeline the Oyster Girl — aka Betty West, who grew up in Mississippi — transformed herself into a sea goddess on the half-shell. Rosita Royce trained doves that disrobed her. Lili St. Cyr, a sexy statuesque blonde, became known as the queen of burlesque.

"Now there was a star. My idol. She billed herself as 'the most beautiful woman on earth.' Her thing was unattainability, but she put a lot of effort into her acts. She trained in several forms of dance. Her acts had themes, beautiful props, and costumes. She had such a grace and ultrafeminine quality about her. She was probably second only in success to Tempest."

Then there's Dixie Evans, "the Marilyn Monroe of burlesque," a blonde look-alike who acted out various sexy situations Marilyn might find herself in. She now owns the Exotic World Burlesque Museum in Helendale, California, where the Miss Exotic World Competition is held every year. Eve loves — *loves* — her.

But for Eve and any other woman who has attempted to remove clothing in a sexy manner, Gypsy Rose Lee set the standard. Her gimmick, which made her rich and famous, was class, sheer class with a little humor to spice up her act. She wore sexy evening gowns and over-the-elbow opera gloves, which she peeled out of in the most seductive manner.

"I had the glove-peel down to an art by the time I was ten. My grandmother would let me play in her mink and opera gloves; little did she know what she was training me for," Eve recalls.

Studying these women, Eve, with her all the savvy of a politician, realized that in the modern porn-chic setting at the start of the twenty-first century, burlesque was so ridiculously colorful and had such an undeniable satirical feel that she had to become part of the scene.

Enter Torchy Taboo, the Human Heatwave.

Torchy is Eve's evil twin, or is it the other way around?

Here's Torchy's bio: Torchy Taboo is a confessed Blanche DuBois living a Mata Hari delusion who performs her own crazy concoction of jazz and Eastern dance, delivered with all the trappings of classic burlesque. Her ever-flickering fingers hypnotize her audience, drawing them to her mysterious, lascivious agenda. Just try to resist!

Let me tell you, it's hard.

Torchy was born when Eve was still stripping but staring at the ceiling tiles while dancing. Bored, she decided to stick her sparkly painted toes into the burlesque waters by transforming herself into Bettie Page. She poured over vintage strip reels and read the *Betty Pages,* a glossy fanzine dedicated to the Southern legend who knew how to wield a wicked riding crop. In the mid-1990s, Eve competed in a Bettie Page look-alike contest, where she met Greg Theakston, publisher of the *Betty Pages,* and the two became fast friends. They collaborated on the magazine *Tease!,* with Eve posing for pictures and then contributing writing and design work.

It was during this time that Torchy Taboo became reality. A rocket-fuel concoction, Torchy (her last name is an ode to Eve's grandmother's favorite perfume, Tabu) sets her act apart from anything else out there in showbiz by playing with snakes and fire and, at the end, allowing her bra to burst into flames. Knowing she had discovered her calling, Eve quit stripping in the late 1990s, dedicating her life to the vintage art form.

Eve's picked the smoky Chamber to tell me about her "naked agenda" for burlesque, but she waits for surly boy to head to another part of the bar to discuss it. It's as if Eve doesn't want to show she's too smart around him.

"I have this background and really I have about twenty years of rehearsal time. I have all of the skills; they are honed to the max. The tease and the sexy part and the stagecraft — that's all there," she says.

Eve wants to express onstage the things that bug her day in, day out. And what does she think about the most: Why do male-female relationships suck so badly? And what's up with feminism in the twenty-first century?

"At strip clubs women are in charge, and they wield their power with a little bit of recklessness," Eve says. "But they don't have anything to say, but 'Give me more money.' I think I can use that same stuff, but add good theater and some comedy and longer eyelashes and better costumes and I've got something."

Back in the 1950s, it was quite common for women to accompany men to burlesque shows. Somewhere along the line, women started staying at home and strip joints became men's territory. It shouldn't be that way. Eve's goal: to give people — men and women — some fun, to let them relax, fantasize, and let their minds roam to naughty places. Then, while they are in a gauzy state with their everyday defenses down, watching Torchy Taboo, Eve plans to give them a new thought or two. She wants to give the audience a wink, wink, nudge, nudge.

"I want the girls to get inspired. I want the men to say, 'She's not in a nurse's outfit but she's still sexy.' Then I want them to go home and do whatever nature leads them to do," she says. "A good thought seals the deal."

Eve's plan is more dense than that, almost as complex as a peace treaty between two countries in the Middle East. Question everything, break the bubble, and touch those around you. That's Eve's mantra.

"If everyone were ten percent more open, a lot of issues would be solved," she says.

Burlesque, says Eve, is the whole point of the feminist movement, which wasn't about overcoming men, but becoming equal.

"Basically it was all about figuring out how to get along with the damn creatures. I'm a researcher in this field. Obviously it's not going to happen if women are all uptight. I want to make women comfortable with their own sexuality. Women can be wild, passionate, get-it-on creatures but still have a brain. You can mold the brain, mind, heart, and soul into one thing, but introducing this in the South is like introducing something from Mars."

Eve has created a burlesque troupe called Dames A'flame, a savage group of women who take no prisoners unless they want to, to further her agenda. Torchy, naturally, is the troup's ringleader. Four women — Gin-Gin the Wild Woman, Madly Deeply, Maji Minx, and Luna Luxx — join Torchy in the burlesque jungle of madcap erotic hijinks.

It's possible, she says, to bring burlesque to a whole new level in the South because the Gloria Steinem mentality of feminism never played well down here.

"It took a lot of time for that shit to settle down here in the South," exclaims Eve. "There's a point where in the South you skip over a certain amount of developments and progress of the feminist movement. That's because women down here are taught to be at least a little feminine and use some sort of seduction to get a man down the aisle, and burlesque is totally about seduction. It's the men I've gotten resistance from down here."

Seduction is a hard sell in Atlanta when titillation is on every corner. There are strip clubs, lingerie-modeling studios, dominatrices with their own dungeons, Jack shacks, escorts of every shape, size, and gender, swinger clubs, adult movie theaters, and the everyday common hooker on the street.

In the 1990s, Atlanta's sex industry contributed more money to the local economy than all the professional sports teams in the city. One reason Atlanta hosts hundreds of large conventions each year is because the town has so many adult entertainment services to offer convention attendees. A friend who lives in Atlanta tells me the city may not be as raunchy as New Orleans or as exhibitionist as Miami, but there is still a steady drumbeat of sex. Atlanta is only one of a few cities in America where alcohol can be served in places with total nudity. That makes the city a haven for clubs that cater to conventioneers.

"Guys are so used to getting whatever female anatomy they want in their face. They just have a jism-related agenda. It's objectified sexuality," Eve says, getting angry.

Staying focused on her naked agenda, Eve, her green cat eyes gleaming with mischief, returns to her message. She's no Barbie doll and that's a point in her favor.

"My softer, curvier frame is more appealing to men and women," she says. "Burlesque challenges the position of the titty bar in terms of adult entertainment. There will be a lot more males and females that let go of that TV serving of Barbie-doll sexuality once they see burlesque."

While she says titty bars are fine, and that she has nothing against them, Eve does know those very establishments where she once worked and still visits are her main competition to luring men, and women, to the seductive side of sex.

Can she do it? Eve bursts into laughter. "It's a grand plan. Brew-ha-ha-ha-ha-ha-ha," she says, rubbing her hands together like a maniacal she-devil. She grins and when she does she looks like the Cheshire Cat.

But don't call Eve a cat. She's a poodle.

When Eve's not in Torchy mode, she becomes a fluffy pink concoction named Mon Petit Shoe the Pink Poodle, which evokes a cotton candy 1950s aura in a surreal manner that would have made Salvador Dali beam with pride. Mon Petit Shoe is French, but of course. She wears a black corset and pink fishnet stockings with another pair of black fishnets over them. A pink pouf ball with poodle ears covers her head while another erect pink pouf-ball tail juts from her ass. Eve wears the same hue of faux pink fur around her ankles and wrists with a pink lace and chiffon French maid skirt that she made herself.

On her ultratiny hands, she wears gloves with claws. Highly dramatic makeup with pink and silver glitter creates an otherworldly look that isn't quite human or animal. Then, to finish off the creation, Eve wears one six-inch platform boot and carries the other one in her mouth.

"I'm a dog after all. I chewed up my own shoe," she says, as natural as if talking about paying the electrical bill. This one-shoe idea also stems from one of Eve's long-standing stage fears — going on to perform but missing a shoe. "Confronting fears, that's a good thing," she says, laughing.

Because she only wears the one platform, the asymmetry allows Eve to keep one leg hiked with her toe pointed, resembling the very stance my childhood picky white poodle Bobo use to make when he didn't want to walk into wet grass. Wearing this attire gets Eve plenty of attention. If it doesn't, she'll generate it as she runs around like a frenzied poodle that needs a Xanax, saying in a French little-girl accent, "I'm out of ze yard. Will vous feed me? I'm out of ze yard. Will vous feed me?" She likes walking up to women, who don't know what to make of this fou-fou creature and saying, "I'm off ze leash, and vous?"

"They do not know what to make of me. I'm hammering wedges, tapping into their consciousness. It's great."

And the men?

"It's makes them insane. It gets me laid. Have I said it gets me laid? It gets me laid," she says, chuckling.

Eve likes to keep people guessing, stirring sexuality in a big cauldron. She plans to take the Mon Petit Shoe character and add performance dialogue, mixing in monologues from Zsa Zsa Gabor's autobiography. Eve's fascination lies in the type of women who talk of falling in love, getting a man to marry them, and then leaving them for the next tastiest choice that comes along. It's the romantic, if a tad scheming, boy-driven agenda, once again, of Scarlett O'Hara.

"The next poetic man I fall in love with should have a shitload of money and I wouldn't have to bust my ass anymore. I want to wear the dresses and be hyperfeminine," she says, moony just like any Southern belle who still seeks her Ashley Wilkes.

In one of Eve's most popular acts, she sings Cole Porter's "My Heart Belongs to Daddy" in a sexy but eerie siren tone. During the song's musical bridge, Eve sashays up to a fella in the audience whom she previously selected and set up before her show. A conniving vixen on the prowl, she likes to pick a man who has brought a date with him. Slinking up to him, she crawls onto his lap, wraps her arms around him, and whispers in his ear. All the while, the audience sees the lascivious glint on Eve's heavily made-up face while she and the man's date shoot each other the evil eye.

With precision and more drama than Bette Davis in *Whatever Happened to Baby Jane?,* Eve reaches into the victim's shirt pocket and tears out the man's heart — a pre-placed prop. He collapses, and the date freaks the hell out. With a maniacal grin, Eve holds the heart up over her head and squeezes it; blood runs down her pale arm and all over her white, lacy bustier. She slams the foam heart down on a waiting silver platter and takes it to the band leader — Daddy. He takes the heart and in exchange gives Eve a glitzy piece of jewelry. In an animalistic move, she licks the "blood" from her arms. She finishes the song and finishes stripping. The end of the show brings Eve's twirling tassels. The audience doesn't know what to make of the blood-licking pixie doll who leaves them with kisses, a tassel toss, and a wink, all the while sprinkling "better sex dust" on them. But one thing is certain: They like it.

Late in the wee hours, Eve sips on a cocktail and tells me she plans to stay a tad longer at the Chamber.

"I'll take a taxi," she says in a throaty drawl like a 1940s starlet.

When I turn for one parting glimpse at this spark in the smoky haze, she appears to be fading. The last thing I see is Eve batting her long eyelashes at her surly boy.

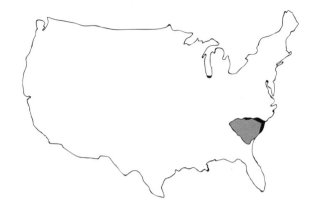

south carolina

big beautiful belles

BBWs, BBQ, and B. B. King

COLUMBIA, SOUTH CAROLINA — Big girls — chubby chicks, huge humpers, heavy hotties, ample beauties — want love, too. And trust me, there are plenty of men out there who will give it to them. These men like big butts and they don't apologize for it. Jennifer Lopez? Not enough junk in the trunk. Please, J. Lo, eat some more red beans and rice, say these men. They don't just like *some* ass, they like a whole lotta butt.

There are men, like Dylan for instance, who joke about how they like a nice, round onion (boy slang for butt) and that a woman couldn't have one big enough for them. However, I think a BBW — that's big, beautiful woman — would be too much for even Dylan to handle.

According to info gathered from many sources, the term BBW was coined during the diet-pill-happy '70s when *BBW* magazine debuted. Who qualifies as a BBW? Everyone from the petite woman who is under five feet and weighs 120 pounds to the towering Amazon who weighs in around 1,200. (Where I come from we call that a baby elephant.)

Pamela Anderson, that curvy blonde bombshell of a woman, is often cited as a role model for BBWs. Monica Lewinsky is among the beloved, and BBWs praise Bill Clinton for choosing one of their own as his White House delicacy. Let us not forget Anna Nicole Smith. She, too, could be in the BBW Hall of Fame, if one existed. It's no surprise that plenty of BBWs call the South home, where fried foods are served for breakfast, lunch, and dinner. While South Carolina has more than its share of wafer-thin Junior Leaguers who live for liposuction, there's also a bevy of buxom beauties who fear that losing a few pounds will make them less sexy and attractive to the men who love to snuggle up next to a BBW at the end of the day.

Sitting in a diner on the outskirts of Columbia, Bonnie Newman, a thirtyish BBW, isn't shy about what she's eating or what she's wearing. There's not an ounce of apology in her. The waffle, eggs, pork chops, and coffee — black — is a good start for a healthy girl like Bonnie, and she seems all too eager to eat them. Her wardrobe consists of cut-your-breath-off tight faded jeans and a red halter top that shows her stomach peeking out and rolling over the jean's waistband. A toe ring glints in Bonnie's green sparkly sandals. She has a big smile and full red lips. Her makeup is bright against her blonde hair. Bonnie's sexy in a strange, over-the-top curvy way, and she knows it.

"Sure, I know I'm no Kate Moss or Lara Flynn Boyle, but why would I want to be?" she asks.

Good point. She's confident and men like that in a woman. Some women fret about gaining a pound or two over a decadent weekend of vanilla ice cream and pecan pie. Not Bonnie. More calories just means more loving for her men. But it wasn't always that way.

Bonnie, a good ol' South Carolina girl in her early thirties who still loves Bon Jovi like it's 1987, used to worry about her weight, especially how it played in the boudoir. She often didn't feel sexy and more times than not, Bonnie felt self-conscious about her 275 pounds. It didn't help that her first serious boyfriend, we'll call him Frank, often nagged her to put away the chicken wings and pick up a bunch of carrots.

"He was always telling me what to eat," she recalls. "It bugged me — a lot. Common sense tells you I won't ever ever be as thin as the average woman. I'm just not built that way. But I was afraid if I said anything he'd break up with me."

Needless to say, the relationship didn't last. Frank eventually said adios and left Bonnie for a thinner woman. Bonnie, heartbroken, didn't know what to do until one night a friend referred her to a BBW Web site. Clicking on that link changed her life. She realized she wasn't the freak Frank made her feel like, and that a sisterhood of women who basked in their supersized sultriness existed. Her life has never been the same.

In the past few years, Bonnie has met many men on BBW Web sites and connected with several of them. The sex, with men who appreciate a bodacious broad, has been some of the best she has ever had, she says. She's explored the world of sex toys, BDSM, and even anal sex, which Bonnie admits enjoying immensely.

"I do love it. Crazy, I'd never thought I would, but boy I do," she says.

I'll pass on a comment. Okay, maybe just one: Your kink's not my kink, but your kink is okay.

Know what BHM means? It stands for big handsome man. FA? Fat admirer (a man who admires larger people). FFA? Female fat admirer (a woman who likes larger people).

Joe, an average-size man with a toothbrush mustache, is an FA, and he admires Bonnie in a big — no pun intended — way. Taking a gulp of coffee, Joe, who weighs a shade under two hundred, beams when he looks at Bonnie, and Bonnie returns the admiration with a pinch on Joe's cheek. I have to ask: Is Bonnie ever too much woman for him? "Good God, no," he says. "You kidding? I've been waiting for someone like this for a long time. She's the perfect girl. Perfect. I like cuddling up in the middle of the night to a woman who feels like a woman."

Joe says he can pinpoint exactly when he became attracted to curvaceous women: He was seventeen. His first girlfriend was a rail of a girl, a bony sixteen-year-old that had a body more like his little brother's than a teenage girl's. But at the time, Joe was in love, as much as someone at that age can be, with Rachel. Since she was his first girlfriend, and he was just happy to have a girl to call his sweetie, Joe didn't think too much about her body shape. That changed when Joe packed up and set off for summer camp. There, in the woods of northern South Carolina, he met Kelly, a plump girl with brown hair and wide green eyes. The first time Joe hugged her, he knew something was different.

"I immediately knew that hugging my old girlfriend was like hugging a coat hanger. With Kelly, everything felt more girly, more right; she had tits and hips that swayed like the girls I saw in the movies," he says. "I knew I'd never want to be with a skinny girl again."

And he hasn't been.

Joe says skinny girls don't have what it takes in the bedroom either. At least not for him.

"When you fuck a skinny girl, you are afraid you are going to smush her," he says. "It's not sexy when you can feel her pelvic bones up against you."

I'd imagine not. Yuck. Can you really?

"Yeah, you can. You really can. It's not a good feeling. I like a woman I can bury myself in — pardon me if it grosses you out — rolls of warm flesh. I like to just bury myself in Bonnie, in every part of her."

Joe's smoky blue eyes glaze over at the thought of the couple's latest romp, I leave him in that world.

Bonnie has invited me to a late lunch with her and two girl-friends, Paula and Mandy. The restaurant, a popular regional chain, features ribs and chicken wings as its greasy, heart-attack-inducing specials. A B. B. King tune blares in the background. The restaurant's logo is a smiling pig in sunglasses and a flirty chicken. Bonnie likes this place and so do her two BBW friends, who are Southern, friendly, and loud. These girls like the zest that comes with life and they aren't shy about showing it. While we wait for a table, Paula, a thirtyish blonde-haired blue-eyed nurse who would easily top out at three hundred pounds, whoops and hollers about the hot guy she sees across the way.

"Double-dog dare you to go over there and ask for his phone number," Mandy, a short brunette with a jagged shag cut, says.

Paula, who wears a lot of brown eyeshadow and a neutral shade of lipstick, laughs. "Girl, you don't think I will, do you? You should know me better than that. I see something I want, I go for it." Paula snaps her fingers like she is some sort of black sistah.

"She's crazy," Bonnie says to me.

"Oh, yeah, I'm a nut. Should be locked up . . ." Paula trails off as she heads over to the man who is looking at all four of us.

In the time it takes to say "hot-wing basket," Paula has sashayed up to this preppy John in his polo shirt and khaki pants and talked him into buying her a drink. She looks over at us and winks. Amazing. Most women over two hundred pounds, especially in the South, would think themselves not pretty enough or too fat to just make a move on a stranger in a restaurant. But not these gals. No way. They are big, bold, and beautiful and they capture the bull of life by his horny horns.

Mandy claims to have slept with seventeen men, several of whom discovered her on the Internet. From their online rendezvous, romance, or at least sexual attraction, bloomed and before long Mandy found herself falling into bed with an array of men as if she were a James Bond babe. She likes to be spanked, and for me, flashes of Alabama pour into my mind. I try to shake the images of large women getting their flabby butts spanked as we move toward our table. Paula doesn't join us. She's still too busy flirting with Mr. Polo.

Bonnie sits across from me at the table and smiles.

"We like to have fun, what can we say?"

It's nice to be around women who are not always second-guessing themselves and who show extreme confidence in their sexual skin — acres of it.

Paula finally joins us.

"So you going home with him?" Mandy asks.

"Hardly, he's married," Paula says. "But I think he liked what he saw."

I get the feeling Paula may be saying all of this for my benefit and, as soon as the Death by Chocolate dessert is eaten, she and Mr. Polo may hook up at the Ramada Inn to do the nasty.

These women enjoy the hell out of sex, and they are some of the most frank women I've ever met. Yes, they like the occasional one-night stand, at least one of them has cheated on her boyfriend with another woman, and one of them makes it her goal to attend Sunday school at least three times a month. They say that for too many years they lived in the narrow shadow of skinny women, but those days are long gone. No doubt these women are a handful in more ways than one.

BBW parties are new to South Carolina. Such events have been trendy in Atlanta for several years, but not in this small state that launched the Civil War and holds on to quiet tradition and romantic myth. What is a BBW party? Let's take a look.

First, a BBW party consists of, well, big beautiful women who don't obsess over the scales so much as they do over who brought the yummy calorie-laden spinach dip and pita chips. BBW parties are held in hotels, backyards, local bars, and homes and sometimes feature a theme of sorts — '80s retro night, luau with leis, disco divas. Of course, a BBW party filled with plump princesses won't work without FAs — lots of them — worshipping the Round Royalty. Because of the Internet — yes, the common thread in the far-reaching galaxy of fetishes and sex — women and men discover love, or lust, a lot more easily than in the days of personal ads and phone sex. One admirer wrote on a Web site that the party atmosphere of one BBW group is a safe haven for BBWs, BHMs, and their corresponding admirers. He said his heart belonged to the group for creating such wonderful social activities.

Some of the parties are innocent, simple gatherings with just BBWs chatting, meeting new friends, having lunch, or swapping clothes they don't want in their closets any longer. Other BBWs go to great lengths to plan parties that consist of blocked hotel rooms. To go one step further, some BBWs have created parties on water: cruises. Yes, three-day cruises from Florida to the Bahamas for BBWs and their admirers, where they let everything hang out.

Bonnie has attended a few BBW events in other states but hasn't yet been to any of the local parties. She's not sure if she will go to them or not. She enjoys cutting loose at the occasional wet T-shirt contest without having to worry too much about her actions haunting her later on if someone she knows should see her.

"I trust my friends, but I'm not sure I trust other women. Sure, it looks like a sisterhood, but you can never tell down here," she says. "You steal someone's honey or flirt with him, and they'll come after your head."

To get the lowdown on the sexual world of BBWs, I decide to track down Mendi Teats, a well-known thirtyish goddess in BBW circles. Her Web sites entice a loyal band of men, and many larger women look to Mendi as a role model. She lives in Florida, the daughter of a preacher man, and now has two children of her own. Mendi, who has modeled sans clothing in *Juggs* and *Big Butt* magazines, isn't reluctant to dish the scoop about the secrets of a BBW sex kitten.

Let's talk stereotypes for a moment. Who likes big women? Black men. The larger the better for some. Hispanic men. They prefer large hips and tiny waists, with a twist of vamp. Twiggy men. What's a twiggy man? An ultrathin dude who doesn't have an ounce of body fat on him.

Who doesn't? Jocks and insecure men.

"Typically, men who like BBWs are more the businessman type, the men who have really gotten to know what they like and are comfortable with themselves, thus are able to be comfortable in a society setting with a large woman," Mendi explains.

Prince Charming, however, isn't always strutting up to BBWs to rescue them from a society that often treats large women like unsexy piles of dirt. Many BBWs actually find themselves in verbal and mentally abusive relationships with men who push them into a downtrodden state. Often, these weakened BBWs find themselves in a "feeder situation." A what?

The feeder scene is a fetish in its own right, usually consisting of a man who likes big women and a small woman who can be fed. This, Mendi explains, goes beyond just admiring an overweight woman; a feeder likes to watch a woman grow bigger and bigger — sometimes reaching six or seven hundred pounds. Feeders buy their women, or as they like to call them, feedees, clothes that are two or three sizes too big so the BBWs can grow into and out of them quickly. The bigger the better. A measurement around 61-53-72 is a good average. Feeders like their women to eat high-calorie meals. Creamy, luscious desserts are never off-limits, and exercise is always discouraged. Eat a big meal and go to bed. For a long time. Gain weight, please.

Oh. My. God. I've never heard of such a thing.

"Oh, yeah, there are women out there who love it or say they love it. In my opinion, they love it because they are getting the attention of a man. I don't think it's healthy. A lot of these men want these women to be six or seven hundred pounds. That's getting in overboard, and that's the point where it's getting scary. But there are people who love it whether it's safe or not."

I thought I had heard it all but this is a new one on me. An all-you-can-eat buffet takes on an entirely new role in my mind.

Mendi has always been a big girl.

During her first and only marriage, Mendi's life took an interesting turn. One day, while pregnant and living in New Jersey, she discovered her husband's porn stash in the bedroom.

Outraged and wanting to dump him for the betrayal, Mendi had a talk with him. Have an open mind, he said. She agreed to look at some of the nudie mags. What she discovered shocked even her. She looked as good, or better, than some of the models, especially the pregnant ones. You should model, the husband said. She replied, "I don't have a body like that. If I ever have a Pamela Anderson type body I'll pose."

Pregnant and round, Mendi realized she did have a body that might work in the magazines. She and her husband snapped some erotic pictures and Mendi took them to the offices of *Juggs* magazine. One morning she received a call.

"Can you be here next week for a photo shoot?" an editor asked her.

Mendi's reply: Sure.

On her way to the magazine, Mendi had a car wreck. Mendi, who believes in fate, karma, destiny, and all that good ying-yang, took the accident as a sign. Shaken, she decided it wise to visit the hospital rather than show up for the shoot. She went to the hospital, and she and her baby were fine. She couldn't forget about the possibility of a modeling career, though.

"I had gotten myself worked up to do it and wanted to do it," she says.

She called the magazine but received this message: Don't call us, we'll call you. The editors thought Mendi was lying, trying to find a way out of the gig. She didn't take no for an answer. She faxed them the accident report. This time, they believed her and set a date for a photo shoot.

Nerves consumed Mendi, then in her early twenties, when she arrived at the studio. She was sure the photographer was a deviant, a pervert with an agenda. But when some women in garters and heels walked by and he didn't give them a second glance, Mendi realized this was just a job for him.

"I had so much fun, an absolute blast, but I wasn't going to do it again. Once was enough," she says.

But the magazine rang again. "When are we setting the next date?" the editors asked.

"Whenever you want it," she replied.

That was the beginning of Mendi Teats, housewife, becoming Mendi Teats, voluptuous adult fantasy. Mendi has risen through the ranks of adult entertainment. She has appeared on many television talk shows, sometimes discussing BBW life, other times performing tricks like squashing Twinkies with her butt.

"Some of it was demeaning, but I say any publicity is good publicity. My message: You don't have to be a BBW and be negative. You don't have to take everything as a put-down. A lot of BBWs need to understand and not let people get to them just because they are fat. A fat chick can have any man she wants; it's just about attitude. With a good attitude you can get what you want. You dress well, you put your makeup on, and you don't care about what people are thinking — you just get out there and have fun."

Said like a true diva.

Call me lily-livered but I don't have the guts to ask BBWs how fat people have sex. I've always wondered about this, but the thought especially occurs when I see one particularly fleshy couple having lunch in a Little Rock bistro. How do they do the horizontal tango? My mission is clear: Find out how oversized people have sex. Do their bellies get in the way? Is there a perfect position? Is it better if one person is a twiggy?

Thank goodness for *Dimensions* magazine, the bible for all things BBW. According to *Dimensions,* sex can be a logistical nightmare when dealing with a certain amount of blubber that gets in the way. Still, fat people do have sex, even in the missionary position. Say the woman is larger than the man. The missionary position still works. I'm trying hard to imagine this. Sexologists say if the woman will just completely expose the goodies between her legs, it should work. Oh, and if the tummy is too big? She can lift it up from her nether region so her man can get positioned. This is not something I want to see in a porn video.

A BBW can be on top without crushing her partner like a cockroach. Some BBWs top the scales at five or six hundred pounds. Their secret? Tuck the BBWs belly up around her partner's neck like a blanket. Now there's an image that'll stay with me for a long time. Doggy style? Yep, it works for BBWs. All the lover has to do is position himself just so and hold up his tummy while thrusting. Also, the woman can stand up and raise one leg for better entry. But if the lover has a short unit, forget about it. Sex for BBWs and BHMs is all about pushing, pulling, tucking, and tugging a few inches here and there before the mutton dagger can seize the happy valley.

NeeCee Belle, a BBW and Southern Charm who lives near the third hole of the Bible Belt, says that she prefers being on top, but it has nothing to do with size.

"I feel like I am in control, and I love to be in control," says NeeCee, a five-foot-one, 240-pound buxom blonde housewife with a Southern drawl. "But, I like all positions, except sixty-nine. I love giving oral sex as much as receiving it, but I prefer to just give as I can concentrate more on my partner. I am not being distracted about what is going on with me."

NeeCee, forty-four, says she prefers a larger man to a twiggy for two reasons. First, her preference goes back to a sexual encounter with an older man when she was sixteen. The man was tall, six-foot-seven, with a large frame. The experience stuck with her, and to this day, she prefers a larger man. Secondly, NeeCee does confess that she fears hurting a smaller guy. Understandable. She pauses: "I wouldn't rule them out completely 'cause if I did I might miss some really great sex."

It's not just men, though. NeeCee likes girls, too.

"It's not that I prefer a woman for her size," she says. "It is usually the personality that clicks, not how much she tips the scales But, I do prefer an all-natural woman."

In other words, plastic surgery babes need not flirt with NeeCee Belle.

"I like real women, physically and personality-wise, too. I like an honest woman. One that is playful, bubbly, and out-going but isn't overbearing," she says.

Regarding size, NeeCee says, "Two full-figured people have sex the same way as non-full-figured. I haven't run into any problems yet."

NeeCee Belle and Mendi could teach Bonnie a lesson or two in driving in the BBW fast lane. Bonnie has aspirations to pose naked for some pictures. She says that she and Joe have taken a few already. They may or may not post them on the Internet. As we say good-bye in the restaurant's park-ing lot, Bonnie and her friends pile into her two-door red sports car. Until now, I hadn't noticed the glittery blue license plate on the front — WholeLottaLove. With attitude in drive, Bonnie and the girls speed off in search of chaos and the certain debauchery that is sure to always follow this trio of BBWs.

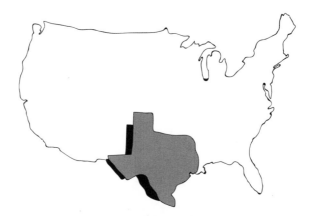

texas

two sisters
teaching love

Stripping, Seduction, and Suburbia

FORT WORTH, TEXAS — I feel like the wise oracle tonight.

Whenever I've watched *Sex and the City*, I've imagined myself as Carrie Bradshaw — also known as Sarah Jessica Parker — the hip sex writer. Okay, so I'm not that skinny, I wouldn't wear some of the things she does, and I don't have that many boyfriends. Still, that's how I usually imagine myself in my group of friends.

But not tonight.

This evening, call me Samantha, the sexy curvy wild character who is all the wiser thanks to age. I'm not sure I like that last one but as I sit here surrounded by three young twentysomethings, Alexa, Karen, and Suzanne, I'm clearly playing the role of elder stateswoman.

We've gathered in a funky mod Little Rock apartment with a wicked view of the Arkansas River to watch a video I've brought. Karen, a short brunette with wide brown eyes, is so excited, she's twirling around like a little girl seeing the *Nutcracker* for the first time. Alexa, a sexy blonde with to-die-for legs who fancies short skirts and high heels, is busy chatting on the telephone. Suzanne, a no-nonsense kind of woman with short brown hair and au naturel makeup, isn't sure what she has gotten herself into but looks happy enough. The video, produced by The Women's Institute of Learning in Fort Worth, Texas, will teach us everything we need to know about stripping for the men we love. Or at least are in lust with.

"I can't wait, can't wait to see this," Karen says. "This is going to be so much fun."

The gist of the video is this: You, ordinary woman, are good enough to strip. You don't need to be the great worrier about intimate encounters. You don't have to fret that your hips are too big, your thighs too dimpled, or breasts too small, big, or saggy. Wrinkles and gray hair worries be gone! After this, we should all feel like Delilah, seductive and alluring as we chase our Samsons.

There's even a booklet and compact disc accompanying the video. The booklet tells us that men like all sorts of women, tall, short, fat, thin, dark, light, boyish, Marilyn Monroe curvy. It also advises us to never apologize for the way we look naked and never reject a compliment. Good advice — he's probably happy that you're naked.

The founders of the institute want their strippers to look good and not perform a striptease in flannel pajamas. That's the obvious reason why they include suggestions on what to wear. Recommended: high heels. Why? Women who wear them jiggle. That's a good thing for a man. Men love red high heels. Va-voom! If you want to go Middle Eastern and dance barefoot, by all means give those tootsies a pedicure before the big event. Toe rings add an exotic touch.

From there, slip on some sheer hose, but remember one rule: Hose should never be a darker shade than the shoes. Don't wear big earrings or necklaces. They get in the way and will hit you and him in painful places at the wrong time.

Go dainty: pearls, black velvet choker, a locket. Or wear the big diamond he gave you. After all, when it's all said and done, that's all that you'll be wearing.

Oh, boy! Lingerie. Men love it. No news flash there. Don't worry about matching too much. Men care more about what's underneath. Let's go!

Free your mind, sistah, and the rest will follow.

The video has begun. Ssshhh. The trio of young women won't hush, though, but that's okay. Nothing major is happening on the video. An overly perky woman with brown hair in a business skirt and blouse tells us in a soft, caring voice that she and her two assistants will teach us how to make a seductive entrance — it never hurts to make a head or two turn. She's very conservative-looking; she could be a Republican intern. From there, we'll learn teasing and blouse removal, sexy skirt removal, and sensuous bra removal. Watch out Torchy Taboo, here I come.

The woman struts in, swiveling her hips with her two back-up dancers following her every move. Karen starts to giggle.

"What is this?" she asks incredulously.

"Who would do this?" Alexa asks to no one in particular. They both take sips of wine.

Hmmm. I might do it. Never know when you may be asked to dance on a table somewhere. From there, we learn how to tease with a strut and remove our blouses. Now, I don't think you can ever be too sexy, but of course, I grew up reading a lot of *Cosmopolitan* magazines and Judith Krantz novels, so glam, glitzy, seductive romance makes me a happy girl.

"Look at how cheesy these women look," says Suzanne. "Do people really do this?"

I try to explain to them that if a woman got married at, say, twenty-one, a very common age to tie the knot here in Dixie, that by thirty-one, she might really need to do something to spice up their bedroom activities.

"I wouldn't do this, though," says one of them.

They think it's sad and pathetic if a relationship comes down to having to perform like this. Ah, young minds. If only they had heard some of the tales that I have: wives holding out on sex for two years, husbands seeking solace elsewhere, both spouses complaining, almost in tears, about missionary-position boredom. For them, a striptease might be just what the love doctor ordered. But my young friends aren't buying it.

Karen says her boyfriend would laugh her out of the bedroom. "If it took this long to get out of my clothes, he might be asleep by the time I finish," she says. If he gets bored at looking at a naked woman, hmmm . . . might want to get out the gaydar.

The women on the screen make it look so easy to remove a business skirt while rolling their heads and cha-chaing. Not sure if I could do it without the zipper getting stuck or some other disaster occurring. When the bra removal part rolls onto the screen, the women reveal nothing because they're wearing flesh-colored bras underneath. Complete nudity would offend the women viewers, I'm guessing, especially in the South.

"This is so tame," Karen says. "They aren't even going to strip."

True, it is tame — innocent, at times, more reminiscent of

a workout video. If it were hardcore, though, women would be intimidated. Certainly, it would make them feel uncomfortable and a bit shameful.

"No way would I do this," Alexa says firmly.

"Uh-uh, who buys this video?" Karen asks.

"Probably schoolteachers, or women who have been married a long time, but I can't imagine standing in front of the mirror practicing this," Suzanne says.

"I've heard about women having parties where they actually practice stripping with each other so they can see if they are doing an okay job," I say.

No way. I've got to be kidding, they say in unison.

Nope, somewhere in someone's living room, probably at this very moment, a group of women are attempting to take off their bras while rolling their shoulders and batting their eyelashes.

At the end of the night, the consensus vote: This is pathetic.

For twenty-four hours, I ponder the *For His Eyes Alone* video in its sleek, well-designed black and pink cover. Sticking it in the VCR, I practice a few of the moves, hoping to get down the strut and the turns. Cracking myself up, I practice raising my hands over my head in a seductive manner before mastering the buttons on my shirt. I twist and shimmy to the salsa music. This could, given the right atmosphere, be fun. If no one took it too seriously, and if I didn't get my high heel caught in my sheer hose and rip a runner the size of the Panama Canal.

The wise woman in me can't help but think I am right, and the trio of twenty-somethings is wrong. Men would like it if a woman stripped for them. Wouldn't they? With time on my hands, I decide to take a poll. First stop, Dylan, who knows all things male.

Question: What would you think if a woman you liked or was involved with performed a striptease for you?

Dylan responds just as I suspected a man would.

"If I walked in and a girl did a full-on striptease for me, I'd be fired up about it on two levels. One, it'd be kind of touching that she thought about me long enough to put together a routine. It's kinda cool to think that she's thinking of me even when I'm not around. Two, I'd be fired up because it's pretty much a lock that I'm getting laid. It was *her* idea — how often does that happen in real life?"

Like Perry Mason, I can't say the case is closed just yet.

Next up: Nick, the foot-fetish enthusiast. Not surprisingly, Nick says, "Not my bag."

Louis, a burly guy who has been married for nearly seven years, inquires eagerly, "Are you asking if my wife teamed up with other women to do a striptease for me?"

Eh, no, that wasn't the question, Louis. Just your wife performing for you after you spent a long day languishing at the office.

"Oh, that would be absolutely awesome. I mean, I am not a huge strip-club guy but that would be extremely arousing."

Bill, my divorced friend who hated the Miss Kitty's experience, chimes in with his answer the next day when I ask him. "Oh, I think it would be good if she was any good at it. Otherwise it could be embarrassing."

Eek. That's scary. What woman wants to be judged when she is attempting to slip out of stockings and a garter belt? I can see why some women would be scared to attempt this. Of course, I'm pretty fearless about most things, most of the time.

My good friend Christopher, whose marriage isn't always the happiest, says he isn't so sure about the whole stripping idea. "I think, unless she's a professional dancer, I'd be less than comfortable. I mean, if it's not something she's done before, I'd be worried about her being worried about what I was thinking. Well, I suppose that'd be the case if I were sober. Things could be entirely different after a few drinks."

In the end it depends on the woman, he says.

Just like anything sexual, a striptease is a gamble depending on the two people. Right time, right place, right mind-set, right couple. Still curious, I decide I've got to meet the people behind The Women's Institute of Learning.

Fort Worth is a city that is one part modern, with state-of-the-art glass museums and skyscrapers, and one part cowboy central, where cows and horses still mean as much as they did during the days of the Old West. It's more friendly and folksy than nearby Dallas, a place that has become an artificial metropolis filled with designer clothes, cosmetic surgery, big money, and even bigger hair. Fort Worth has a lot of things: The National Cowgirl Museum and Hall of Fame, the Stockyards, a history of cowboys and oilmen, and spicy hot salsa. It doesn't have a Women's Institute of Learning, at least in the bricks-and-mortar sense of place. It's all about ideas, existing in the abstract.

Meet the minds behind the video: Paulette Belmore and Kitty Eckardt, two sisters who happen to be mothers and grandmothers. Their mission: to teach women a few lessons in plain old common-sense seduction.

Paulette suggested we meet on a March morning for Sunday brunch at the Colonial Country Club, a historical plush spot in Fort Worth surrounded by an incredible and famous lush-green golf course. It's appropriate I've ended up at a country club, considering such places are sexual hotbeds for well-to-do Southerners who thrive on social events like garden parties, elaborate balls, and weekly cocktail parties.

We sit in an informal room overlooking the golf club and chat as church-attired people begin to filter in for lunch. Paulette is dressed conservatively, casual in nice, rich-black slacks and a vivid blue plaid jacket with a turtleneck underneath it. She has short blonde hair streaked with placed-just-right highlights. Kitty wears brown slacks and a green sweater. Both sisters carry expensive designer handbags. Enough chitchat — I want to know how two former Tri Delt sorority girls decided to make a video to enhance women's sex lives.

The project was hatched two summers ago beside a swimming pool just down the way from where we are sitting. Paulette was lying out in the Texas sun gossiping with her girl-friends, and the conversation continually looped back to — what else? — sex. Paulette, a divorcée who shattered the glass ceiling of a telecommunications firm years ago, and her friends found themselves talking about ways to spice up their love lives. One of the common complaints focused on a women's magazine that suggested a woman strip for her man but didn't give details.

The lightbulb zapped over Paulette's head. Why not create such a video, so that women of all ages could watch and learn? Always one to lure her older sister into plots and adventures, Paulette called Kitty, who lives in a small town between Dallas and Houston, and explained the project.

"I didn't hesitate. I said, 'Count me in,'" Kitty says.

But don't think the sisters just pooled their money, called a videographer, and started filming. They thought about their project — really thought about it.

"Women can be offended," Paulette says. "They will buy stuff, though, that is under the guise of education. A lot of women go and buy striptease videos, and all they center on are boobs and bottoms. You never see feet. Women don't care about boobs and bottoms if they are trying to learn a striptease; they need to learn a dance. I wanted to make this video in such a way that women would want to learn and perform it."

Their target? Not the skilled stripper, but rather the soccer mom who wants a new way to initiate a bedroom romp.

"A professional stripper would never use this," Kitty chimes in. "This is for people who don't have poles in their living rooms."

Paulette didn't waste any time with her project. She decided to visit strip clubs, watch the strippers' movements, and see what the men liked the most. Paulette visited so frequently that some of the girls in the clubs started to wave at her. I'm trying to imagine this Donna Karan–wearing grandmother visiting a sleazy joint like the one Dylan and I ventured into in Memphis. It's hard, but if I squint enough I can sorta imagine it. But only sorta.

"Sometimes men want to see things in a club that they would never want their wives to do at home," she explains. "Some men like to keep their wives on a pedestal, but that doesn't mean they don't want their wives to indulge them with some tease and dance, though. That's the kind of stuff we took into consideration."

Flashing back to Platinum Plus in Memphis, I can see how some men might not want their wives to wrap their legs around the heads of their golfing buddies. But would the husbands want their wives to try to wrap their legs around *their* balding heads after a long day at the office? What man wouldn't want to see his wife enjoy a little girl-girl action? But maybe there are more men out there who are prudes than I thought. Naturally, I think, most Southern men want their wives to behave like Melanies, but they will pay to see strippers act like Scarletts.

Fact One: Men like to see women touch themselves. That is hammered home in the video and the booklet, but it's subdued touching, safe touching. So many women, though, are apparently scared to touch what God gave them, especially in the company of a man. Paulette hopes that with simple lessons teaching women how to do this, blended with mysterious teasing moves à la Gyspy Rose Lee, women will discover a new comfort level in their sexuality.

Let's hope so. For the sake of suburbanites everywhere.

Richard Simmons probably doesn't know he had anything to do with inspiring a stripping video, but he did. Kitty, a retired teacher who earned a master's degree in special education, studied Simmons's classic *Sweating to the Oldies* tape and counted how many dance steps were in each segment. She actually used her teaching methods, normally for students with developmental disabilities or attention deficit disorder, to break down the steps in an easy-to-follow tutorial for the hapless housewife.

From there, the pair discovered a Chicago choreographer who could put the movements to the steps in a sequence. It's easier to remember that way. The sisters created a package that provides a comfort zone for the shy woman who craves for her husband's eyes to ravish her as she removes lacy undergarments.

Fact Two: The tape isn't to be watched, it is to be done. Like an aerobics tape.

"It's not boring if you are doing it," Paulette says. "This is not to be watched; it's not pornographic. Get up there and shake your booty and do it."

Ahh. That's what went awry the night I watched it with the three young babes. No one dared stand up and shimmy their hips. As if reading my mind, Paulette says that one woman wrote and said she was bored when she watched it.

"Of course, she was bored . . ." Paulette says.

"Who says I'm going to go entertain myself and watch Richard Simmons?" Kitty chimes in, laughing.

Paulette attempted to get a business loan for the project at the bank, but found that a lot of banks wouldn't finance something that teetered on "pornography." Excuse me? I've seen porn; I've even seen R-rated movies. This video isn't even as racy as some Disney cartoons. Still, any time the word "stripping" is mentioned, especially in the South, you better know that many minds go straight to Gutterville.

At the last minute, a family member swooped in to save the day and loaned Paulette the money for her venture. From there, Paulette hired a film company in Dallas to shoot the video. Paulette and Kitty had to keep a sharp eye on the all-male production team, who tended to lose focus on filming the feet and inevitably shifted the camera to the dancers' breasts.

"I'd say 'A woman can't learn to dance if she's looking there,'" Paulette says with a chuckle. "They'd go, 'Oh yeah, oh yeah' and then remember to start shooting the feet again."

The instructors on the tape look like women from the grocery store or from a neighboring cubicle in any office. That's on purpose. According to Paulette and Kitty, some women feel insecure and intimidated if they have to watch beautiful thin Barbie dolls teach them how to strip.

Women never cease to amaze me. In the booklet that accompanies the video, there's point #17 for the woman who may not exactly understand what she's doing. Point #17 says, "You will notice that the dancers in the video are wearing body stockings. It's doubtful you don't already know, but just in case: You will *not* be wearing a body stocking when you perform the dance for your man."

Surely women aren't that dumb. But maybe. Melanie in *Gone with the Wind* was quite the modest mouse.

This is not porn, but try telling that to some newspaper editors in the South. Since the tape premiered, many editors have shied away from reviewing it, fearing the backlash from readers who might be offended that the morning newspaper is telling them to strip for their man. Paulette and Kitty think it might be hard for me to believe this, but I tell them I was deposed about sex and thrown off public television for writing about it. I feel their pain.

Porn doesn't save marriages, nor do sex toys, or blue aphrodisiac drinks from Sweden. Neither will this video. Paulette and Kitty make sure I know this. Stripping, no matter how many times you do it, will not save a marriage that is already sinking into the muddy waters of divorce court. Women can roll themselves in Saran Wrap or swing from the chandelier in a latex catsuit, but if a marriage is over, it's kaput.

Fortunately, the sisters have received some positive media reviews from around the country, even in the South. They've also gotten a few cutting remarks from feminists. Alert: If you are a feminist, don't try to tell Paulette she's taking the movement back thirty years by telling women to strip for the men they love.

"That's like saying women don't like, or women shouldn't like, sex," Paulette says. "That's denying that whole part of womanhood. We have worked very hard to have the freedom to do what we want to do, to go through the loan process — fifty years ago that wouldn't have been possible — to go into any kind of occupation we want to, to be able to rise as high as our ability allows us to in a company, to be able to buy a house and live on our own. We couldn't do that twenty or thirty years ago. We have gone through a lot to do that, but that we have done that doesn't discount the fact that we are women, and women love relationships and women care about relationships. Women are sexual animals and they deserve to have exciting, fun, liberating sex. That need in a woman doesn't prevent her from being a feminist and accomplishing everything out there. Once you talk to them that way, they look inside themselves and they see that."

The irony surrounding the videotape for Paulette is that she has yet to find a beau for whom to perform her striptease. Life! Kitty, on the other hand, is married to a lawyer and former mayor of a small east Texas town. The more conservative of the pair, Kitty kept her project a secret from her friends for a while. But she eventually told them. After all, her friends had worried about the frequent trips Kitty made to Dallas, never really explaining why she was going.

" 'Thank God,' they said. 'We thought someone in the family had a terminal illness and you just didn't want to tell us.' " Southerners — we always fear the worst, and inevitably receive the strange.

Kitty admits that she was scared about what people would think in her small town if they found out she, a proper Southern woman, was producing a video about stripping. "It's still very ladylike down where I live," she says. Kitty is the type of Southern woman who still cooks lunch every day for her husband, throws little lady luncheons at her home, and hosts intimate dinner parties. She worries that someone in her small town may go bonkers and protest what she has done. But Kitty says she doesn't lose a lot of sleep over it. She's a big girl and a Texas woman and she can take whatever is slung at her.

These women grew up in an idyllic Southern world. Their parents were madly in love with each other. Their dad, a night pilot, would come home from flying early in the morning and sweep their mom off to the bedroom for a few hours. Sex was never discussed but the young girls knew what was going on. Their parents, who are still alive, weren't always affectionate in front of the girls, but that was because they were Southern and very proper.

"It was all so romantic and very healthy," Paulette says.

"We were very lucky," Kitty says.

At Kitty's recent fortieth class reunion, classmates routinely asked about her parents, who had left an impression on them at a young age. They remembered the happy couple taking them waterskiing and drinking Grapette by the gallon, which her parents bought on a regular basis.

That kind of relationship is what Paulette and Kitty want to spread through the South and the rest of the country and world. It's working. The shyest of Southern women are buying the video and writing to tell the sisters about their attempts at outperforming the most experienced stripper. They won't say explicitly what's going on when they try out their act in the bedroom, but one customer said that she stripped for her husband and "when it was all over, well, let's just say he was 'ready.' "

Ahh, Southern women and their euphemisms.

Back in my living room, I'm at it again, trying to master the passe pointe, head roll, cha-cha-cha. I took ten years of dance, and this is hard. I laugh, imagining some of the Junior Leaguers who lunch at my favorite restaurant trying this in their interior-decorated homes. I won't give up. I'm determined to perfect the seductive entrance, the tease, the blouse and skirt removal, and the most important: the sensuous bra removal. It might take a while, but I won't give up. My goal: not to strip for a man but just to know that if the fifty-five-year-old wife in Plano, Texas, can do this, so can I.

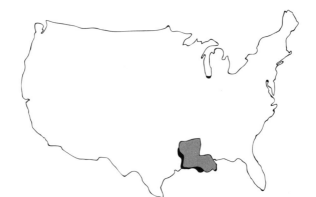

louisiana

saints and sinners talk sex

Gennifer Flowers and Radical Faeries

NEW ORLEANS, LOUISIANA — Free condoms with funky wrappers always, always catch my eye. Did I say always? I'm not sure why, but they do. Maybe it's because condoms represent illicit sex. When I see a basket of Saints and Sinners condoms, I know this is the event for me.

I arrive at O'Flaherty's, an Irish pub with the quintessential French Quarter courtyard, when the workshops are already in progress at the Saints and Sinners Literary Festival. Getting my registration packet — and free condoms — I stroll into the courtyard where a saleswoman peddles books, and piles of gay literature and information sit on a table. A hot pink bookmark catches my eye. It's advertising *The Gay Herman Melville Reader,* a new anthology of Melville's gayest moments. Huh? I'm no Melville scholar so I confess I'm ignorant about the gay moments in *Moby Dick.* Although, on reflection, Bartleby always seemed a little light in the loafers.

In the courtyard, I spot a tattooed waif in a yellow dress. She wears mod glasses and chunky shoes, de rigueur for the creative type. She introduces herself as Michelle from San Francisco. I'm mesmerized by her tattoos, especially a complex rendering of an intergalactic world with planets and UFOs. The hot New Orleans sun beats down on our heads. I'm more used to it than this West Coast wafer in front of me. She's sweating already, and it's only morning.

"Oh, oh, you have a feather on your glasses," she says, leaning into me to pluck the feather that has fallen on me from the sky.

Another part of the feather lands in my hair. With careful grace, she strips away the tiny plume. I acknowledge the kindness with a grateful smile.

It's only later that I wonder: Was she flirting with me?

The Saints and Sinners Literary Festival is the first one of its kind — gay, lesbian, bisexual, transgender — in New Orleans. Shocking to me that it's the first, since I always imagine this city, often referred to as the Sodom of the South, as both the gay and literary mecca of Dixie. My gay friends who live in the small-town South think that New Orleans is a twenty-four seven gay smorgasbord, loaded with lots of public displays of affection and gay bars on every corner. They are mistaken about the Crescent City.

The only time, besides Mardi Gras, that it's really like that is at the bawdy Southern Decadence festival, a yearly late-summer event that sees gay and straight revelers celebrating gay life. Halloween also offers a respite from conservative lifestyles, when the gay community comes alive with circuit parties. Tourists can indulge in a gay heritage tour hosted by a Southern gentleman named Robert Bates, who wears a silk white suit and a white fedora. A poster of him at this literary conference bears a strange resemblance to a country lawyer I know in south Arkansas who has a love for seersucker suits in the summer.

But day in, day out, the gay community of New Orleans is not a force to be reckoned with, certainly not in a league with San Francisco's. If I go to the local grocery store in the Garden District, I'm not going to see lots of out-of-the-closet gays or lesbians holding hands and shopping for paper products. Surprisingly, only one gay literary bookstore — that isn't a cruising type place — even calls New Orleans home, and it's on its last leg.

Being gay in New Orleans is just as hard as in any place else in the South. Maybe more so. Not only does it have the Bible Belt looming around its edges, the city proper has more than enough Catholic churches and cemeteries — to remind one of eternal damnation — to make anyone feel guilty.

In the dark upstairs of O'Flaherty's, gay poets and writers prepare to take the stage. I've never heard of gay witchcraft in my life, but that's what's on tap to kick off this reading session. Christopher Penczak, a dark-haired, dark-eyed recovering Catholic gay pagan from the Northeast, hits the small stage. This is his first reading ever, he says, explaining that he normally teaches spells to crowds like us. He teaches spells? Outside of Hogwarts? My Harry Potter radar has kicked in. Alas, I am soon wishing for a longer attention-span spell.

I tune out at some point between finding my soul mate in this life or a past life and walking from the light into the dark or something like that. Penczak tells us about a spell he used to lure his husband to him eight years ago. Something about one red rose and dragon blood. Wacky.

Next, an older South Carolinian tells us how he usually writes hardcore erotica but today has chosen something more sentimental to share. The story is about a teenage boy whose father has caught him with another boy. The father is distraught and angry, the son devastated. The only understanding, rational person is a grandfather who sits down with the teenager. Come to find out, the grandfather, for years, had a torrid secret affair with a fellow shipmate from their days in World War II. They swore to be true to each other and stayed in touch after the war ended. They married and while they loved their wives, it was never the same as what they had together.

The two men visited each other often, although they lived in separate states. Their wives thought they were fishing, but they often snuck away to a nearby motor inn to spend the afternoon making love. Grandpa even named his son — the father of the teenager — after his lover. The reason, explains the Grandpa, that the father might be so upset at his son is because history repeated itself. The father had walked in on his father and the shipmate one afternoon during a romp at their house. The father and son never discussed what had occurred. At the end of the story, the author is visibly upset and tears brim in his eyes. That's like no Hallmark moment I've ever experienced. Now, I can't stop thinking about my uncles who were in the military and the possible secret stories that they took with them to the grave.

My new friend Michelle stands in front of us in her yellow dress to read a story about too much flag waving and patriotism after September 11, 2001. Earlier, I heard her say that her boyfriend was transgender. I'm trying to get a handle on how that works as she reads, but my mind continually replays past family reunions, thanks to the previous reader's story. My head hurts, I'm so confused.

My mental slide show of uncles and aunts is still running when a short guy with a shaved head takes the microphone. It's Brad Richard, celebrity poet of this powwow. He's won many prestigious literary awards and everyone in the room seems to know him. The minute he speaks he sounds exactly like Kevin Spacey in *American Beauty*. Exactly. If Kevin Spacey came down with laryngitis, Brad Richard could fill in for a voice-over. He reads amazing poems about how everyone has a little secret. He shares with us that his favorite Greek mythical character is Hermes, a complex figure who isn't just a messenger god but also a guide for souls in Hades. His poems have cool titles like "Go-Go Boy Circle Jerk" and "My Sixth Grade Sex Life." Damn, if this guy were straight, I'd have a crush. Can you have a crush on a gay guy? (Note to self: Watch more *Will and Grace*.)

After he speaks, my mind has forgotten possible gay family members and now skips and sashays with dancing poetic images. Soon the readings end and I find myself following Mr. Richard to the next event — From the Erotic to the Divine: Poetry as Sacred Song of Sexuality — at the Shim Sham Club, a popular venue for burlesque. I'm not sure what this will center on; something about poetry as a sacred song by gays. But at least I can keep an eye on my new crush.

A silver lamé curtain shimmies to create a crazy hologram behind the speakers. The psychedelic drape and the chatter about Socrates hanging out with groups of gay guys talking about levels of sex and love and how one can see glimpses of the divine in other people makes my head feel woozy. Then, something catches my ear: a radical faerie gathering! What in the name of Zeus is that?

Before I can even wonder, a poet is reading his own creation written at one of these gatherings. Sounds like *A Midsummer's Night Dream* complete with anal sex, full mouths filled with kissing, and boys' magical seeds dripping over pieces of fruit. Something tells me this wouldn't play well back in Little Rock.

A Radical Faerie Gathering has no rules or schedules. They can last from a weekend to a month at campgrounds located in the boonies or on private property. Faeries like to call "circles," which let the men have group meditation, pass around symbolic items, or talk about feelings or dreams.

I'm told that a big gathering of faeries happens somewhere in rural Tennessee in the spring. Makes sense: The flowers are pretty that time of year.

Like the hippie communes of yore, these gatherings are all about forgoing inhibitions and exploring every aspect of being gay. Men dress in drag or casual clothes, or bask in nudity. Some make their own faerie wings — I kid you not — which serve as symbols in the faerie world, where they also christen themselves with new names.

I wonder silently when the next one is, and if I could pass as a gay man. Probably not. But it might be fun to try.

After that workshop, Mr. Richard (I feel like I have to address a poet of his caliber this way) and I sit in the dark Irish pub chatting about gay life in New Orleans.

"It revolves around bars, and well, sex. There aren't a lot of cultural events like this around," he says.

Mr. Richard grew up in New Orleans, left to earn his degrees, and returned twelve years ago to accept a job offer. Plus, he says, the South lured him back. The habits of living and the habits of thinking in the South, the comfortable laid-back feeling, even if it is often a repressed society with secrets bubbling underneath, often compel native sons and daughters to return and stay. Some, like myself, never leave. The sultry humidity, the genteelness of the people, the sexiness of illicit behavior, the food, the slow drawls, even the rich soil, make Southerners hard-pressed to seek life elsewhere. Mix that with the voodoo sensuality of New Orleans, a historically cosmopolitan city steeped in sexual arousal, and it's hard not to think of the Crescent City as one of the most erotic cities in the world. The crossing of cultures — Creole, French, Caribbean, African, European — makes this place seem connected in the most intimate of ways — the mixing of bloods, the sense of the forbidden.

With so much hoodoo lovin' going on, it's easy to think of New Orleans as the most liberal place on Earth. And it is in some ways, as the poet of the hour explains. But not like a big city with the same history would be if it were outside of the South.

"You have these conservative energies that are trying to push against liberalism," the poet explains in his Kevin Spacey tone.

The churches, especially black and Catholic ones in New Orleans, feed into the conservatism, generating a tension that breeds both repression and seduction. It's very similar to the entire nature of the South.

While Mr. Richard writes amazing poetry about sex, sin, and sensuality, he tends to temper the submissions about gay life that he sends to the state's arts commission when attempting to get grants.

"I know I might not get a grant if I write about the gay lifestyle. I'm so sick of not sending them, because that's the work that is closest to me now, but that's how Louisiana is in general," he says.

He also tells me, much to my surprise, that a lot of gay teachers in New Orleans' public schools have either lost their jobs or at least been harassed by principals because of their sexual orientation. Still, he says, gays in New Orleans don't really get worked up about a lot of issues like they should.

Mr. Richard has a good handle on his state, and especially his city. He weaves stories about gay politicians in New Orleans that fascinate me more than any talk of radical faeries does. He tells me about a politician who had grand plans to run for city council, but wouldn't come out of the closet because he feared he'd lose the election. His district? The French Quarter of all places, the most liberal area of New Orleans.

"I can't imagine New Orleans having a gay mayor, not in my lifetime. I can't even imagine a gay mayor in any major city in the South, can you?" A sly one, he turns the question on me.

Nope, I say, telling him the story about how Arkansas had a chance to elect a female governor and liberals and conservatives repeatedly said that the state wasn't ready for a woman to be in charge of it. So, sadly, I don't see much hope for a gay politician winning anytime soon in Dixie.

Speaking of politics . . .

"She looks like Debbie Harry in this picture, doesn't she?" Michelle asks me.

Yeah, weirdly enough, the woman in the black-and-white airbrushed picture in the Saints and Sinners program does look like Debbie Harry, just a little bit. But that's not who she is. She's Gennifer Flowers, the very one who nearly derailed a presidential campaign in 1992 by claiming a twelve-year affair with Bill Clinton. Gennifer Flowers is the hostess with the mostess, welcoming an evening of risqué readings at her club, the Gennifer Flowers Kelsto Club.

I've brought my mom along for this adventure. She doesn't care about the erotic literature. She wants to see Gennifer Flowers, whose very name personifies sex, especially if you hail from the Land of Clinton. It's true. For months when Clinton ran for the presidency, her face popped up everywhere in Arkansas, on the nightly news, in weekly newspapers, in the daily newspaper. Everyone had a Gennifer Flowers story, and my mom and I latched on to the titillating tabloid tales. Covering politics, I have met many of the Clinton babes, but Gennifer with a "G" has always eluded me.

Kelsto is a small venue with dark chocolate-brown walls and dimly lighted sconces that look like warm vanilla candles. Around the bar's windows, Mardi Gras tinsel woven with purple, gold, and green lights shimmers. Pictures of panthers surrounded by jungle-print mats in large black frames adorn the walls. In two corners near the large bar hang pictures of our lady Gennifer. A large floral arrangement sits on a mantle in front of a mirror. There are autographed pics of

Phil Donahue, the Spice Girls, and Morgan Brittany of *Dallas* fame. My eyes roam to the framed cover of the *Penthouse* magazine with Gennifer Flowers on it. That says it all: She ain't apologizing for nothing. Ever.

Mom and I sit down at a corner table near a window and a baby grand piano. The French Provincial gold chairs are accented by black silk upholstery with woven golden flies. Freaky. What an interesting use of an insect motif. And I thought she was only interested in presidential flies. Wink, wink.

"We'll be able to see everything from here," Mom says.

Never shy, Mom's always right in picking a prime spot to see the action. On our table, an advertisement entices us to have a drink called "The Flower of the South." Maybe it's all the travels, but I am seeing way too many double entendres these days. The small bar fills up with chattering literary folks.

"Hi there," says a tall, lanky man who is the ring leader of this weekend. He sits on the edge of the large windowsill next to me.

"Hey," I say.

"Look," he says in a serious whispered tone. "I'm glad you brought your mom and all but she won't be offended, will she? I just don't know what some of these people will read or how racy it'll get."

I chuckle and reassure him that she won't be. He still looks nervous. Surely, there's nothing here my mom hasn't read or heard about in all of her seventy-something years, especially these last few months of my wacky adventures. If there is, then I could probably be just as easily shocked. I don't have the heart to tell him that after living with my teenage musical cacophony, if Mom doesn't like what she hears she can amazingly just tune it out.

Another little sign on the bar around the piano catches my eye. "No photographs of Gennifer Flowers may be taken by customers."

One word: Diva with a capital D.

Then, I see it all. White T-shirts for sale sporting Gennifer's image and red smooch logo. The same sign I had been reading a second earlier informs customers that they can buy the Gennifer *Penthouse* magazine for two hundred dollars or her book *Passion and Betrayal* for fifty smackeroos. She also peddles shot glasses, pictures of herself, and compact discs. Who knew fucking the president could yield such an empire?

Mom and I are super fidgety. We're anxious to see Gennifer Flowers. You'd think we were strict Catholics waiting to see the Pope. Meanwhile, as we wait, some granola girl in the corner is checking me out. At least, I think she is. I can't help but wonder if some of these people think that I go for older women and Mom is my date. The room becomes more packed, a heated buzz suddenly enters it, and I know: Gennifer Flowers has entered the room. I'm not wrong.

Gennifer walks through the crowd in Kelsto and takes the microphone. Her blonde hair is still as suicide platinum as ever, and thrown up in a come-hither pony tail with her trademark poufy bangs. Wispy strings of fallen hair edge Gennifer's neckline. Her heavily made-up complexion is smooth, her pink coral lips pouty. Almost too plump and pouty, as if she's had a kiss or two of collagen. A velvet and chiffon shawl with long fringe drapes over her black dress. A vintage bronze necklace with large turquoise stones adorns her neck and directs focus to her plunging neckline. Gennifer wears funky black glasses with rhinestones on the frames. In some weird way, the woman standing in front of me seems to be, well, sex personified, a Jackie Collins vamp come to life.

Mom and I look at each other but say nothing. We both know the erotic snippets of her affair with Bill Clinton. Neither one of us ever really believed that she was lying about the fling. It's just strange finally seeing her in person. She greets the crowd and wastes no time getting the evening started by introducing Michelle, who will read a story about how Mötley Crüe broke her cherry. As Michelle talks about cunts and cocks, blow jobs and Vince Neil, I almost have to laugh at my life. It's Saturday night, and I'm in Gennifer Flowers's bar listening to lesbian poetry with my mother. Not exactly a Norman Rockwell moment, but it works for us.

It was around this time, as Michelle described some sort of girl-girl action backstage at a Crüe concert, that Mom and I begin to notice something outside the window. Every pedestrian who passes Kelsto pauses. They look at the pictures of Gennifer or point to the sign above the club's door. Hardly anyone ignores the fact that this is that woman who slept with that president. More than a decade later, and we are still not over it. When Michelle ends her story, Gennifer only has one word: "Wow."

The next reader shares a story about some man, a model, who has hooked up with another man, an artiste. I don't follow the story at all, because my mind has wandered back to the women in Bill Clinton's life. It doesn't discourage my thoughts that a cigar store sits diagonally across from Kelsto. My mind leapfrogs from one Clinton woman to the next:

Gennifer, Paula Jones, Monica, and several others I know in Little Rock.

For a political connoisseur and Clinton addict, concentrating on gay literature is hard when Gennifer is in the room. Strangely, sitting here listening to writers string words together to make the room hot and bothered, I realize that none of this turns me on. Not at all, and it has nothing to do with the people in the room being gay and my being straight. It's just that at this very moment, after a long journey through the South, I've discovered my fetish. Wow. I have. And here it is: Politics is my fetish. Clearly. While other workshop attendees want to meet writers like Dorothy Allison, I'm tingling with the thought of meeting Gennifer Flowers. Some people would say that's weird. I say my kink isn't your kink, and that's okay. But you've got one buried somewhere, too, so just hush.

The passers-by continue to stop, peer into Kelsto, and try to steal a glimpse of Gennifer. Are they curious about her or simply shocked that this is the same woman who almost ended Bill Clinton's political career before Monica ever entered the picture? Or are they thinking "Huh? Gennifer Flowers owns a bar?" Because in the end, people who stroll by this window know Gennifer Flowers not as a smoky-voiced chanteuse but as a sex kitten who nailed a president.

The diva continues to introduce readers. At times, Gennifer looks a little shocked by some of their explicit words, and this makes me smile. It's good to know someone who has seen a politician up close and personal can still be just a tad shocked. Mom tuned out the reading a long time ago. Such writing with sexual words but without a real plot doesn't interest her. She keeps stealing glances at a man who is perched on the window ledge wearing leather hot pants and a black and red striped tank top. He's gay and he's proud of it. My mother — I can read her mind — thinks he should go back into the closet and get another outfit.

Finally, an intermission!

Too much Coke has left me needing the ladies' room. Going out into the foyer, I cross to an area behind the bar right behind an older red-haired woman with a black boa wrapped around her black cocktail dress.

"Hey, babe," she says to a woman coming down a staircase near the powder room.

Gasp! It's Gennifer herself. What to do? Mind you, I've met a lot of people in my journalism career, including Bill Clinton too many times to count. I'm never jittery. Who cares, I figure? They roll out of bed every morning just like I do. But for some reason, unexplainable intimidation washes over me. What the hell? I plunge in and introduce myself.

Somewhat stuttering, I tell her I'd like to talk to her about, well, sex. I even throw in I'm from Little Rock. She seems unimpressed, but gives me her card. She tells me to call her next week. Now, I'm no dummy, I can tell when I'm getting dissed, especially by a diva, and this is it. It's the equivalent of "Have your people call my people." If only we both had people. She hands me the card and I walk to the rest room. The door won't open, so I stand in the hallway, with Gennifer three feet away, and look at her card.

A close-up picture of half her face adorns the front of the card. Her bedroom eyes stare at me. Her partly pouty lips would tempt even the most loyal husband. If she's selling sex, it's working. The card flips open with a list of fine scotches and vodkas. On the other side, a pair of red lips with these words: "Gennifer, these are special guests of mine. Please offer them a complimentary beverage." On the line for a signature, she's written N/A. Lovely.

I feel like an idiot. The bathroom door wasn't locked at all. I just didn't push it hard enough so now I've been standing in the corridor looking at the card and then at Gennifer like some love-sick stalker chick attending a gay and lesbian festival. She probably thinks I have the hots for her. This is not turning out well.

When the readings resume, Mom and I try to refocus but our attention spans are shot. We don't want to hear about any more kisses that are sweet like plums or ménages à trois that turn out wrong. Then, finally, it's time for the man in the leather shorts to read. During the intermission, I spotted him chatting up Gennifer, almost bowing in front of her. Even I didn't do that. Has Gennifer Flowers become a new gay icon in a post-Clinton world? Maybe.

I tune out his story about a dominatrix and two gay guys because I'm watching Gennifer. She seems bored, too. Looking at my watch, I realize these writers are cutting into her performance time. That can't be a good thing. In the time it takes a cat to meow, Gennifer wraps up the evening, invites all the GLBT literati to stay if they want to hear her sing, and exits the stage. Only two, plus Mom and I, choose to do so. The rest bolt like there's a sale on housewares at Pottery Barn.

The woman I'd seen earlier in the black boa is Gennifer's pianist. She's joined by a man with a shaved head who plays an assortment of brass at Kelsto. No Gennifer, though. The cocktail waitress returns and tells Mom and I that there is no cover charge to hear Gennifer but there's a two-drink minimum. If we only want to stay and hear a little bit of Gennifer, then she'll waive the two-drink deal.

"We'll have a couple of Cokes," I say.

"Yeah," Mom says. "Who knows, we may want to stay awhile."

The duo plays classic New Orleans jazz tunes, the rhythm picking up, the piano getting just a little louder; no doubt, Gennifer is in the house. Sure enough, she is. She's changed out of the Dorothy Parker velvet shawl and into a classy black tuxedo coat. I wish I had it in my closet. She belts outs a couple of jazzy tunes and points to special guests in the audience. I'm not one. She says something about a relative sitting in the audience. Gennifer glances around the room and makes quick eye contact with me. She looks away.

"Where are you from, honey?" she drawls to a woman on the other side of the room.

She asks a few more people where they are from. Fingers crossed, I hope she asks me. I'd love to say "Little Rock" and get the room worked up in a frenzy. But she doesn't ask me.

In a sultry deep throatiness, Gennifer growls Peggy Lee's "Fever." Did she ever sing that to Clinton, I wonder? She's not half bad. It's not like she slept with a politician and then decided to parlay that into a career, like a model who decides to try acting. She can sing and gets applause from the room of about forty people who have filtered into the club. Like an experienced nightclub act, she tells a joke.

"Know the difference between a golf ball and a G-spot?"

she asks a shocked man sitting next to the piano. He shakes his head no.

"A man will spend all day looking for a golf ball," she says, laughing and raising an eyebrow.

Oof.

Gennifer croons "Ain't Misbehavin'," which could be her theme song. She cracks some joke in the middle about how much fun it is to be a bad girl, which forces the room to share a collective thought about the little things she used to do with Bill Clinton in her boudoir. Gennifer says she knows how to work two pieces of equipment late at night, the radio and well . . . you know the other one. Gennifer can be a very, very bad girl.

Four songs and she's outta here. Time to take another break. A diva shouldn't work too hard, especially after she's earned her prima donna stripes on the world stage.

It's Sunday morning, and I'm again confused. Dorothy Allison, who wrote the award-winning *Bastard Out of Carolina*, sits on the stage in front of me at the Shim Sham Club. Lesbians have gathered to discuss how to write and express themselves beyond the boundaries — race, class, gender — in which they live. I've hung out with lots of gay men and have often been the only woman with them, but a room full of lesbians is a different matter entirely.

First, I don't speak their language. Like they are talking about a Shirley MacLaine–Audrey Hepburn movie called *The Children's Hour*. I've never seen the movie, but it's all about two closeted lesbians who love each other. Dorothy

Allison rants about how this was before the days that women could leave the closet, or the attic, in the case of this movie. The movie is set in a time when people did not say *lesbian*, did not say *dyke*, did not say *pussy-licking hounds of hell*, so sayeth Dorothy Allison. But that doesn't mean the fight for lesbians has ended, no way; it's up to all of us sitting here in this room at this very moment to go out on the balcony, strip off our clothes, and scream our names, and the collective one — lesbian — loudly. If Dick Cheney were in this room right now, he'd have another heart attack.

Second, I'm not sure I have anything in common with anyone in this room. Okay, maybe the older woman next to me reading a fluff entertainment magazine. Other than that, I don't think so. I don't wake up every morning asking myself if I am a white woman first, or a straight woman. I don't think about my sexuality very much. I don't have to, because I'm in the majority.

Okay, I was wrong. I do have something in common with them. Many are talking about how they have been treated like dirt by former lovers and treated like scum by society. Amen, sistah. I can raise a cup of café au lait to that.

A few days after I leave New Orleans, the gays and lesbians fade from my consciousness, somewhat. But not Gennifer Flowers. She told me to call her, and I have. I've left messages for her at Kelsto and even on some answering machine at the Gennifer Flowers Company that has her seductive trill on it, telling me to leave her a message and she'll call me back. She hasn't. But now my political fetish has kicked in with full force and my voyeurism is out of control.

Maybe I wasn't as curious about Gennifer with a G as I should have been in the 1990s.

Late at night, I order a used copy of Gennifer Flowers's book online for seventy-five cents. Really, she is charging way too much for that book in her nightclub. A few days later, my book arrives in a plain brown envelope. I snuggle in for the night to read about her lust and love for Bill Clinton. By morning, my eyes are bloodshot and weary but I've learned a lot of hair-raising titillating tidbits about Miss Flowers and the former president that I never knew, and which certainly didn't get a lot of play when the book came out in 1995. Bill once let Gennifer put makeup on him. Gasp! He liked to be spanked! Oh, my. He wanted her to tie him up. Hello! Bill Clinton is a son of the South, after all. Reading it now, after my journey through Dixie and knowing what I know about randy politicians' sexual habits, all I can say is I need one hell of a cigarette. Or a cigar.

post-coital bliss

What I Learned as a Voyeur

I'm standing at the coffee counter in Little Rock, half-asleep one early morning. Groggy and in need of caffeine, I notice the woman in front of me with a book about horseback riding. My mind instantly flashes awake. Is she buying it to learn how to ride a bio-horse or a man-horse? What's her kink? Egad, I muse, maybe she actually does just want to ride a horse. Or maybe not . . .

A man stares at me from a table. His T-shirt says: WEAPON OF MASS ERECTION. A tough-looking chap with a cell phone snapped on his waistband like a gun, I'm certain he must be into Iron Belles swinging him around like a piece of rope.

After the cup of coffee has kicked in and my reflexive kink-radar has stopped chirping, I think about a few things I've learned from my erotic romp through Dixie:

1. You never know what someone's got up her doo-lolly.
2. Never underestimate the thong-crafting ingenuity of a man who prefers skirts.
3. Drag-queen boys have much better taste in music than straight boys.

4. Muscle women can squeeze cereal boxes into bow ties.
5. That collar-type necklace your mom is wearing may be more than just a sweet gift from your dad.
6. Whenever you're with a squirter, always stay at least five feet away because you never know when she's gonna blow.
7. Your hotel desk clerk may in fact be a big nelly bottom.
8. Never eat a lollipop at a strip joint.
9. If I suddenly develop a craving for nude, submerged, wrestling mermaids on video, there's someone out there who can help.
10. When dismounting from a man-horse, be mindful of his tail.
11. When someone says "swing your partner," they might not be square dancing.
12. Eva Wynne-Warren, the pixie burlesque goddess with the vintage stripper's wardrobe, needs her own agent. Fast.
13. I can never listen to Led Zeppelin's "Whole Lotta Love" the same way again.
14. I have, after much practice in my living room, mastered the Sensuous Bra Removal.
15. Lesbians + stage + reading dirty words aloud does not necessarily = poetry.

As I cast my gaze around the coffee shop, I see a familiar cast of characters. The frat boys. The businessmen. The Junior Leaguers. The senior citizens. Yes, all the same folks that sipped coffee here with me before my journey, but now they're all different.

Actually, they're not different at all. It's me. I'm different. When I see a grandmother, I'm wondering if she's into pony play. When I see the frat boys, I'm curious as to how often they frequent strip joints. That businessman in the corner with his *Financial Times*? If I had to guess, he's got aqua porn written all over him.

After visiting ten states, I realize one thing: I've changed into more of a voyeur than ever before, certainly looking into places I shouldn't and awaiting with a tingle my next voyeuristic caper. One thing's for sure: I've watched some crazy stuff in Dixie. I've been shocked, amazed, wowed, impressed, repelled, and cracked up, but not turned on. If anything, I've learned to never look at anyone the same way again.

resources

If you'd like to do more research into the secret worlds populated by the *Sex in the South* characters, I've provided a starting point. Here are links to some of the true-life, wonderfully wacky Southerners who shared their stories for this book. Happy surfing.

* Linda Brewer — Passion Parties
www.mypassionshop.com/lindabrewer

* Dale Miller — also known as Skirtman
www.skirtman.org

* Miss Gay America Pageant
www.missgayamerica.com

* Iron Belles and Cheryl Harris
www.ironbelles.com

*Ms. Cindy Charms
www.southern-charms4.com/mscindy/bio.htm

* Southern Charms
www.southern-charms.com

* Angelo Dixon
www.dixonbooks.net

* Aqua Fantasies
www.aquafan.com

* Trigger the Humane Equine
www.thehumanequine.com

* Dr. Eddie and the Intimacy Institute
www.home.earthlink.net/~drziggy00

* Torchy Taboo and Dames A'flame
www.damesaflame.com

* Mendi Teats
www.menditeats.com
www.bbwdivas.com

*NeeCee Belle
www.southern-charms2.com/neecee/index.html

* The Learning Institute for Women
www.learningwomen.com